THE HEALING HOUSE

How Living in the Right House Can Heal You Spiritually, Emotionally, and Physically

Barbara Bannon
HARWOOD

Hay House, Inc.
Carlsbad, CA

Published and distributed in the United States by:
Hay House, Inc., P.O. Box 5100, Carlsbad, CA 92018-5100
(800) 654-5126 • (800) 650-5115 (fax)

Edited by: Jill Kramer   *Designed by:* Jenny Richards

Library of Congress Cataloging-in-Publication Data

Harwood, Barbara Bannon.
    The healing House : how living in the right house can heal you spiritually, emotionally, and physically / Barbara Bannon Harwood.
        p. cm.
    Includes bibliographical references.
    ISBN 1-56170-427-X (trade paper)
    1. Architecture, Domestic--Psychological aspects. 2. Interior decoration--Psychological aspects. I. Title.
    NA7125.H39   1997   728.01
    728' .01--dc21   H2R   97-13377
                            9.01   CIP

ISBN 1-56170-427-X

00 99 98 97   4 3 2 1
First Printing, September 1997

Printed in the United States of America

This book is dedicated to my husband, Richard.
But for his solace and comfort, I would not be who I am.
But for his teaching, I would not know what I know.
But for his patience and help, I would not have been able
to take time to write this. For his love, comfort,
and guidance, I will be eternally grateful.

Places and Spaces

This place is an emotional wilderness
Where feelings run and hide
    fearing the light, the sound
    of their own voices alive in air
Pleading for a drop of water
    in the desert's void
    longing for a solitary breath
    of release
    of comfort
    a single word
    of confirmation
    aching to hear the pure music
    of a single voice of acknowledgment
    the faintest recognition
    that truth lives as much in hearts
    as in heads
    or other things one can touch and hold.

Is it this Place?
This town?
Do I believe in the vibrations of place
    of a certain space in time?
Is this spot on the planet
    somehow absent of an energy
    a synoptic flow
    with the human soul?
Are there really places more suited to
    machines
    maybe robots
    than living beings?
Or is it only that the vibrations of this
    sterile place
    are a void
    an emotional cemetery
    filled with a generation of those yet
    young and undeveloped in cosmic years?

Whatever it is
    there is a spiritual battle
    when I am here in this void.
A Battle for breath
    as in one who has been struggling
    against the weight
    of the stormy sea with a body no longer
    able to swim.

Perhaps this void is here, in this place
    which then draws to it
    people who do not wish to feel
    like houses which
    when entered
    give off pain
    or vacant joylessness;
    a reflection of the empty human shells
    still not completely gone from their
    walls and floors.

Perhaps . . .
    in the same way there is joy which can
    only be felt vividly
    in the same place where pain has
    carved its space
Perhaps in the same physical pattern that
    for every action
    there is an equal and opposite reaction
Perhaps for every place
    there is an opposite and equal place.
For every place of contentment and peace
    there is a place of turmoil and torment.
For every place of love and spiritual beauty,
    there is a place of vacant cold materialism
For every place of verdant, luxurious
    growth, there is a desert void.
And as like is drawn to like
    so do the people resemble the place.

Or perhaps not.

Perhaps the aberrant can be found
    wherever there is life.
Perhaps so, but I think not.
For it truly seems to me
    that vacant souls seek vacant places
    to find their own purest reflection
    and when the reflection no longer
    appears true
    they leave
    to find themselves again
    in another place
    in life's great mirror.

— Barbara Harwood

Contents

◆   ◆   ◆

PREFACE

Can We Expect Healing Where We Live?

Inevitably, those who know me ask how a woman with a journalism and music background came to write a book about housing, so I should, as I begin, tell you the story of how I got into the homebuilding business. I think, most simply, that I was led there, almost from the time I was a child. I was adopted from an orphanage in Lincoln, Nebraska, by a western Nebraska couple, both educators, who later turned to operating the family farm and ranch. You will hear details of my early years in stories throughout the book, but suffice it to say, for now, my favorite relationships as a child were with my horses and my piano. The cold, barren plains and the sheer, spectacular wideness of the skies often left me feeling small and alone, which, in turn, probably fed my voracious curiosity. I also had a knack for what might loosely be called "making a healing connection." I seemed to adopt injured children, the elderly, horses, and, without knowing exactly how I did it, I made them feel better. I also loved science, so, after grammar school and high school where I graduated with honors, I decided to try premed.

As you will learn later on in the discussion on Multiple Chemical Sensitivities, I discovered in college that I was deathly allergic to the formaldehyde used to preserve bodies in science labs. That was the end of my dreams of becoming a doctor, but I also loved writing, so I switched to journalism. All through college, I had a music minor, primarily voice, but with some piano. Both journalism and music played the major part in my careers, which took me from Colorado to California, and, ultimately, to Texas. I worked in music, and broadcast and print journalism until the early '80s, but through it all, somehow, my "observant self" always saw me as a teacher. As I look back, that's what I've been doing all my life: alternately learning and teaching. There has always been a "presence" around me, pushing me this way or that, leading me where I'm supposed to be, placing those who need me in front of me. Only when I began to meditate did I begin to understand it all.

The Birth of a Book

I have meditated daily, usually only once, but sometimes twice, for about 20 years. When you meditate, you link yourself with some power far greater than yourself. Filmmaker George Lucas called it "The Force," and for lack of a better term, and because the general public always knows what you are talking about when you say it, I use the same, albeit limited, phrase. Ancient Hebrew tribes called it "Yahweh," meaning the unknowable and unnameable in Aramaic. And indeed, it is that and more. When you meditate, you feel it although you never understand it. Not only are you led to new thought paths during meditation, but all through your life you find miraculous connections just erupting from the hidden recesses of time and space, meeting you on the paths you walk and opening brilliant new horizons before you. I will discuss this more in the last chapter. For now, let me tell you the story of how this book came to be.

The winter of 1980 to 1981 was one of the coldest that Chicago has ever known, and it was my introductory winter back in the north. I had married Richard Harwood, a major Chicago developer, the previous spring. It was then that three things happened, almost simultaneously, which led me to the homebuilding business, and eventually and inevitably, to this book, although I would have been dumbfounded if someone had told me in 1980 where all this would lead by 1997.

Our family was involved in a program to take food to the poor during the holiday season. One bitter cold, snowy day we walked up a half-flight of rickety wooden stairs into the apartment of the Medisky family on Chicago's near-North Side. Mr. Medisky was lying on a couch, probably clothed in everything he owned. He looked like a white-haired matzo ball with legs. When he sat up, the tired old tan blanket fell off his legs, and we noticed that his ankles were blue.

Although all of us were bundled up in our warmest coats, hats, and snow boots, at that moment we began to realize that the air on our faces wasn't *that* warm. We looked around the room and realized that wind was blowing the curtains *through closed windows*. About that time, Mrs. Medisky came into the room. An elderly woman who looked rather unkempt and very tired, she said she had been sitting in the kitchen with the oven open and all the burners going, trying to keep warm while she read a book. She explained that her husband had diabetes and heart disease. It was already obvious to us that he was blind as well.

She thanked us profusely for the armloads of groceries that my husband and I and three of our five children were carrying. She said they had no money for food and medicine *because their entire Social Security check of about $500 was going for rent and utilities*. It became obvious to me in a half second that they couldn't have kept warm in that apartment if they had spent a thousand dollars a month on utilities. It was impossibly leaky. We left the groceries and our best holiday cheer and good wishes that day. But we told the Mediskys that we would be back to make their apartment more livable.

A couple of Saturdays later, we all returned. My husband, a prominent developer and builder in Northbrook, had brought carpet he scrounged from one of his subcontractors, and I had bought caulk and plastic and a space heater at the hardware store. We first cleaned up the apartment, obviously an impossible task for the elderly Mrs. Medisky, who couldn't leave the warmth of the stove to do anything. To the shock of our children, when we picked up a battered old brown recliner chair to take it outside for disposal, the bottom fell off and a zillion cockroaches came pouring out of what was obviously a nest. Teenagers can be quick, especially when they are motivated by an oncoming hoard of repugnant pests, so for a few minutes, the room was all-a-flurry with flying feet and swatting newspapers as we chased and destroyed most of them.

Our children swept, washed, and cleaned while I caulked, and Richard put plastic over the windows. While we laid and tacked down the carpet, Mr. Medisky went into the kitchen to sit by the stove with his wife. When we were finished, they came back into the living room. He couldn't see our satisfied, smiling, exhausted faces as his wife could, but he could feel the carpet under his slippered feet, and he got down on his hands and knees and kissed it.

There wasn't a dry eye in the room.

On the way home, our youngest daughter was still crying. "I can't believe people as nice as the Mediskys have to live like that," she said through her tears. "Thank God our grandparents have it better." I could tell from the tortured expressions on our boys' tear-streaked faces that they felt the exact same way. And with the inevitable uncanny and unexpected wisdom combined with incredible naïveté that teenagers come up with occasionally, our youngest boy said, "Mom, I know you will be able to do something to help them find a better place to live."

He's always been something of a mind-reader, that one. And indeed, I had already been thinking along those same lines. So I began an occasional search (in between my work and my family) for a better apartment for the Mediskys.

Is It Coincidence, or . . .

At the same time, in one of those "coincidences" that can't possibly be a coincidence, the *Chicago Sun-Times*, for whom I was then writing, sent me to a little town in southern Illinois to do a story on an earth-sheltered house. I had never been in one before, and contrary to the cold, damp cave I expected when someone said it was a house built into the earth, I entered a bright, sunny little house about the size of the Mediskys' apartment. On that sparkling-cold winter afternoon, sun was pouring in the south windows. The north, east, and west walls and roof were sheltered from any infiltration of the bitterly cold winds by thick layers of earth. The happy, healthy couple who lived inside, about the same age as the Mediskys and with about the same monthly Social Security income, told me that *their entire utility bill for a* winter *was $30 for half a cord of wood.*

The lights inside my head went on. *The difference between this smiling, happy couple and the cold, sick, and unhappy Mediskys was the energy efficiency of their housing.* Of course, at that time, I had barely heard of the words *energy efficiency.* But the concept was clear and obvious: The Mediskys were not only spending money they didn't have in order to pay utility bills that were wasted, they were freezing and miserable in spite of paying for utilities that *should*, in a properly insulated and sealed building, have kept them warm.

Now I was really compelled to find better housing for the Mediskys. But one more thing happened soon after. One Sunday morning in January, we woke to unbelievable winds and no power. We learned later from neighbors that the chill factor that day was *80 below zero.* The real temperature was something like 20 below. That day, I learned how "passive solar" makes you *feel.*

We lived in a house designed by Bill Deknatel, a partner and associate of Frank Lloyd Wright. We loved the feelings it generated for us when we first saw it. It looked like it was part of the earth beneath it and the forest behind it. The house circled around the pathway of the sun, had almost an entire south wall of windows with four-foot overhangs, and fewer windows on the north. The interior was pure Wright: redwood siding up to six and a half feet, then a harvest-yellow textured finish above, sliding doors throughout with alternating glass and redwood panels aligned perfectly with the natural redwood on the walls, a concrete block fireplace, and built-in redwood cabinets and cubicles as room dividers. That icy cold day, we learned to appreciate the energy considerations in its construction. I won't say, in retrospect, the "energy efficiency" of its construction, because it wasn't sealed well enough, but it was certainly the right design, as we, and all our neighbors found out. Without power, their homes were miserably cold. It was a special hardship for our neighbors immediately to the north, who had a baby girl.

With the sun shining, even though there was no power to run the furnace, *our house was 70 degrees by 10 A.M.* I still marvel at that whole day. So many truly unusual things happened that if I look back, it was just as if there was some hand on my shoulder pointing to something, saying, "Now look at this and think about it," over and over. First, the unbelievable wind. Second, it was a weekend day so everyone was home, and third, the *sun was shining.* Anybody who has lived in Chicago in the winter knows how rare that is. When you live there, you feel like the cloud cover comes in October and doesn't leave until April, although that's not entirely true. But to have both those things happen in one day while we were all home so all of us were *aware of how cold we could have been* was a miracle.

With the foolhardy bravery that teenagers are famous for, our middle son *had to go outside* to see what it felt like to be blown over by 80-mile-an-hour winds. He made it as far as our next-door neighbors. When he almost literally blew in their door, they could only talk about how cold they were, and how worried they were about their baby girl. Not quite realizing yet how different our house was, he started asking questions about why theirs was so cold. Then he told them, "No matter, just come home with me. Our house is toasty warm." So they did. Then he went to the neighbors on the other side and found that they, too, were very cold, so they arrived next, and on and on until we had a houseful. It was our first passive solar party. Believe me, everybody there understood the concept the minute they stood in front of the south windows and felt the warm sun radiating its heat onto them. We built a fire in the fireplace, hung a teakettle on it, dragged out our iron frying pan that we used for camping trips, and made pancakes and eggs. We felt like old-time pioneers, and we were incredibly grateful to Frank Lloyd Wright, the teacher, and Bill Deknatel, the student, for their design genius.

Back in "College"

At that point, it was becoming more and more clear to me that energy efficiency and passive solar design were the keys to a lot of things: winter comfort, insurance against power outages, low utility bills, and, therefore, a healthier life. So I began asking myself why *all* houses weren't built that way. And I knew I had to learn more. Some of that learning was already being programmed for me, probably by the same forces that were introducing me to all the rest of this. The *Chicago Sun-Times* kept sending me on stories about energy issues: clean-burning methanol fuels produced near Champaign, Illinois; an earth-sheltered house in Riverwoods; an active solar system somewhere else. All the people doing these projects talked enthusiastically about why energy was so important an issue for as long as I would listen. Fortunately, as a journalist, you get paid to learn. All you have to do is ask the questions. I asked them where to find out more, and they told me. I wrote, studied, spent hours in libraries, and asked questions at home—popular questions for a wife who knows almost nothing about her husband's building business, such as "Why don't you build passive solar, energy-efficient houses?"

Then, even worse, I started mixing in my husband's business at the National Association of Homebuilders, where he was on the Executive Committee and chairman of a committee dealing with building-code issues. I began asking what *they* as an organization were doing about promoting energy efficiency to all their members, and learned that one man, Ivan Woolworth, had the same idea and had formed a "Standing Committee on Energy." When they told me the name, I immediately pictured a group of stuffy, gray-suited men *standing up* around a table talking about energy. The first part was largely right, but they did sit down. And they mostly talked about how to *avoid* something called Building Energy Performance Standards (BEPS), a new energy efficiency standards program developed by the Department of Energy (DOE). I decided to go to the source.

So one fine spring day, an eager young woman out to change the world—me—walked into the concrete bunker building they call the DOE, on Independence Avenue in Washington, D.C. At that time, they didn't have a receptionist or a metal detector with guards greeting you at the door. They just had empty, barren, gray concrete hallways merging at the entrance. When you entered, you had to *guess* where to go next.

I walked into the first door I saw and said I wanted information on passive solar, energy-efficient construction. The woman sitting at the desk inside the door looked up at me as if she was plenty tired of playing receptionist for the whole building on top of her regular job. "This office is . . ." whatever it was, she said. "I think solar is in . . ." whatever. The hallways are labeled with letters, then numbers. A211 is thus a very long walk from Z920. I arrived in the building at 10 A.M. By 4 P.M., I was still going from office to office, from one end of the building to the next. Everywhere I went was the wrong place, and they sent me someplace else. I was tired and hungry and disgusted. The next office I went to was wrong again, and I was fed up. The poor woman inside the door caught the entire six hours of my frustration in one noisy bundle.

"Let me tell you something, lady," I shouted. "I am a U.S. taxpayer. You work for me, and so does everybody else in this building. You all spend millions of dollars of taxpayer money doing research, and I need to see some of it. Now get some all-fired bloody person over here who knows where passive solar information is. I've been shifted from pillar to post in this bloody building for six hours, and I haven't even had lunch . . . ." and so forth. As I shouted, she backed up farther and farther, her eyes got wider and wider, and colleagues began to gather around her. One woman said, "Okay, ma'am. We'll find someone to help you. Just have a seat over here." He pointed to a distant chair without getting any closer to me than was absolutely necessary.

Soon, John Milhone appeared. This kindly, almost white-haired gentleman who had recently been hired by the DOE had just been handed his most difficult assignment: Take a raging, starving, obviously demented woman away from an office she has terrorized and get her out of the building! But when I told him my story, he was completely sympathetic. He got me to the right place, put the information I wanted in my hands, and even bought me lunch in the basement cafeteria. We talked about BEPS, about the inaccessibility of information at DOE, and about the necessity for more energy-efficient, passive solar construction in America. A friendship and professional relationship was begun that continues to this day. John rose from there to become head of the Buildings Systems division of the DOE, an Assistant Secretary. He is now doing the same good work in Poland, and several wonderful people have succeeded him in that position.

My work in the early '80s went from "pillow-talking" my husband into making the homes he built more energy efficient, and working out a marketing program for him that offset the increased cost of energy-efficiency measures by making them more saleable—to becoming an advocate and teacher. Also, I was continuing to learn more about energy efficiency in buildings and renewable energy, as all the energy resources that naturally renew themselves (such as sunlight, fuels made from plants, and wind) are called.

A Return to the South

By 1983, it was clear that a woman who had lived in relatively warm places such as California and Texas for 20 years would not last in the Chicago winters. I felt trapped indoors by the cold, and by March, when the azaleas bloom in Dallas, I was ready to go home. I told my wonderful husband he would either have to come with me, or I'd see him on the weekends; because the long, cold, white, brown, and gray winters were too much for me. I returned to Texas, and he soon sold his company and followed.

My most immediate goal when I arrived was to produce low-income, energy-efficient, passive solar housing. When I had searched for better housing for the Mediskys, I had found that not only wasn't there more energy-efficient housing available to them, there was *no housing* they could afford that was better than what they had. Then I heard President Reagan saying that we didn't need a Department of Energy, we didn't need a Housing and Urban Development (HUD) office, or any more low-income housing. I saw hundreds of apartment buildings for low-income families being gentrified and turned into condos. I thought that this loss of low-cost housing, resulting in Medisky-type living conditions, was a scandal in a country as rich as ours, and I told myself, so naively I can now hardly believe it, "How hard could it be? I'm smart enough and energetic enough—I ought to be able to build some of this housing that's so desperately needed." And that's how my business began.

A Murder in the Night

However, the final event that led to this book came about in 1987, when the 14-year-old son of very close friends was murdered in his bed at midnight by a stranger.

That day, his stepmother, Helena, a commercial photographer, had been taking pictures of the latest dance performance at Southern Methodist University. Someplace en route home, she was spotted and followed.

Through the back screen door, which she had quickly locked when she saw the young man who had followed her home approaching, she heard him ask, "Can I see what's in your bags? I just want to look at your camera."

Helena, not unkindly, said she didn't have time just then, closed the interior door, and promptly snapped the three locks. She still remembers the dark eyes that stared eerily back at her as she pushed the door toward him to latch it. They spooked her enough that even after she closed and locked the back door, she checked all the other doors and windows and picked up the phone to call her husband. Moments later, as the man walked off down the street, she put the phone back on the receiver, mentally dismissing him as some neighborhood kook. He was young, she remembers, and, as she said then, "There are plenty of weirdos hanging around a university."

That night, asleep next to her husband upstairs in the two-story bungalow, Helena thought she heard noises downstairs. When her groggy husband crept down the stairs to check, he found a man bent over his son's bed, violently, angrily stabbing a knife in and out of the boy. As Howard wrestled him off the child, the attacker slashed his arm and hand, then ran out the back door. Helena got to the bottom of the stairs just in time to see that it was the same man who had asked about her camera that morning.

Their only son died in Howard's arms before the police and ambulance arrived five minutes later. He had been stabbed 24 times.

It happened in the spring. Howard and Helena spent the next three months—all summer—sitting on the back patio of our house. They almost never moved from our canvas sling rockers. Day after day, night after night, soothing, peaceful, and comforting Windham Hill recordings played on our outside sound system. Sometimes Howard and Helena sat so still that wild canaries, cardinals, sparrows, and jays that inhabit our backyard perched on the table between them and listened, too, flicking their little heads from side to side, staring at them. They were probably trying to figure out whether the two bodies in the chairs were alive or whether they were yard sculptures. Or perhaps these creatures of the earth and sky could feel the pain radiating out of their fellow living creatures, as animals often do, and wished to offer them some comfort.

In the evening, the couple ate with us and whichever of our college-aged children were home that night. Sometimes we would laugh at the silly voices our boys used, imitating some professor or the other, or calling radio station DJs with different foreign accents, the kind of high-spirited harmless antics boys love and girls roll their eyes at. Howard and Helena laughed, too, but their laughter always rolled off into anger or despair—Howard's into lengthy, angry tirades at the negligent criminal justice system; Helena's into a very uncharacteristic, denser, darker intensity. We listened. We waited.

And the house, they said later, healed them. *The house.* Our house. Perhaps included in "the house" are the people who live here. Most certainly, the exterior environment, the music—including what we call the natural music of the heavens—the birds, the water in the pool and the fountain, combine with the spaces themselves to assist that healing. But whatever was included, Howard and Helena still call it "The Healing House." And none of us doubt that this house, as well as the one we lived in before this one, has a profound impact on our well-being. But until then, I don't think we ever consciously thought about the physical structure and the *feelings it could generate,* whether it heals or causes discomfort and sometimes even pain.

Howard and Helena never set foot again in the house where their son died. (**See the Appendix to the Preface at the end of the book.) That fall, they bought a house a mile or so away and began adding to it and rehabbing its original rooms. It took almost a year. The healing took much longer, and there are still moments when we realize that it's not completely over yet. They had a son a year and a half later, and a daughter two years after that. Their new house feels wonderful to me when I visit. I've done a little healing of my own there—from nothing as drastic as a murder, just some physical problems and business problems—life's normal ups and downs.

But what is it about buildings that cause people to feel that they are "healing places"? Can we *create* healing places as we design houses and build buildings? Do most of our buildings, our homes, as Frank Lloyd Wright said in his 1954 book *The Natural House,*[1] "lie to us" about what we will find inside? Is it simply *comfort*—solace, refreshment for our souls, and serenity—that we want in buildings when what we often get instead is what Wright called "grandomania," exaggeration of height and architectural detail to impress others? Have our buildings become an extension of our turn-of-the-century mania to prove that we can be all things to all people, successful to all who observe? Do builders and designers play into our culture's schizophrenic pursuit of possessions as a panacea for the emptiness we often feel in our lives? Are we looking for love *"in all the wrong places,"* as the song says, when we think that a place with pillars and grand entryways and fancy furniture will make us feel accepted and content? Or is it possible that we have been led down the garden path once again by the hyper-selling of grander and grander new homes with their pretentious possessions? Is it possible that what we are *really* looking for in a home is a way of healing ourselves from the battering of the outside world and a place of bonding with those who are close to us?

Since the summer of Howard and Helen's tragedy, I have struggled to understand what it is that buildings do for us, or *to* us. The answer is complex, yet simple: A *Healing House* can be created, and, if simple principles are followed, it can be available to people in all income ranges.

I hope this book will lead you down new pathways, first to show you why I think homes are like they are today, and then to show you, with several easy-to-remember rules and examples, how to get a Healing House yourself and keep it that way. Because, if you don't have a home to go to that heals your spirit, this world can never feel comfortable for you, *no matter what else you have*.

Welcome to the journey!

◆   ◆   ◆

ACKNOWLEDGMENTS

Thanks are due to so many people in my life who have helped make this book possible. First, the Mediskys. I bless their souls, wherever they are. Secondly, Holly and Hugh, whose terrible pain has, hopefully, been given some measure of comfort by knowing that others have gained understanding and help through their great loss. Then, not necessarily in this order, my splendid children, all of whom have taught me, perhaps, even more than I have taught them, and who have always been there when we needed their varied professional skills. To my wonderful, lively grandchildren, through whose eyes I catch a glimpse of the next century and better understand my responsibilities. To Sharla, whose weekly acupressure has kept me going. To Jack, whose assistance at my right hand is always invaluable. To my gracious and patient editor, Jill Kramer; and my undyingly enthusiastic publicist, Kristina Reece. To my many friends who helped edit this material. First, my husband who read every word twice and offered very wise suggestions. Then to Oliver Drerup and Elena Westbrook, who kept me from going too far into left field.

And to the literally hundreds of others from whom I have learned what I know over the last 18 years and who have always supported my crazy, sometimes eccentric efforts—particularly Jim and Patty Rouse, Pliny Fisk and Gail Vittori, Dr. Art Rosenfeld, John Milhone, Joe Lstiburek and Betsy Pettit, Amory Lovins, Bill Browning, Perry Bigelow, Craig Eymann, Gail Lindsey, Bob Berkebile, Liza Bowles, Ned Nisson, Tom Farkas, and all the members of the Sanborn Team. I thank you all for knowing. You bring me joy and guide me with love and wisdom. And I thank you for being in my life.

The Blueprint

For your ease and understanding as you read this book, I have divided it into five sections:

- *Part I*:   Housing As a Tradition of Personal Shelter
- *Part II*:   The Circles of Life: Re-energizing Through Your Own Healing House
- *Part III*:   Awareness As the First Step to Self-Renewal
- *Part IV*:   Adapting the Physical Realm to the Spiritual— How Do We Change the Way We Build Houses?
- *Technical Appendix*

The first part will tell you about the birth of our housing tradition, why we have the houses we have, why our choices are often limited, and how we decide where we will live. Part II will lead you to an understanding of the links to the natural world and why they are necessary to a Healing House. Part III will open new doors of understanding to the natural world, and Part IV will talk about how we can help in the healing of that natural world so it can sustain life infinitely.

The Technical Appendix is for those who want to understand more clearly some of the technical elements in a Healing House—for example, what passive solar heat is, how it works, and how to design it to get its free advantages. It also describes materials, heating and cooling systems, and other elements that make a house energy efficient and increase its comfort, in more depth than was given you in the chapters themselves. None of the technical information is so complete that you could build a house from it, but it is enough for you to understand all the terms involved and to know whether you are talking to a builder who understands how to create a Healing House for you. The last section of the Technical Appendix deals with Multiple Chemical Sensitivities on a very abbreviated level and gives you a list of products that are less harmful to humans and the environment than many that we all use now on a daily basis in our homes.

Appendix references will be denoted by superscript numbers followed by letters, within the chapters. For example, in Chapter 5, the references to the Appendix would be [5A], [5B], [5C], and so on. Footnotes will only be designated by superscript [2] numbers, and all footnotes will follow the Appendix at the back of the book.

Following the Notes section is a Bibliography for those who wish to learn more and perhaps access some truly technical information about how to build energy-efficient, resource-efficient, environmentally friendly, passive solar homes using some of the new technologies.

PART I

◆   ◆   ◆

Housing As a Tradition of Personal Shelter

C H A P T E R   1

◆   ◆   ◆

Our Homes As Extensions of Our "Selves"

"We shape our buildings, and afterwards our buildings shape us."
— Winston Churchill[*]

It is important to understand that our homes are truly extensions of ourselves in perhaps an even more profound way than we realize when we say that people buy homes to fit their needs (or at least to fit the way they see themselves and their needs at that moment in time). We buy our image of what we "belong" in; then we add our own particular mix of interior color, material, furniture, and art that feels comfortable to us.

So often I have worked with clients who wanted far more than they could afford, and houses that didn't seem to fit their evident personas even a little bit. I fell in love with one such young couple the minute I saw them because they looked so "un-Dallas." He had a couple-of-days' beard, a mustache, glasses, and longish hair, and was dressed in a workshirt and jeans. His passive, smiling, and adoring wife was in a simple T-shirt and pants. He worked for a railroad, and she worked for a bank. Bouncing around them with a million questions a minute was a bright-eyed girl of four or five. They told me they had been prequalified at a bank for a $125,000 house, then they showed me plans for a Georgian-style 3,000-plus square foot (sq.-ft.) mansion with a colonnaded front porch, large living room, dining room, family room, kitchen, and master bedroom/bath on the main floor, and three

---

[*]Churchill liked this statement so much that he used it twice, first in 1924 at the English Architectural Association, then in 1943 upon the occasion of requesting that the bombed-out Parliament be rebuilt exactly as before. The first time, he said, "There is no doubt whatever about the influence of architecture and structure upon human character and action. We make our buildings and afterwards they make us. They regulate the course of our lives."

◆1

bedrooms above. The father, who did all the talking, said he would require a "few" changes because he wanted an office on the first floor, but they would cut costs by not finishing the second floor. When I asked where the office would go, he said he wasn't sure, but he wanted it somewhere immediately behind the elaborate, colonnaded porch. When I asked where the little girl would have her room, he said she would probably share their room or have a bed in the dining room for the moment.

I gently tried to tell them that they might be happier with a smaller, better designed house, and volunteered to find them one in a plan book that we could alter. I did the research and faxed them some designs a week or so later. When they returned, the man brought the picture of his original house back again. None of the ones I had found were right, he said, in spite of the fact that they met the physical needs he had described. When I finally asked exactly what it was about that house that he liked most, he said, "It looks like I want a house to look. I've been poor all my life, and I want to feel like I've really made it. We've saved most of my wife's salary for ten years to get a house like this."

That was hard to argue with because I knew that the man wouldn't realize that it didn't do for him what he thought it would until he tried to *live* in it. If he had the kind of job that required entertaining a lot, or if he lived a daily lifestyle in which he circulated to parties in similar houses, maybe it would *live* the way he thought it would. But I knew that when he realized he could skateboard with his daughter in the gigantic family room, he might wish he'd left that space in the backyard and used some of that ten years' worth of savings to take a trip around the world—or just kept it for a rainy day.

So the first thing you need to do when you look for a house that will *heal* your spirit is to think about yourself and *who you really are—not who you were in another life or who you think you would like to be in this one*. Then, remember that the house, in order to feel good to you, must allow you to "play" in it and around it. "Play" means let out *your own happy child* and relax, as children do when they play. What is your happy child inside going to feel like if you're saddled with more debt than you are comfortable with, with a house you have to spend every spare minute cleaning because you can't afford help? My guess is that your happy child would rather go fishing!

That sweet, unassuming man in the previous example works 12 to 14 hours a day. When he gets home, he wants to crash in a comfortable chair and read the paper while his wife puts his dinner in front of him. Is he going to be able to do that in his grand house? Where is a comfy old lounger going to go in it? He's probably going to feel as if he should hide *it*—as well as himself in his work clothes—in the unfinished upstairs area. The house takes up most of the lot, as these grand houses in Dallas do more and more lately. Where is he going to play with that charming, inquisitive, and active child? Where is the kid going to look for snails and worms in a garden or build a playhouse out of an abandoned shipping box? Where is she going to wiggle her toes in the grass and watch for birds in the trees? Not in *their* backyard, and not even in the nearby area, because every block is filled with great big, pretentious houses on small lots. No spacious backyards. No parks.

Who are these houses serving? Dare I say that it is the building industry only? The homebuying public has been sold a bill of goods that bigger is better, grander is more impressive, and impressive equates to happiness. We need the right kind of brick, the perfect flooring system, lighting designed by professionals inside and out, the designer colors of the day on our walls and in our sheets, and above all, the approach must be a frontal assault of finery not only better than the Joneses, but *better than ourselves*. It must be *the person we think we want to be*. It must be our *new self-image*.

Why It's Hazardous Buying a Home That Way

Is the above situation dangerous? Of course. If the place we call "home" isn't a *homey place* for our real selves, then we will never feel comfortable. If we never feel comfortable, we will never be able to truly relax. If we can never really relax, then we certainly can't heal, because our bodies will never be in balance. *Balance* is such an ancient word, yet it is so little considered today. The ancient Chinese philosophers called it the *yin* and the *yang*—balancing the two sides of selves, balancing the inner and the outer, the right and the left. To find this balance in our lives, the yin of our soul self—that which we really are when we are alone in the dark with no one at all to answer to but the most basic part of ourselves—must be able to blend with its yang external environment so each—our yin and our yang—can give each other nourishment.

An example of our environment giving us nourishment (which you can do yourselves) happens with trees and people. Sometime when you are very tired and burned out, go outside to a fairly large tree in a quiet environment. Lean your back against the tree with your feet slightly away from the base. Put your arms back and to your sides, embracing the tree. Close your eyes and just relax. Silently, slowly, ask the tree to give you energy. Wait, and feel its flow pour into you. It doesn't happen in seconds, but it does happen in five or ten minutes. You'll be amazed. You will never again think of a tree as "just a tree." *That* is precisely the kind of energy a Healing House should give you. It is, after all, made of the wood of a living being—a tree.

The second danger in buying or building a house *for the person we think we want to be* is that when that image we are creating is not real, it will change often. There is always the chance that, after that self-image changes, you will be in a home that you then have a hard time getting out of, in which case Shakespeare's admonition "To thine own self be true" has even more far-reaching implications than a simple student of literature might have thought. Perhaps that is why the national average occupancy of a new home is seven years. We take seven years to find out that the "image" we bought for ourselves wasn't really comfortable, so we continue to look for what we think we want, and the cycle begins again because we have never really understood that what we want is a *house that heals our spirits.*

© 1997 Barbara Harwood

This house, slightly out of proportion to the needs of two people, actually caused the eventual demise of its owners. The so-called House of the People, built in Bucharest, Romania, by former president Nicholai Ceaucescu and his wife, Elena (often called greedy and materialistic by her "subjects") caused a revolution. They were captured and eventually shot by a firing squad, and even though no blood was spilled on the castle's imported carpets, nobody still knows what to do with this "house."

◆   ◆   ◆

Homes and Their Histories—
Extensions of Human Traditions, Cultures, and Climate

If our homes are "extensions" of us, then it might be logical to assume that the way we *create* buildings must be organized using the analytical model we humans use to "produce" other things. That is, Step One: What is the desired result of our creativity? Step Two: What materials are needed? Step Three: How do we assemble these materials to achieve the desired result?

Perhaps, to a certain extent, homes are still planned using that analytical model by individuals and families. Certainly in a rural countryside anywhere in the world, you see the equivalent of a "barn-raising" when a home or barn needs to be built. Friends gather materials from the forest or the soil and get together to put them up in some pattern that has been established as the acceptable norm for that culture. When they're finished, they hook up the local version of a pot-bellied stove to its flue pipe exhaust, light a fire; and sit down in its shelter to eat, drink, and celebrate.

Often, when you enter a home or barn built that way anywhere in the world, whether a wood-frame art studio to replace a burned-down one in Texas, an underground house in Romania, an adobe house in New Mexico, or an igloo in the Arctic, there is a feeling inside it that somehow the human spirit has been ennobled by that endeavor. Present there, in some rudimentary form, is that which Indian shamans call "the healing spirit," because the love and concern that brought that group of people together to accomplish that task for their friends is left behind as an integral part of that building. But perhaps that's not all.

There is a combination of factors that, individually, would not lead us to an understanding of how to create a *residence* of healing, but which, taken together, can let us experience within our homes the *integration* of those three legs of the footstool we call living to the maximum: the physical self, the emotional self, and the spiritual self. It is often a bit impractical for all of us to have "house-raisings" for ourselves, so in our search to understand what it is that gives a house magical energy, we have to figure out exactly what that combination of factors is. Before we can find it, we have to define it. Before we can do that, we have to understand how healing buildings have been created by those in our long-forgotten past.

Our Ancestors and Their Building Sites

In ancient societies, as well as in our own, placement of buildings on the land was the first consideration, but for considerably different reasons. No Realtor or builder said, "Location, location, location," but, nevertheless, they understood that it was one of the most crucial parts of ensuring that they would have a house that was compatible with their spirit, that nurtured their innermost depths. Primitive cultures that are still scattered throughout the world give us a hint of the methods that have been used to select building sites through hundreds of thousands of years of human history; and research into ancient buildings and their relationship to the earth, sun, and moon is providing even more clues.

In Paul Devereux's captivating book *Symbolic Landscapes*, he describes the intimate relationship between existing aborigines and the earth, as well as the traditions they have carried down through the centuries with them, which, sadly, are now fading away. The land they live on, cross through, and occupy, he said, is *part of themselves*, and many of their rituals involve renewing contact with that part where they and the land are inseparable. Those traditional rituals involve certain specified places during what he calls "Dreamtime," or time before recorded history that people in those societies now often recall in dreams.

During that Dreamtime, Devereux said, the aborigines believed the earth to be "just a flat, featureless and uninhabited plain." Then at a certain point in this mythic past, giant, semihuman totemic figures emerged from beneath the surface of the plain and started to wander in various directions. As they did so, they carried out the everyday tasks familiar to the aborigines of today. "They camped, made fire, dug for water, defecated, performed ceremonies, and so on. In doing this they left traces which formed the topography, the flora and fauna that can be seen today." Once they departed, they left behind those features as "sacred sites." He went on to say:

> The very paths the Dreamtime beings took across the land were sanctified. The events of the Dreamtime imbued the landscape with a metaphysical power or "life essence"—*kurunba, miwi,* or *djang.* It would be easy but dangerous for us, with our cultural background, to think of this in simplistic terms of "energy." "Numinosity" gives perhaps a better sense.[1]

Lest anyone fear that this esoteric language about Dreamtime is an indication of people who didn't live in reality, let me quote a well-known 20th-century writer, Lawrence Kushner, who also wonders whether humans can imprint the land they cross in some way:

> Late one Friday evening, I walked home through a . . . late March snow. I had the universe to myself and that unequaled joy of making the only footprints in the new snow. Occasionally, I turned and walked backwards so I could watch the tracks I had just created. Later that night it warmed up . . . and the next morning there was not a trace of white to be found. But as I walked back retracing my steps, it was as if the footprints remained. Perhaps there are traces people leave behind them in space and time as they make their way through the universe. Traces that cannot be eradicated. Through kings and wars and volcanoes. Traces that tell all.[2]

Our Mystic Awareness

"Numinosity," or just a mystical sense—whatever we call it—covers the span from prehistory to today. And it doesn't mean that people who *feel* these mystical beginnings, whether an aboriginal Indian or a working rabbi from New England, are somehow slipping 'round the bend. Paul Devereux thinks that it means the opposite:

> The Aborigines distinguish between the physical and metaphysical landscapes they inhabit, and have a clear and vivid knowledge of the physical process in nature around them. Their mythic awareness should not therefore be confused with naivete in any way. It is rather that the mythic land is interfused with the physical landscape and they *know how to relate the two aspects.*[3]

In modern medical terms, this ability to "relate the two aspects" could be translated into right-brain, left-brain differentiation. In modern *meta-physical* terms, it could be related to techniques of meditation in which the person is able to meld the conscious self with deeper unconscious processes and bring them to revelation, or to feel a companionship with all creation. But one way or another, this "mythic awareness" is part of the human memory and impacts decisions we make and the way we feel about our lives in crucial areas of functioning, such as where we live.

In prehistory, and in some cases, during recorded history, sanctified pathways and mythic sites became sacred sites, imbued with powers that humans who lived on or near them believed could influence their physical and spiritual selves when they were in contact with them. "Because the physical land embodies their spiritual life," Devereux says, "aborigines have a relationship with their home territories that looks like, but is utterly different to [sic], Western concepts of patriotism or ownership. Rather it is a life-giving participation."[4]

That relationship between human "energy" and well-being and a relationship to the earth is not unique to Australian aborigines. Indeed, it seems to be multiculturally imbedded in mythology. Our native ancestors, the American Indians, viewed the land in much the same way—as shared ownership of all mankind with the Great Spirit. In 1854, the "Great White Chief" in Washington made an offer for a large area of Indian land and promised a "reservation" for Native American people. Chief Seattle's reply has been described as the most beautiful and profound statement on the environment ever made. I quote from it:

> How can you buy or sell the sky, the warmth of the land? The idea is strange to us. If we do not own the freshness of the air and the sparkle of the water, how can we sell them? Every part of the earth is sacred to my people. Every shining pine needle, every sandy shore, every mist in the dark woods, every clearing and humming insect is holy to the memory and experience of my people. The sap which courses through the trees carries the memories of the red man. The white man's dead forget the country of their birth when they go to walk among the stars. Our dead never forget this beautiful earth for it is the mother of the red man. *We are part of the earth and it is part of us* [author's emphasis]. The perfumed flowers are our sisters; the deer, the horse, the great eagle, these are our brothers. The rocky crests, the juices in the meadows, the body heat of the pony, and man—all belong to the same family.[5]

Holy Buildings on Sacred Sites

As humans felt the sacredness of the land, so it evolved that they felt this holiness should be consciously transferred *inside the buildings they created*. In Greece, the parent civilization of most Western mythology, homes were located by two principles: First, they were placed in a relationship to the sun that allowed temperature control of their interior environment throughout the year (which will be discussed in more detail in the Technical Appendix in the section on passive solar heating). Second, they were located near sacred sites because their temples were there. This is not unusual. Throughout the world, temples of many religious traditions have been placed on sites that adherents believed possessed a physical force or power to influence their lives. Those places were often also marked by specific land formations: mountains, hills, bodies of water, or ancient pathways. A classic example is the Parthenon in Greece, located on a rocky hill, now in the center of Athens; but once in the center of a ring with hills to the north, east, and west, and water to the south.

Vincent Scully, a Yale University architectural historian, went to Greece and Crete to study these ancient building sites and to document the structure and nature at those places that represented the deities to whom they were dedicated. It is clear from Scully's studies, Paul Devereux said, that "ancient Greeks clearly inhabited a mythologised landscape just as surely as did the indigenous peoples of Australasia."[6]

In a fascinating story of how a healing building was intimately and requisitely related to a sacred site, Devereux tells the story of Asklepios, the "god" of medicine; and Chiron, the good centaur. It is worth repeating here:

In Greek myth, Zeus is said to have fathered Apollo, a shamanlike mythical personage who seems to have been brought into Greek mythology from a remote northern source, and whose key Greek shrines were Delos and Delphi (where he supplanted the worship of Gaia, the earth mother). Apollo, in turn, was the father of Asklepios, the god of medicine. The cult of Asklepios eventually became more popular than that of Apollo. His major shrine and birthplace was understood by Greeks to be at Epidaurus, on the Poleponnese Peninsula across the Saronic Gulf from Athens, where his worship had commenced possibly as early as the sixth century B.C. Asklepios resulted from the union of Apollo with Coronis, who was killed by Apollo when she was unfaithful to him, even though she was pregnant with Asklepios. Apollo, himself a god of medicine, saved the unborn child and had him suckled by a goat and guarded by a dog. He entrusted his child's upbringing to Chiron, the good Centaur. Chiron taught medicine to the child, who perfected the art. He used snakes to find healing herbs, and these, and a rod and dog, became his symbols. (In many depictions, the rod has a snake or snakes wound round it forming the symbol of the "caduceus," still used today to symbolize the practice of medicine.)

Asklepios supplanted the worship of Apollo at Epidaurus, and it became a major center of healing and worship. . . . The temple and healing center at Epidaurus was only one of over 300 such sites in Greece. They were places where "temple sleep" took place. This involved those seeking divination (usually concerned with an ailment) going through a series of ablutions and purifications at the temple (such places always seem to have been associated with water sources) and *going to sleep in special cells called abatons* [author's emphasis] . . . which were special sleeping cells built adjacent to an ancient well . . . in the temple healing center.

Also included in this temple complex, Devereux said, were baths, a mysterious round structure called "Tholos," a place of lodging, and a theater and stadium.[7]

Holy Buildings, Sacred Sites, and Health

If it were the 1990s, this kind of complex would be called Esalen, or a full-service spa resort. The only difference that is we now seek relaxation, physical fitness, and what we are now calling, not coincidentally, "reconnectedness," not the approval of Asklepios, at these sites. It seems that even the Greeks, who had much less technical medical skill, fully understood that to heal illness of the body, a holistic approach was needed that would bring wellness to the entire mental, physical, and spiritual being.

Almost every ancient culture has its mythology linking land in some form with human beings and their health and well-being. The Celts had their "Hag's House" in Scotland, which means house of the Earth Goddess, and the Irish have "Navan Fort," which is not a fort at all, but a ritual enclosure or sanctuary outside Armagh, an important Christian ecclesiastical site. One of the myths behind Navan Fort will warm the heart of any '90s woman challenged to be all things to all people. It tells of the arrival at Emain, a nearby holy place established by an earlier queen, of the Goddess figure, Macha, and of her marriage to a local farmer. She asked him not to tell anyone she was divine. However, his tongue was somehow mysteriously loosened one night, and he bragged that his wife could run faster than the king's horses. His folly got him arrested and threatened with death. So

Macha had to race the king's horses to save his life. She not only won, but gave birth to twins along the way. The myth does not recount what she had to say to her husband when she got home, but Navan remains a center for special cultural festivities down to the present century.

Perhaps the most famous historical mythic site for Westerners today is Jerusalem. Which religious group it is most sacred to has been the subject of wars ever since its founding by King David 3,000 years ago. At the moment, at least two different religious groups wish to claim it as their own and settle their people there: the Jews and the Muslims; and Christians from around the world make spiritual journeys to it.

It is often the *buildings* in Jerusalem that have been the focus of the holy wars—*buildings which, to be sure, are on sacred sites*—but buildings, nonetheless. The Western Wall, sometimes called the Wailing Wall, of Solomon's last temple could justifiably be called the most sacred of all building remnants to Jews. The Church of the Holy Sepulchre is the holiest of holy sites to Christians, and the Dome on the Rock is one of the three holiest sites in the world to all Muslims. It is also situated on the same site where both of Solomon's temples were located, and many believe that it stands on the site named Mt. Horeb in the Biblical Torah story of the sacrifice of Isaac. There are literally hundreds of other sacred sites in and around Jerusalem: the Church on the Mount of Olives, where Jesus was thought to have prayed; the town of Bethel (Bethlehem) where Rachel's tomb and Jesus's birthplace are both located; and Nazareth, where Mary and Joseph's house probably stood. The Via Dolorosa, or pathway Jesus might have taken on his way to the crucifixion from the Temple Mount to the Church of the Holy Sepulchre is the site in Jerusalem that perhaps most closely resembles the aboriginal sanctified paths across the land. However, there are other pathways associated with the Holy City, including the road to Jericho.

Other sacred pathways have recently been demonstrated at various points around the world; including Nazca, in Peru, and Chaco Canyon, in New Mexico—home of the Anasazi Indians and now the Navajos. Many of these Chaco Roads, straight 30-foot-wide features branching out from the religious center at Chaco Canyon, have recently been revealed by infrared air surveys done by NASA, even though they have not been visible to the naked eye for many years, perhaps centuries. The mystery of the purpose of these roads has also been speculated upon by NASA scientists. They are thought to have connected structures called Great Houses, large buildings that functioned as ritual centers where people gathered periodically for festivals and ceremonies. It is speculated that the natives' homes were located along these societal blood vessels.

Shamanic Tradition

If these ancient traditions all across the globe are correct, then humans throughout history have had at least a subtle, if not profound, awareness of an innate connection with the land and places that their group had labeled its own special spiritual sites. They believed that their shelters, required at times during the year to shield them from the elements, could not separate them from these places on the land without cutting off a basic well-spring from which their energy derived. They took great pains to make sure that the memory of that connection was passed from generation to generation. This was formalized in most societies, according to anthropologists, by intermediaries, called shamans, who have been around for nearly as long as human beings have existed. Shamanism has taken many forms and existed in varying traditions, but when it exists, it is always at the heart of a culture, and is usually identified metaphysically with the nonhuman creatures who provided the first food, clothing, and shelter for humans.

The shaman, then, perhaps forged the first link between shelter-producing materials and the ritualistic traditions bound to the land. Those materials included the animal skins used in teepees; the earth used in primitive earth-sheltered buildings, including Navajo hogans; bundled grasses and straw used as building material; the limestone and clay of Indian cliff dwellings; the wood, branches, and grasses used in tropical area shelters; and birds, bones, feathers, and earthen colors used to decorate dwellings in all regions.

Beyond linking shelter-producing plants and animals to the land, shamanic culture typically also found and described for a culture a "center" of focus for the society, or more literally, an "axis" that was a conceptualized transport system from one level of consciousness to another. From this center, they moved between the other world and this plane and linked the humans here with their psychic or spiritual origins. According to Devereux:

> By symbolically traveling in trance states along this axis, the Shaman could ascend to heaven or enter deeply into the body of the Earth. . . . A mythological expression of this occurs in the Norse legend of the sovereign-shaman, Odin, who hung on Yggdrasil, the World Tree, or in the story of Christ, who was crucified on the cross.[8]

And the cross on which Jesus was crucified was located on a hill in the place that is the most sacred site in the Western and Middle Eastern cultures: Jerusalem, the center of the ancient, non-Asian world. This world axis of the shamanic culture is the point from which the sacred circle is originated and was often recorded in placement of the first stone of a building. The Muslim's Dome on the Rock illustrates a building at the center of a world axis, called an *omphalos*. Inside that building is the famous rock thought to be the same one on which Abraham was prepared to sacrifice Isaac.

Throughout the primitive world, there remains evidence of original omphalos. From the Indians of North America and their tent poles and totems; to the Etruscans in Italy with their *mundus*, or first fruits put into a hole and covered with a stone as the beginning of creation of a new city; from the Yakuts of Siberia, who believed a tree with eight branches was the golden navel of the world; to the Semangs of the Malay Peninsula, who believed their huge rock was and is the center of the world, this omphalos was the *"mental, non-material reality symbolically given a physical location."*[9]

Teotihuacan, larger in area than Imperial Rome during its peak period from 200 B.C. to A.D. 750, and a pilgrimage site for many of the ancient peoples of Mesoamerica, was laid out around a great central axis. Streets and plazas flowed outward from the axis marked by an omphalo*s,* and they were punctuated by great pyramids and palaces.

However, the omphalos location with which we in the West are *most* familiar is Stonehenge, a sacred site in England for over 5,000 years. Recent research has found that this spot was sacred from the time of its first use, when at its center stood a wooden circular structure Around the outer perimeter were gravesites of highly respected members of the privileged class, whose artifacts have recently been uncovered Eventually, the ancient Druids built the great circle of saracens (giant rocks standing on end) we now recognize as Stonehenge about 2,600 years ago. It is believed that the circle itself functioned as some sort of calendar, and it is known through observation that on summer solstice, the setting sun shines between two great pillars and exactly over the top of another, farther placed saracen outside the center circle. This huge circle of stones within a sacred site, although closed and guarded on the summer solstice, is still an inspiration for travelers from around the world.

That phenomenon of seeking sacred sites continues today in places such as Haleakala, the volcanic crater on the island of Maui, Hawaii. There is a whole cosmic energy pop-art form that treats the crater as a power source, according to Kathy Pulley, associate professor of religious studies at Southwest Missouri State University. She says, "Different groups can worship the earth in differing ways, and Haleakala acts as a centering point. The volcano represents a power center. Geysers may be considered impor-tant in the same way."[10]

This physical location, imbued with cultural significance and blessed with some sort of omphalos, was the origin of the building, town, or city that became linked to the human consciousness via unconscious mytholog-ical memory. Lawrence Kushner further explores place-memory in his entrancing book, *Honey from the Rock.*[11]

> Once we made our way down the hundreds of steps leading to the old cemetery of Safed. High in the Galilean hills, the town was for centuries the center of Judaism's greatest mystical revival. Buried on the side of the mountain lies Rabbi Isaac Luria, the Lion, The Ari, creator of the Lurianic Kabbala. So many visitors have come to light a candle here and deposit a pebble that the place is covered with stones and melted wax. And scrawled notes and crumpled prayers. And except for the unending breeze from the valleys below, there is stillness. Next to Luria is Alkabetz, author of *Lecha Dodi,* the great Sabbath love hymn. On the other side is Joseph Karo, author of the *Shulcan Aruch,* the great Code of Law. It was here that we found ourselves. Although we were not sure why we had come. And then after a few moments, we understood.
>
> The memories of the place had become part of it. Places and things never forget what they have been witnesses to and vehicles of and entrances for. What has happened there happened nowhere else. Like ghosts who can neither forget what they have seen nor leave the place where they saw it, such are the memories tied to places of ascent. Temples. Trees. Melodies. Objects. Words. Whatever they have witnessed is chis-eled into their substance.

Beneficent placement of buildings on the land is an integral part of the Asian system called *feng shui* (pronounced *fung-shway*), which emphasizes protection from bad influences and invites in the *chi,* or positive cosmic breath of the benevolent celestial dragon. Good chi assures health, wealth, success, and friends. One school of feng shui advocates the "green dragon" hill to the east, a "white tiger" slope to the west, and a range of hills sym-bolizing the "black tortoise" to your back. Advocates of this school believe that nestling your home in this geological surrounding gives the proper col-ors and protective masses to secure the proper yin and yang for your home.

Bless This House

After the ancients built their shelters following these natural practices and traditions to foster the in-dwelling centering of that mystical energy source, they required a next step—the blessing of their work. Most cultures have a consecration or "housewarming" ritual. The most important of these in Navajo culture is called The Blessingway. In a lovely traditional story sung and told by the Navajos of Arizona to Nancy Curtis in 1875, the origin of one such ceremony is told.

> Two blessed hogans, the first that ever were made—one in the east, the hogan of Hastyeyalti, god of sunrise; one in the west, the hogan of Hastyehogan, god of sunset. Long ago, the gods had no dwellings but met in the open, they say. Then they decided that they must have houses wherein they might hold their sacred rites and sing their holy songs. So the blessed hogans were made, and this song was sung to consecrate them. Even so, the same song is now used by Navajos to consecrate a new dwelling.[12]

Navajo hogans, even though they are only temporary buildings, abandoned when the flock moves on, are still consecrated to their owners in this manner. Each time the Navajos perform a sacred ceremony, they believe that they are breathing new life into their ancient traditions, summoning up spirits that have dwelt in their stark, spectacular landscape since the earliest dwellings were created.

They knew this mystical link of shelter to ancient ceremonies celebrating life passages and their connections to natural order had to be recognized and blessed by their compatriots, their culture, for that shelter to, in turn, bless them. Where has this search for the indwelling spirit in our homes been lost? Or has it? Does our common method of home construction and site planning play a part in destruction of those healthy links to the natural order in our buildings and towns and cities?

What Is It That Has Gotten in Our Way?

In today's "hurry up and build me a house" American culture, we invest scarcely a glimmer of consideration in the site upon which we build our home, compared to the efforts ancients made to ensure "blessed" sites. We often pick our lot based on price, the look of the neighbors' houses, the nearby school or shopping areas, proximity to our jobs, or a freeway that will get us there as fast as possible. If we are truly demanding, perhaps we will require a site with trees, but ecologically, that is about all most people are concerned about. Most consumers know little about orientation—that is, the placement of a home in relation to the sun or winds for maximum comfort and energy efficiency—let alone finding a sacred site and utilizing it to the maximum to ensure the inhabitants' connection to the earth's energy.

(In an earlier poem of my own, I explored the significance of places and the spaces that develop on them, how they impact us, and whether they cause *us,* or we cause *them.* You can find this poem in the front of this book on page vii.)

And so we say: Perhaps there is more to the way we select where we live than we consciously know. Maybe we need to be very careful about the locations in which we place our buildings. And, it's entirely possible that there are more reasons than the obvious ones that demonstrate why we need to understand how the places we settle—the places we build our shelters— relate to our bodies.

Our Bodies, First Cousins to Our Homes

"If a man is created, as the legends say, in the image of the gods, his buildings are done in the image of his own mind and institutions."
— Lewis Mumford[1]

Perhaps, in truth, the paradigms we have established for our shelters are in some way related to the flow patterns of our bodies. Maybe in some long ago mindset, our ancient ancestors "saw" buildings, villages, and cities in the same patterns that they recognized in their own bodies and transferred those blueprints to the development of their larger environment. Is it possible that, in truth, all we are able to do is see things in the same patterns over and over again? After all, we see the same pattern in the solar system and the galaxy as we see in the atom. We see the same pattern in a river flume as we see in a leaf or a tree. Maybe finding a pattern that *fits our particular selves,* understanding our own place within those larger patterns, is what we must do to find happiness and security in our surroundings, in our own lives.

It wasn't at all common for anyone but naturalists to see those kinds of patterns early in this century. The young Frank Lloyd Wright was the exception. He made the revolutionary connection between the body and the building when he first began as an architect: "Bowels, circulation, and nerves were new in buildings. But they had come to stay, and a building could no longer remain a mere shell in which life was somehow to make shift as it might."[2] Imagine talking in 1954 about flush toilets and sewer systems as the "bowels of a building," or the electrical system with its lights

and radios as the "nerves." Over time, we have used more and more biological terms to refer to building parts, anthropomorphizing, if you will, our
buildings.

The term now often used to describe the exterior shell of a building is
"skin." Famed Greek architect Alexander Tombazis of Athens said at a
recent World Renewable Energy Congress:

> We can learn a lot about how to build our buildings by looking at the
> skins on ourselves, plants, and animals. Our skin is the threshold between
> outside and inside space. The skins and leaves of plants and fruits are relat-
> ed to climatic parameters and other functional considerations, as the shell
> building is both its skin, its protection, and a threshold between the exte-
> rior and interior. I compare the skin of buildings to different kinds of skins
> of plants, animals, and human beings and contemplate on their similarities
> and differences, because we should always remember that many of our
> habits and patterns of living come from nature and were established there
> many thousands of years ago.[3]

If we are going to make ourselves comfortable in our living environments and create homes that are restorative and regenerative, then we need
to understand more about how our bodies and our buildings relate to each
other. To do that, we must think about how our ancestors, the earliest
humans, developed rudimentary shelter.

Connectivity

Of necessity, primitive peoples had connectivity with the earth and its
plant and animal life in their shelters. They had to use materials from the
earth to build their homes because those were the only materials available
in the Stone Age. They placed them directly on or in rock or earth, con-
necting them organically to their earth environment. They connected with
the sky by leaving holes open in the tops of their homes for air circulation
and to exhaust smoke. They walked on earth inside their buildings.
Sometimes that earth was kiln-dried brick or tile made from native clay.
Sometimes it was the rock in the cliff. Sometimes it was just packed earth,
tamped down and covered with woven rugs. Whatever it was, they *felt* that
connection between their feet and the soil, and sometimes, depending on
where they slept, they felt the connection between their whole bodies and
the soil. It wasn't necessary to recall their connection with the earth because

they were part of it, and it belonged to them. They were completely dependent on it and tied to it in the most fundamental sense.

An old stone, log, and thatch roof house in Romania.

© 1997 Barbara Harwood

© 1997 Barbara Harwood

The interior of an old earth shelter in Romania. The floor is natural earth, the furniture is all home-made, and the candles provide light.

Timbers from the site have been used to frame this building in Romania.

© 1997 Barbara Harwood

Over time, this traditional shelter became refined and ceremonialized to honor the building's organic connection to the earth. Those ceremonies stabilized in traditions that recognized the mystical relationship with earth that these people sensed, although probably not always cognitively, that their bodies needed to re-energize. As early shelter-makers struggled with the evolution of shapes and sizes of their shelters, those ceremonies were formalized to be certain that succeeding generations maintained the traditions that honored those mystical connections to the cycles and materials of the natural world, as in the Navajo creation story told during the Blessingway:[4]

> Of all these various kinds of holy ones that have been made, you the first one will be their thought, and you will be called *Sa'ah Naghai,* Long life. . . and you who are the second one, you will be their speech, and you will be called *Bik'eh Hozho,* Happiness. All will be long life by means of you two, and all will be happiness by means of you two.

We know the materials primitive cultures used and the natural cycles they honored. We see the same cyclical signs they did: the burst of new life on foliage in spring; the evening's setting sun; the smell of moist, clean air after a rain; and the refreshing coolness of a green arbor of trees overhead on a hot summer day. These are same the things we crave when our minds and bodies are fatigued by the hassle and pressures of everyday living. But what *exactly* was it that this mystical connection with the earth gave them?

Frank Lloyd Wright tried to describe this craving for the natural even as an 11-year-old boy:

> The first feeling was hunger for reality, for sincerity. A desire for simplicity that would yield a broader, deeper comfort was natural, too, to this first feeling. A growing idea of simplicity as organic, as I had been born into it and trained in it, was new as a quality of thought, able to strengthen and refresh the spirit in any circumstances . . . All around me, I might see beauty in growing things and, by a little painstaking, learn how they grew to be "beautiful." None was ever insignificant. I loved the prairie by instinct as itself a great simplicity; the trees, flowers, and sky were thrilling by contrast.[5]

Defining the energy that ancients sought and which we have so neglected is amorphous and difficult to articulate so it is little addressed in human discourse, but it is all around us and, from time to time, we are consciously aware of it. William James wrote about it in this famous passage:

Our normal waking consciousness, rational consciousness as we call it, is but one special type of consciousness, whilst all around it, parted from it by the flimsiest of screens, there lie potential forms of consciousness entirely different. We may go through life without suspecting their existence; but apply the requisite stimulus, and at a touch they are there in all their completeness.[6]

If natural materials and cycles re-energized them, perhaps the natural *evolution* of those materials was also a factor. Christopher Alexander, architect and professor at the University of California at Berkeley, says it is natural *processes and their slow natural evolution* that we are missing. He is quoted in Stewart Brand's remarkable book, *How Buildings Learn:*

Things that are good have a certain kind of structure. You can't get that structure except dynamically. Period. *In nature you've got continuous very-small-feedback-loop adaptation going on, which is why things get to be harmonious* [author's emphasis]. That's why they have the qualities that we value. If it wasn't for the time dimension, it wouldn't happen. Yet here we are playing a major role in creating the world, and we haven't figured this out. This is a very serious matter.[7]

In addition to the loss of those connections with natural materials, cycles, and evolution as we entered the industrialized age, there were other pressures at work. As we "perfected" our shelters and standardized more and more of the parts, we saw the need for conformity so the parts would fit. As we achieved more and more conformity, it gained a kind of existential importance. We wanted to make sure "our house" had the same "new good things" as "their house." It was, in the '50s, referred to as "keeping up with the Joneses." From "keeping up," it became oneupsmanship: "I make more money than Mr. Jones, so my house has to be better than his house so you will be sure to know that I am better than Mr. Jones." Values shifted. No longer was the connection to the earth that revitalized the soul and body seen as the overriding criterion for shelter selection. It was now a social issue—would the house I lived in present me in the light in which I desired to be seen? We allowed our self-worth to be defined by our shelter, instead of permitting our shelter to assist our naturally worthy selves in our own growth and our continued search for identity. We completely forgot the ancient traditions of maintaining our "selves" by restoring that link to the earth on a daily basis. And when we did that, we disconnected ourselves from the source of our greatest inspiration, the well-spring from which our physical wellness is derived, the true origins of our own wholeness.

A New Urban Myth

Somehow we sense we have missed *it*. When we don't have *it* in our homes, we are constantly fixing this or that to try to find it, even though we have not always defined what "it" is. There are scattered clues showing that some have understood what this connection to the earth that we need in order to be physically and emotionally healthy is all about. The Tucson Medical Center (TMC) was built in Arizona early in this century, originally as a rest sanatorium in the middle of what was one of the most beautiful and complete cactus gardens in the world. It has in-patient rooms that are *all*, without exception, on the ground floor and have large windows facing an outside courtyard patio. Birds land in miniature trees, hummingbirds flock to the sugar feeders hanging there, and tiny lizards run among the cacti. Daylight floods the rooms every day. Sun heats the hospital in winter, and overhangs keep out the sun in summer.

Marie Booth, one-time assistant administrator, described the value of these patios in "Patios for a Purpose," published in the August 1973 issue of the hospital's newsletter, *The Spokesman:*

> TMC, in its unique history and setting, has always used the benefits of the Arizona sun and air to supplement patient care. Believing in the aid to recuperation of relaxation, our patios have been designed for our patient's comfort . . . a place where they and their families can enjoy their togetherness much the same as at home. Every unit has its own patio and gardens. . . . We receive many compliments on the beauty of our patios and although we hope they add to the esthetic sense of the viewer, this is not their primary purpose. Tension during illness is a deterrent to healing. We sincerely believe that the serenity of our grounds and these quiet areas help our patients meet their medical care with calmness and confidence.[8]

My son was a patient at TMC for over a month one summer while he was attending the University of Arizona. His leg was severely fractured following a bicycle accident. It was a repeat of a similar break the year before when the car in which he was an occupant rolled, shattering his right femur and tearing his left leg apart at the knee. When his bicycle skidded on gravel during bicycle-team tryouts, the injured leg, secured with a long metal plate, flew up, causing a new fracture all the way to the top of the femur. Both accidents required bone grafts. One day I was discussing his medical situation with a surgical nurse there, explaining that he seemed to be healing faster at TMC than he had the summer before in a high-rise hospital in

Dallas where he had spent two months. She told me that nurses at TMC believed patients felt happier and healed better because they were exposed to the outdoors every waking minute. The woman who founded the hospital, she explained, had made a stipulation when she granted the land to build the hospital, that *every room had to have an outdoor view and be at ground level.*

I was very impressed and was determined to learn more about this remarkably prescient woman. My research, however, did not bear out her story. The sanatorium was largely created by Alfred W. Erickson, founder of Congoleum, who financed its initial construction as a tuberculosis sanatorium in about 1915. With the assistance of Erickson's funding, young New England physician, Dr. Bernard Wyatt, M.D., who had bought the land for $25 an acre along with two other doctors, built the administration building and four units he named for Indian tribes. Each unit was built around an open courtyard and contained eight patient rooms with individual screened porches. When Wyatt's funds ran low, he brought in Erickson, who offered to continue to finance the project, and he employed Wyatt as president and medical director. The major, and only, stipulation Erickson attached to his funding was that all proceeds from the hospital would flow back into research and patient care, not to stockholders. He said: "If any profits are made in one department, they will be used to carry on work in another, the real goal being a dividend in medical knowledge which will generally be distributed throughout the world."[9]

When Erickson died in 1936, his widow operated it until 1944, when she donated it to the city of Tucson with the single stipulation that the community raise enough money to convert it to a general hospital, and then operate it for five years. They did. The city assumed ownership in 1944.

After I learned of TMC's history, I was even more interested in what had been told to me: that Mrs. Erickson *required every room to have an outdoor view and access.* Where did this myth—for it was clearly an urban myth—come from? Nobody there knew, but yes, many had heard and believed that story to be true. Did hospital staff tell patients this tale? Many said they did, often because patients *first* commented on it. Did the story, and the atmosphere, help them heal? Most staff I talked to were convinced that patients, upon hearing the story and then being exposed to the natural elements outside their hospital rooms during the recovery period, healed more quickly and were happier during their stays. Perhaps these myths, like many ancient ones, originate in what we *innately sense to be true*, even though its beginnings are poorly understood by us. Maybe Dr. Wyatt believed that. Or, perhaps it was all accidental and he simply liked one-story adobe buildings—which were much cooler in summer in the days before air conditioning. Thus, he built TMC that way, and afterwards, people noticed that patients thrived there, which fed the myth. Perhaps we shall never know—any more than we will know the origins or most other myths, but that does not prevent us from recognizing their wisdom.

Building "Science"—Or Is It?

The basic need of our bodies to connect to natural elements in our shelters is, however, understood or discussed by few professionals in the building industry. Rare examples—architects such as Pliny Fisk of the Center for Maximum Potential Building Systems; Charles Durrett and Kathryn McCamant of *Co-Housing* fame; Frank Gehry; Antonin Predock; Sym Van de Ryn; Peter Calthorpe; Andres Duany; Elizabeth Plater-Zyberk; and perhaps others, follow the Frank Lloyd Wright tradition of blending the interior with the exterior and using natural materials to create a holistic relationship between humans, their shelters, and their planet. But there is little intercommunication between those who understand this natural connection with the elements and people who want and need it.

The building "sciences" are in between. I put "science" in quotation marks because building "science" is no more static and prescribed than medical "science." Both have the same flaws, and both, in their own ways, tackle the same problems. On the micro level, there are disease organisms in both buildings and people: bugs, mold, and rot in buildings that eventually destroy them; and bugs, pain, and deterioration in people that often kill them. On the macro level, the health of both buildings and bodies is affected by their shape, their size, and the exterior skin condition. Proper air circulation is necessary for both to function properly. Internal and external temperatures must be appropriate to the bodies of both. You can't build an igloo in Texas or an uninsulated courtyard adobe in Alaska any more than you could leave an unclothed human body standing in a snowdrift.

"Skin is the threshold between outside and inside space. The skins of plants and fruits are related to climatic parameters and other functional considerations," architect Alexander Tombazis said, "just as the skin of buildings must be."[10]

Nerve systems must be properly designed and functioning. If they aren't, in homes you get electrical shorts or worse. In human bodies, you get paralysis or a variety of neurological dysfunctions. The chemistry of materials placed inside must be appropriate. Human beings suffer when they drink water polluted with chemicals. Buildings (and their inhabitants) suffer when moisture stays inside walls, or when outgassing chemicals are used in material used to build them. Any chemicals and other waste materials inside must be appropriately and speedily removed from both for them to remain healthy.

When you begin to understand why buildings function as they do, you see that for every solution, there is another problem. In medical science, you solve one "illness" with a medication or operation that often causes something else to happen. Just as in medicine, building science researchers uncover new facts almost daily—new "medications" for houses with the kind of problems we have heard about on the television news. Moisture is causing walls to collapse in North Carolina. High winds are blowing houses apart in Florida. Cold drafts are freezing feet inside buildings in Chicago. Do the new "medications" work? Time will tell, but every house (unless it is an exact replica of the one next to it, facing exactly the same direction with the same exact flora outside) is a *unique* creation, just as every human body is unique. Both "house doctors" and medical doctors have to first understand the uniqueness of the "body" they must treat, then have the scientific knowledge to know what basic principles should be applied. They must also have intuitive knowledge about what might work, then know where to go to gather information that turns their hunches into reality. Both require constant study, continual updating of knowledge, and adaptation of old methods.

Not only are there many similarities between houses and bodies; there is also this amorphous, grander connection from one "living" entity to another. Both need a healthy environment outside not only to survive, but to thrive. People need healthy buildings and air and water. When we have neither, we have the high rates of disease (here, a hyphen in the word might also be appropriate: *dis-ease*) now surfacing in places such as East Germany, where heavy concentrations of aging, inefficient industries have polluted air and water to unsurvivable levels. If I saw the kind of pollution-related heart and lung disease that is now showing up in East Germany near a place I lived, it would *certainly* make me feel uneasy!

Buildings need a healthy exterior environment. One need only look at the acid rain decaying France's most treasured cathedrals, or the sulfuric acid fall-out from transport fuels eating holes in the magnificent ancient marble statuary and buildings in Italy. Even in America, our monuments and the older buildings in our inner city cores have been decayed and blackened by polluted air.

And our air, worldwide, needs healthy, energy-efficient buildings. When we burn fossil fuels to produce electricity in our gas appliances and furnaces, we add to the pollution that destroys buildings and people. The less energy efficient the building, the more fuel is consumed keeping it heated and cooled.

If these healthy relationships between our bodies and our buildings and their exterior environment is disturbed, what does it do to us? To our feelings of well-being? To our "comfort" and the solace we seek? Is this "healing spirit" we seem to long for and find so ethereal related to our physical well-being as well as our mental well-being? If it has been for eons, why wouldn't it be true now? And, therefore, shouldn't our society, when it builds homes—and other buildings—follow that medical credo: "At the very least . . . do no harm."

Now that we have identified these forces and relationships, *shouldn't we go even further and build homes that become places of healing for all who live in them?*

◆   ◆   ◆

C H A P T E R 4

◆   ◆   ◆

The Financial Marketplace, the "Golden Rule," and Your House

At the moment, the home you live in, as well as the building industry itself in America, is largely defined outside of the normal consumer marketing channels. It is true that consumers make choices about their housing, thinking that *they themselves* are actually the ones *making* the decisions. But look a little deeper, and you find that they are not. The housing market is truly defined *for us* by the financial marketplace. The financial "golden rule" really does rule in the housing industry: *The guys with the gold make the rules.* If the bankers like the house itself and feel it will have resale value in that market, and they like the borrower and the financial history and collateral he or she provides, the house can be built. If they don't, unless the homebuyer is independently wealthy and can build without borrowing for a home loan, it can't.

So we have a culture in which the larger personal desires and preferences of the individual are secondary to the image of "what will sell," *as perceived by the lender*. If we desire any kind of housing that is different— for example, "green buildings," which are just beginning to move into the mainstream (development that co-exists compatibly with earth and all its materials), then the paradigm in place at the moment that often rejects new kinds of buildings has to be changed.

Never was that fact brought home more clearly than in a situation that occurred recently. A custom buyer with whom our company was working on a very basic, earth-friendly, energy-efficient, passive solar home was rejected by the lending underwriter (who had, ironically, requested that we bring "green buildings" to them) because it had no fireplace, no garage, and a gravel driveway, among other things. She said that it would have "no resale" value without those features. She also felt that because it was on ten acres out in the country and "nobody wants to worry about taking care of ten acres and maintaining a major vegetable- and fruit-producing garden," it would have less resale value.

Last, but not least, the bank's underwriter said that at 2,400 sq. ft., it was "too small" for the area and the ten acres. The fact that the family designed it, wanted to live there for the rest of their lives, and the wife was going to stay home precisely to raise the gardens and her children, meant nothing. Their "comfort values," their need for the kind of healing respite and outdoor activity they had designed for themselves into their own home and site, were not heard, or at least not understood, in the *financial* market-place. Since they needed the maximum mortgage to qualify, they were turned down.

Frank Lloyd Wright, the Bankers, and the Builders

The situation mentioned above is not new, nor is it unique to our time. In 1910, when Frank Lloyd Wright was striking out with what is now rec-ognized as a brilliant innovation in architectural design—the "prairie house"—bankers rejected his plans. To get the homes built, he had to go *outside* the standard financial marketplace. Years later, he said that "bankers at first refused to loan money on the 'queer' houses, so friends had to be found to finance the early buildings."[1]

That same bank that would not lend on our "green" building will lend any day of the week to a 5,000-sq.-ft. home on a 7,500-sq.-ft. lot in a crowd-ed subdivision behind a suburban brick wall. Builders, too, *prefer* to build homes like that because they are *the local paradigm* in the marketplace and, therefore, easy to sell. People move to a new area, and a real estate agent they have picked to help them find a new home says, "Oh, yes, these hous-es are quite different from where you came from. You know, *everybody here* in Dallas wants a big all-brick home with . . . " or "Everybody here in New England wants a New England Cape Cod," or "Everybody here in San Diego wants Spanish style," and that's all she shows them.

So the family finds the house that comes closest to what they want (in the middle of the stressful situation called "relocation"), and they submit their mortgage application to a bank. They, thereby, have perpetuated the mythology that "everybody wants one of these." It might be quite a different matter if there were other options, but since the type of house already prevalent in the local area is *what is selling*, lenders are reluctant to let builders try anything else. Why is it selling? Because it's there. This is not a riddle. Houses are not like cameras or shoes, where there is a wide variety from which a customer can choose. In any particular area, there is one basic type of housing with differences only in size, room arrangements, and interior decor—not in exterior appearance.

That local paradigm becomes, predictably, the type of design with which subcontractors are familiar, so it is also *easier* for the builder to get the work done. At that point, contractors and subcontractors influence what housing is today, because, when there is plenty of work, they are often loath to bid on buildings that are fundamentally unlike the building traditions to which they are accustomed. Wright had the same problem getting them to do anything different.

> Millmen would soon look for the name on the plans when the plans were presented for estimates, read the name of the architect, and roll up the drawings again, handing them back with the remark that "they were not hunting for trouble"; contractors more often than not failed to read the plans correctly, so much had to be left off the buildings.[2]

© 1997 Johnny Walker

House designs we have nicknamed the "Plano Special."

Thus does a paradigm, or accepted pattern of building style, get implanted in an area. The Dallas area is famous for what has come to be called the "Plano Special." This type of house often has a dozen little hip roof details, a turret here or there, a circular eating area at the end of the kitchen, a master bath larger than the bedroom I was raised in, a two-story tall atrium (often with windows facing west), and utility bills larger than most families' mortgage payments.

Somehow we have arrived at a point in our country where we think that these homes—the larger the better—are the mark of a "successful" family, a family of "substance," or, as Garrison Keillor would say, a family "where all the men are strong, the women are good-looking, and the children are above average." It is believed to be the visible sign of a family who has "arrived." In most cases, the only things considered are whether or not the design meets this "status criteria," and whether it fits the prescribed list of qualifications—both at the bank so that it will be perceived as a candidate for quick resale—and at the traditional builder's desk so it will be familiar to subcontractors. *Comfort*, in its most profound sense, the long-term health of the residents, the durability of the building, and the monthly cost to pay its utility bills do not usually enter the initial equation. Add to that the fact that buyers typically have so little time to consider what they might *truly like to have in a home* that they take the path of least resistance, and you have the formula for what I call "home-human discontinuity"—that is, a home to which they never feel spiritually and emotionally connected.

How does a family feel living in that house designed, in essence, by bankers and builders? Does it bring solace to the tired spirit, serenity to a weary soul? Let me relate the experience of one young family in just such a house.

The Northern Nightmare

A young Illinois couple moved out of a small inner-city apartment near their jobs because they were ready to start a family. They wanted, to quote the young wife, "a big yard with trees for the children to play in, a big family kitchen, four bedrooms for future growth, and a play area for the children." Some of their other requirements included being near a place of worship, a grocery store and drug store, and having a convenient commute to downtown via some major artery—either railway or highway.

As things generally happen, their first priority was what they looked for initially—the large lot with trees. They found that lot in a suburb 30 minutes northwest of downtown Chicago called Buffalo Grove. A builder had a subdivision partially finished. The plan choices shown to them included a large, two-story, four-bedroom home with a large kitchen. They picked it, bought the lot, and began.

As the structure began to go up, the couple started to see things that *did not fit* their vision for their new home. The workmen were careless with the trees on the lot. When the builder wouldn't listen to their complaints about the trees, the couple finally had to put their own orange string barrier around the drip line of the trees to protect them. Strange configurations were used in the framing wood. The husband called it "slap-dash framing." When they complained to the builder's office, they were told it was customary practice and there was nothing wrong. They were assured that it would "meet code." Then they noticed that the walls were "thin" for the cold Chicago climate, and had only Fiberglas bat insulation, no exterior sheathing, as they had seen in the houses we build here in a much milder climate than Chicago. When they asked the builder's office about the lack of insulation, he said that exterior insulated sheathing would have been "an extra," but they could no longer get it because it was too late, and that this builder used 2" x 4" walls, not 2" x 6", "because that's how it's done here."

This contentious relationship continued throughout the building process. Trim was not cut properly, and popped out under cabinets. There was a gap under the floor trim in the living room and entryway, and you could feel cold air coming through. And so on. When a final letter of protest was written by the couple's lawyer to the builder, the reply was, in essence, "My banker, the appraisers, and city officials have approved our buildings and our building methods. We cannot afford to 'customize' your home with the special details you describe [this was a $285,000 house!] because this is a tract home." The bank wanted the construction loan paid back as soon as possible by a buyer who had a mortgage to lower risk. The builder wanted to be in and out as quickly as possible to maximize profit and reduce interest carry.

Rush-rush building *is fine if it doesn't get out of control*. I submit that it is out of control when energy efficiency isn't added to a $285,000 house in a climate as severe as Chicago, and when the builder tells you he can't fix things that are wrong because a home in that price range is a "tract" house! Not to mention all the other elements that indicated an out-of-control building process.

Did the bankers complain about the way this builder constructed the building? Did they *worry* about making a mortgage on that poorly built house in the same way they worried about making a loan on a "green" building? Did they consider that the utility bills will keep going up and up from the inefficient point where they started, and perhaps ten years from now when *every home will be built efficiently*, no one will want to buy this one? Will they have as much fun getting it back as they did the properties in the savings-and-loan crisis of the early '80s? I hope so, because, mark my words, this *will be the next loan crisis.* Nobody will want those energy-guzzler homes, especially after deregulation hits, and bills for residential customers soar (to foot the bill for industrial customers who will buy power from new, small power providers with small-scale cheap power). (For more on utility deregulation, see Chapter 17.) No, those things were undoubtedly not considered because that home fit *the bankers' image* of the *kind of house that will sell* in the northern suburbs of Chicago, and the builder had built hundreds of others of the same poor, energy-inefficient quality. So why would the bankers consider anything except the builder's credit standing?

Is this any way to make decisions about what kinds of houses get built? I don't need to answer that for you, but of course it isn't. However, as with many systems that are established and bureaucratized in this country, large banks have become big bureaucracies. No longer can employees *know* the people they lend money to and make decisions based on common sense. Because of that, many mistakes are made for which we, as individual home-buyers and members of a society that is becoming more and more unsus-tainable, pay in the short term. The bankers are the ones who will pay in the long term when the houses they stamp with their approvals are no longer saleable *at any price.*

How do we turn this around? Well, two things have to happen. Builders have to establish a new pattern, first of all. As usual, change happens most readily when a catastrophe jolts someone awake. What may perhaps be a small sign of that happened last year when 2,500 or so stucco houses failed in the Carolinas because of improper sealing from wet weather. It had also happened a couple of years earlier when Hurricane Andrew hit south Florida and blew buildings apart. Builders have been forced, in those areas, to think about *how they build homes.*

Forcing bankers and builders out of long-cherished design concepts is the second task. There is no reason why every house in America should not be designed with passive solar (heat from the sun shining through windows appropriately placed) as its primary heating source. *Passive solar is free—both in the design and the heat you receive.* All you have to do is put the windows in the right place and protect them from summer sun *during the design phase.* There is no reason why landscaping can't be an integral part of the energy-efficient design. And, there is no reason for a large number of the energy-intensive requirements that subdivisions have, such as very wide streets and concrete or asphalt driveways everywhere, except that they are a habit with building departments, and, therefore, with builders and bankers who review the plans. We will get into specific changes and how they can and should be made in Chapter 13 and the Technical Appendix, but in the meantime, you, as a consumer, have to *change the way you think about the home you will live in.* You have to demand something different in large enough numbers so that both bankers and builders will begin to listen.

You have to demand a Healing House.

PART II

The Circles of Life Re-Energizing Through Your Own Healing House

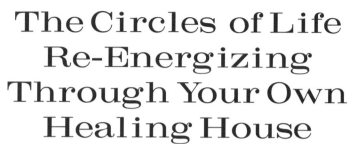

We spin
    at once and always
    circles lead us onward
    from the atom
    to the molecule
    to the planet
    to the solar system
    to the galaxy
    to the universe.

So with the life
    from the tiniest invisible seeds
    to the newborn
    to the family
    to the friends
    to the neighborhood
    to the town or city
    the state, the country
    and the planet.

Like a child's stacking toy
    or the Russian dolls
    which fit one into the other
    until the game ends
    with the smallest or largest
    a child can find.

But in real time
    real life within our planetary
    circle
    is there structure we can
    predict?
Is there a different kind of
    gravity
    holding it all together
    down to the smallest units?
Is a smaller circle distorted by an
    absence
    which in turn
    distorts a larger circle
    and yet a larger one?
Is it for me, then, that the universe
    was created?
What is it I should do
    to hold together
    my unique spot in the circles?
Will I recognize the choice when it
    comes?

— Barbara Bannon Harwood[5A]

The Ultimate Good Vibes—
Integrity in Buildings

"Houses are built to live in, not to look at."
— Francis Bacon, in *Essays*

There are many terms in our culture for defining people who are comfortable with themselves and their world. "Centered" refers to those who meditate, as well as to some who are uncannily focused and balanced even though they don't. When I was growing up, we also referred to those people as "knowing what they're about," or "having integrity." "Being real" was a '60s term. "Good vibes" was an '80s phrase for people or buildings or art—things we *look at or live with.* When we are frantic and anxious, we can't give off "good vibes." When a house is dark or mechanically noisy (as differentiated from the noise nine-year-old boys make, for example) or has bad air, it can't have "good vibes." It can't have what Frank Lloyd Wright called "integrity."

> In speaking of integrity in architecture, I mean much the same thing that you would mean were you speaking of an individual. Integrity is not something to be put on and taken off like a garment. Integrity is a quality *within and of* the man himself. So it is with a building. Naturally, should you want to really live in a way and in a place which is true to this deeper thing in you, which you honor, the house you build to live in as a home should be integral in every sense. Integral to site, to purpose, and to you.[1]

Wright called his houses, where everything was "genuine and harmonious," Usonian homes.

The Usonian house, then, aims to be a *natural* performance, one that is integral to site, integral to environment, integral to the life of the inhabitants. A house integral with the natural materials—wherein glass is used as glass, stone as stone, and wood as wood—and all elements of the environment go into and throughout the house. Into this new integrity, once there, those who live in it will take root and grow. . . belonging by nature to the nature of its being.[2]

© 1997 Barbara Harwood

Usonian homes create a warm, flexible environment, proportioned to human scale, which promote family unity and grow organically out of the surrounding landscape.

Then, astonishingly for a book written in the early '50s, Wright *talks about how* we receive energy *from our buildings.*

> Whether people are fully conscious of this or not, they actually derive countenance and sustenance from the "atmosphere" of the things they live in or with . . . we receive many letters from people who sing praises for what has happened . . . telling us how their house has affected their lives.[3]

Forty years ago, Wright recognized something that people rarely talk about—the fact that we actually pick up what he could only call "countenance and sustenance" from buildings. I call it absorbing energy from the vibrations of materials around us, but I am the first to admit it that it probably goes even beyond that to something we can't yet label. First, why do we absorb energy from materials?

It is a well-known scientific fact that molecules move, even in "solid" materials. They just move slower in stone than in lighter materials, such as air, for example. But they are there. There is "space" around and within molecules, which are made up of atoms. And all of us who have gone past fifth grade have seen the diagram of an atom. It is *mostly* empty space spotted with a neutron, some protons and electrons. The vibrations that set atoms and molecules in motion have also been measured innumerable times by physicists. Why does this molecular motion happen? Because of something called "wave energy."

A simple example of wave energy is the sound coming from your radio. That sound is carried on a "radio wave" that is an electromagnetic wave with a certain frequency, or speed. We have given those "frequencies" numbers, so that we say Station BARB is at an AM frequency of 1410 kilocycles.

A wave of energy can also vibrate other things. So what is the frequency of a wave that would vibrate, say, a wall in our house? This is one you can easily feel even without putting a specific frequency number on it. Just put a teenager with a drum set in a room, and feel the vibration in *all the walls* in your house (and your head, and your body! Hey, kid, get a flute!).

Or feel the vibrations when a plane goes overhead. In the opera, even before the aphorism about "when the fat lady sings," came the one that asked if the soprano could "break a glass." To do that, she had to reach a vibration with her voice that would match the vibration of the molecules that held the glass together. Her vocal vibration and the one that drives apart the molecules in that glass, match, blend, and flow together to do their collective damage (and usually to give her artistic recognition down through the ages)!

Trucks going down a highway near a building will cause it to vibrate. Literally, everything in this tangible world holds together because the frequency that would break it apart has not struck it—because "the vibes are right." An example of what happens to buildings when the "vibes are wrong" is an earthquake. Those intensely destructive vibrations may be the ultimate "bad vibes"!

So what is the equivalent of "bad vibes" or "good vibes" for the human body? What kind of vibrating is the material in our home doing? How are those vibrations reaching our bodies, and what effect do these vibrations have when they hit us?

Vacation Vibes, Getting Away, or . . .

Have you ever gone someplace on vacation where you felt an incredible sense of peace—even beyond that which you could explain by the

simple fact that you are far away from the obligations of the normal worka-
day world? And conversely, have you been on vacations where, for no reason you were consciously aware of, you felt more fatigued when you
returned than when you left?

I believe relaxation in the human body is directly related to being able
to close out unwanted vibrations from unrequested and undesired frequencies. We cannot, most of the time, hear those frequencies. However, our
bodies *feel them* and react to them in various stages of tension build-up.

For many years I traveled to the high mountains of Colorado or to Big
Sur, California, in order to relax. I leave there in three days feeling like I've
had a week's vacation. "There is something about this place . . . ," I used to
say—something that drew me back again and again, in spite of all the other
exotic locations in the world I tried out from time to time.

One day, I was playing in a tide pool at Pfeiffer Big Sur beach when a
man dressed like an old beach bum sat down on a rock near me. He just sat
there, alternately staring out to sea and watching me while I sat playing in
the water, chasing a tiny crab with half of an angel wing seashell.
Eventually, he spoke. "No radio waves. No TV waves. Isn't it wonderful?
Only ocean waves." I just nodded and continued with my sea toys. He got
up and sauntered off. And I sat and thought about what he said. I thought
about the fact that a radio wave or a TV wave has to travel around me,
through me, and past me in some fashion to get where it's going if the TV
or radio station is on one side of me, and the TV or radio set that receives
it is on the other side. I'm in between, or on some pathway that intercepts
it on its way to the ionosphere.[5B] What does it "feel" like? Why am I not
conscious of how it "feels" at some cognitive level? Why was the man conscious of its absence there?

It's true that in Big Sur you can't even get radio waves from Carmel.
The place is silent unless you have a VCR or tapes, because the mountains
block the waves from the inland side, and there is nothing but ocean directly north and south. Very few, if any, waves get to Big Sur from the West,
because China, its westernmost neighbor other than passing whales, is
almost halfway around the world!

The same absence of radio waves is true in much of Colorado's high
country. There are now some radio stations *up there* in Glenwood Springs
and other scattered places. But you can't get any other stations because the
surrounding mountains are so high and *you* are so far up. Some radio waves
are undoubtedly bouncing around up there, but far fewer than you would
encounter if you were, say, in Denver. If you do get any Denver stations,
most are fuzzy and unpredictable. So what does that have to do with my

body feeling rejuvenated in those places? Could it be that I would *always* feel the energy level I do after being in Big Sur *if it weren't for "waves" that I'm not consciously aware are hitting my body all the time?*

Scientists may argue that there is no evidence that wavelengths hitting our bodies do anything *bad* to them. I believe it is just that they haven't gotten that far in their research yet. They do already know that ultrasound waves[5C] are reflected off body bone, fat, and muscle; and that x-rays, at the other end of the electromagnetic wave spectrum, discriminate between densities of body tissues through which they pass.[5D] They have also discovered, quite recently, ionized atoms in the body that do multiple forms of cell damage called "free radicals," atoms with a free electron attached. Some people have more than others, and certain vitamins, they now know, reduce the incidence of free radicals in the body (vitamins C and E, for example).

Could it be that the building I am in either encourages or doesn't encourage conduction of certain of these waves that hit certain vulnerable cells, atoms, or molecules in my body, such as the free radicals, causing them to oscillate and increase the damage they can do? Does conductivity of materials have something to do with whether I relax and am rejuvenated in my own home? (Glass and metal, for example, are more conductive than wood or stone so they would transmit these wavelengths better.) When I go to bed in old mountain lodges made of stone and wood—such as the Grove Park Inn in Asheville, North Carolina, I feel intensely relaxed and restored when I awaken, even when I am working or speaking at a conference. Is it because the heavy stone walls are absorbing or deflecting those waves before they get to my body? Is using all-natural materials that Wright said give us countenance and sustenance, good for more than aesthetics?

At the American Solar Energy Society (ASES) conference in Asheville in 1996, a Wisconsin woman who was involved in retrofitting old low-income housing approached me after my presentation on sustainable societies of the future (see Chapters 16 and 17). She said that she believed completely in increasing the energy efficiency of buildings and in using renewable energy resources, and, indeed, she was doing it in her work. But she said she had serious concerns about buildings that were "too tight" because she seemed to be allergic to them. Specifically, she mentioned that she was allergic to insulation. I asked her several questions about sensitivities I've encountered over the years from my various clients: What kind of reaction do you have? When does it typically happen? Have you ever been diagnosed as "chemically sensitive"? If not, are you allergic to pesticides (my quickest indicator for the probability of chemical sensitivity)? Do pesticides give you headaches? Does the smell of paint give you headaches? Was it buildings with cellulose that bothered you? Was it buildings with fiber-glass? What kind of reaction did it cause?

She could come up with nothing specific from those questions. She said that tight buildings often made her feel "uncomfortable" and "nervous" and "headachy" and "tired." I asked her about shopping centers. She said they were the worst. Bingo! My guess was that the root of her problem was also part of my own personal experience.

Mall-Fatigue: More Than Just Chasing Kids

For years I've hated to shop in large malls. When my children were the age where clothes mattered, they would beg me to go to malls with them. "Mom, let's go shopping," was the weekend watchword, especially from the girls. I would plan a little excursion. "Well, okay, I need to pick up this or that, and then I'll take you skating" or "to lunch" or whatever. Then, *always,* after an hour, I would feel completely exhausted. At home I could work in the house, garden outside, run around like the typical frazzled mother, and never get tired. But take me to a mall, and I'm asleep in an hour. The same thing happened in the large megastores. The kids would say, "Aw, Mom, you just hate to shop." Well, that *was* true, I had to admit. So we left it at that.

A few years later, the first year after I founded my construction compa-ny, I moved into a glass-and-steel highrise. I loved my work. I wasn't bored. Yet the same "mall-fatigue" happened there—not convenient when you have a business to run. I can't tell you how many times I had to ask my assistant to tell people I was "busy" while I took a nap on the floor. I blamed that on air quality, which I'm sure was part of the problem, and on my recently diagnosed "post-polio syndrome." But perhaps there was more.

Five years ago, my doctors said I had to move my office to my house because my mobility was becoming more and more limited. I moved into the room next to my bedroom that our daughter had just barely vacated. It felt strange at first. There were difficult things to get used to. I had to answer my own phones and do my own faxing and filing. But somehow I didn't tire as much. Was it the commute I had avoided? I was working just as hard—even harder without any assistance.

Gradually, I became aware that our wood-frame home, with nothing between me and the earth but a concrete slab; and nothing between me and the sky but wood, cellulose, felt, and shingles, also had a lovely solitude and placidity that seemed to move through the day, almost as the sun cycles did.

As I thought about the possible reasons for that, I consciously considered the fact that the placid rear exterior faces a flood plain and hills dotted with trees about a half-mile wide, so it is very quiet here. The inside of the house was and is filled with green, living things. We don't use toxic chemicals or pesticides in our house and haven't for 14 years. We *do* follow the rules for Healing Homes that you will read later on.

As I settled further into my routine, I observed that I was highly energized until I was specifically ready for a nap, and that the two were easily differentiated. Until nap time, I was never tired. I was far more creative and resourceful than I had been in my high-rise office space, and work was more pleasant. Outside the window above my computer is a big ash tree frequented by all varieties of birds (the most entertaining was a woodpecker with a perspicacious little red cap) and a squirrel I named Squiggly who sat at the tree crotch and stared at me, seemingly fascinated to see a people-zoo with a window where he could watch his larger creature-cousins safely. My eyes, when they glance off the screen while I think, move up to the tree, its multiple visitors, and the sky beyond.

Was my renewed vitality psychological? Was it the view of the outdoors? How much of a factor was that atmosphere? How much was the energy saved because I didn't commute? Was it the "natural" materials in this building versus the huge steel beams in high-rise buildings and shopping centers? Was it the fact that I could walk outside at will and feel the earth, see the sky, and smell the sweetness of the honeysuckle or gardenias? Was it that we never use chemicals in or around the house that could interfere with air quality? Was it the abundance of life around us—wild birds including heron, egret, cardinals, warblers, mockingbirds, blue jays, ducks, and geese—not to mention frogs, toads, snakes, lizards, squirrels, and rabbits? Was it the luxurious flora all around—wild morning glories, wild holly, wild honeysuckle, trees of all kinds—all planted by birds and squirrels and benignly neglected by us? I'm now convinced that it was all of those things—and more!

Sometime during this period of growing awareness of how my body felt in certain buildings, research was initiated on using steel studs in buildings because wood prices started going through the roof (so to speak). I began to read that steel studs created a problem with "conductivity." They conduct heat, and cool intensely, even when covered with sheathing, so the energy efficiency of a structure is compromised. They also conduct sound from room to room and pick up sound from outside. Sound comes in waves, as I discussed above. What other "waves" do they pick up that our bodies react to with tension and fatigue, but without conscious recognition?

That's how I answered the Wisconsin woman's question. I told her that I have no scientific data to prove that metal conduction causes fatigue, nervousness, irritability, or headaches in human beings. But I personally have experienced problems in metal buildings, and when people tell me they have these fatigue symptoms and can't find any other reason for them, I suggest they observe their reactions carefully in certain buildings and then find out what materials were used in construction. The most natural of buildings—those made from straw, clay (adobe), and wood *should be* the least troublesome to these people. Those with a heavy structural requirement for load, which have to use reinforcing rods or steel, including, disappointingly, most earth shelters and insulated concrete form buildings (ICFs), may cause the most problem to them.

If we wish to keep our bodies functioning at the highest possible level, it only makes basic sense to allow them to live in the type of environment in which they evolved; that is, in materials that come from the earth in their natural state.

If Frank Lloyd Wright was correct, and we receive "countenance and sustenance from the atmosphere of the things we live with...," we need to be consciously aware of the natural cycles of the the earth, daylight and dark, hot and cold, wet and dry, cloudy and sunny; and of the other creatures we live with—those in the larger circles of our lives, our families, our neighbors, the natural flora and fauna around us, and the materials *of the earth herself.* That kind of thinking will bring wholeness—integrity—into our lives and our homes because nature herself is whole and we, creatures of the process of natural evolution, are attached to her in the most fundamental way of all. Nature gave birth to us. Learning to live with nature, the mother of us all, and to bring her bounteous abundance into our places of shelter is our task, and our gift.

"The most profound truths are found in the body of Nature,
for when she speaks for herself, she never lies."
— Antoine de St. Exupery

"To him who in the love of Nature holds
Communion with her visible forms, she speaks
A vivid language."
— Bryant-Thanatopsis

◆   ◆   ◆

Our Family—
Succor for Our Spirits

"In dwelling, live close to the ground. In thinking, keep to the simple.
In conflict, be fair and generous. In governing, don't try to control.
In work, do what you enjoy. In family life, be completely present."
— Tao Te Ching

The word *family* has had different meanings down through the ages, and, indeed, has meanings beyond the nuclear family group even now, political rhetoric to the contrary. A "traditional" American family, in the eyes of politicians scrambling for popular images with which to sell themselves, may be "The Brady Bunch," with Mom and Pop and kids; or Ozzie and Harriet and the boys. When television was brand new, captivating us with its novelty, writers visualized for us their visions of what a family *should be.* It stuck. Many attitudes of our present leaders were formed by those '50s and '60s sitcoms.

I have to make it clear, when I talk about "family housing," that a Healing House is not *exclusionary.* It places no *labels* of appropriate or inappropriate family size, shape, or membership when it energizes healing for our spirits. It is a place that is structured for the *family of all living things,* whomever we choose to be with in our own homes. Critical, intolerant people who judge others harshly will draw to them, and into their house, people *without* healing natures, and will thereby place unconscious obstacles in the way of the healing patterns of nature.

> For a house to function as a Healing House, tolerance, compassion, and justice that accepts all sorts of "family" groups must be integral to the thought patterns of the people living there, or the healing vibrations will be destroyed by the critical nature of its inhabitants.

There have been all kinds of families throughout history. In the earliest days of buildings, domestic and farm animals were considered to be part of the household and often lived together with humans in the same building. As objectionable as most of us would find the odors and cleanliness problems of being housed with animals, this situation probably had some benefits. In the far north, before the invention of insulation, animals provided a lot of heat, and people may even have slept next to large domestic animals for warmth. I clearly remember, as a child, curling up for a nap in the barn on a bed of hay next to a horse, feeling the shelter and comfort of its great, furry-winter-coat warmth on a wind-chilled day on the Nebraska prairie.

So it makes perfect sense to me that a mother in Siberia or Scandinavia a few hundred years ago, with the 40-below-zero winter winds filtering through her loosely constructed wood shelter at night, might have taken her babies or children and gone to sleep snuggling up against her farm animals. And while this probably sounds heretical, I don't think there is anything so horrible about taking a blanket, wrapping it around yourself and your child(ren), and lying down to sleep next to an animal. In fact, I hope I can be forgiven for suggesting that perhaps that is the genesis of the story of Mary and Joseph—finding "no room at the inn" and having to seek shelter for the night in the stable with the animals. In those days, curling up with the animals was probably a whole lot warmer and more comfortable than sleeping in a drafty traveler's inn with wood and straw beds in the middle of winter! I know if I were in the advanced stages of pregnancy and had to choose between the two, I'd pick my horse or mule and the stable in an Israeli minute! Eventually, though, people evolved out of houses with animals in them, and created "out-buildings" for their animals in the northern European areas, beginning with those who were wealthier. I guess we could call it "farm gentrification."

Archaeological records have shown no evidence that, in southern Europe and the Middle East where the climate is warmer, animals were housed in the same buildings as people. The best of the early excavations of ancient houses is at Pompeii, where homes were frozen in time—or perhaps we should say, "baked" in time—by the explosion of Vesuvius. Mummified people were found in the same positions in which they had died, doing the same things they did, with the same furniture and artifacts around them that they had lived with in A.D. 79, so we have a clear picture of their lives and their homes. Surrounded by bare outer walls, these houses were built with atriums and a peristyle (a series of columns supporting overhangs to protect atrium windows from direct sun) surrounding the interior gardens. There was no evidence of animals there. But there were other changes that must have affected the family composition. The evolution of men's "business" interests to a location away from their living quarters seems to have happened about that time, because the wealthier men of Pompeii built separate houses at a distance from their work places. (Who knows, maybe this was the beginning of the infamous decadence of the Roman Empire. Get away from the little woman's watchful eye, and . . . well, you know the rest.)

Ancient families, and thus, their homes, were also affected by marriage customs. Where polygamy was accepted, or where a husband was allowed to have several mistresses, whether in the Middle East or among the 19th- and 20th-century Mormons in Utah, the house had to make accommodations. So, in Muslim areas of the Middle East, the house included the "harem" or "seraglio." Since the men with the largest harems were usually the rulers or sultans, in some countries such as Turkey, their entire house, or palace, eventually was called a "seraglio." (Whether using the word that meant "harem" to denote the whole house had any implications on the behaviors inside is not for us to know, but our imaginations can go a long way here.) Homes of the Mormons in Utah often had several identical units under a single roof, like a harem-Motel 6, so each woman and her children had their own specific and equal domain, with the husband as household head, who presumably took a turn under each roof in some equitable arrangement.

In some early European cultures, the religious leaders, musicians, and tutors were part of the "family" and household of the wealthy rulers or land-holders. In most medieval castles and large palatial residences through the 19th century and into the 20th, chapels or places of worship were included in the dwelling, along with residential areas for those extended-family members.

In some ancient Amer-Indian cultures, including the cliff-dwelling or pueblo Indians, many extended family members shared one unit, as the plains Indians sometimes did in their tipis (teepees). This could include family elders, cousins, or others as was necessary to house their "family" group. And the word *family* had a different meaning to an Indian. The entire tribe was thought of as what we label "extended family" today.

In a description I found very unusual and fascinating, Marna Bate described a past-life regression stumbled upon by a doctor (hypnotherapist) who was struggling to find a significant *trauma* in this life, which was causing her current miseries.

> She located me in what I think was a Native American tribe. I was a
> male. She took me through stages in that life asking me to go to a

"significant" moment . . . . At one point, she moved me . . . to my wedding day. Looking for a problem, she asked if I had married the wrong person. I remember the blank pause I went through. I was searching for comprehension of her question. Finally, I was able to find some words to . . . say . . . "Your words have no meaning to me."

In my search, I had seen my village people gathered in the solemn celebration of this wedding ceremony. I had completely understood and felt our group unity. I knew this union was for the benefit of the whole as well as for the benefit of the couple. But to see this union from an individual standpoint was literally incomprehensible. My wife was not to serve me. I was not to decide if she was worthy of me. Our focus was to serve the whole. I knew instinctively that each member of the village was as a link in a single fence. Each link had its value, and each link was to serve the whole. No link was more important than another. No link was looked at for flaws, but rather, was valued for its contribution. The focus was on the whole. I simply could not comprehend a thought as self-centered as "Would my wife be satisfactory to my own needs?"

The thought of judging my wife, or anyone else for that matter, was not conceivable. The focus was not on me. The focus was on the whole, and the energy spent for the good of the whole.[1]

I have another very close friend who has had a similar experience. If you who are reading this think it is all a bit strange, I agree, but I know this woman to be of remarkable business skill, well known in her field, happily married, and with successful, seemingly well-adjusted children. She even thinks it's a bit strange, but here's her experience:

I had a series of revelations over a period of about a year in my daily meditations. This "past-life" memory had only happened to me once before, in quite a different setting, when I was traveling. So to experience what it felt like to be an Indian woman in a specific place was a bit odd for me. I recalled sitting on a blanket by a stream on a beautiful, warm autumn day. Several elderly women from my tribe were sitting at a distance under a cluster of trees on the other side of the same stream. The men were at a distance, probably a mile or so away, at a meeting on a hillside under a cliff overhang. I clearly remembered how *very happy* I was that day, and I have a feeling that this happiness was short-lived and that perhaps I hung on to that day in my memory fiercely to be able to survive whatever came next.

I remember holding my baby, who was probably about four months old, in front of me at arms' length and watching her laugh at me with her fat, round face; her black, black eyes; and her funny hair, black and thick—but completely uncontrollable and wispy, like wild feathers. She laughed at me, and I laughed at her, and laid her down beside me and played with her as I sat on that soft blanket in the late afternoon sun. I knew I had come there as a Shoshoni because my father, who was Chief, had arranged a marriage for me with the son of the Chief of the Ogalala Sioux in order to secure peace between the tribes and an ally to secure the area. I felt *very, very* lucky that this arranged marriage had turned into a passionate love affair and had produced this beautiful, sweet-natured child. And I remember feeling how wonderful it felt to have *two families*—my old Shoshoni one, and this new Sioux one with women who helped me and cared for me, a husband who loved me, and a kind and generous Chief who cared for us all.

Some of us long for a society in which we are closer to extended family members, but most of us are isolated in some form of *nuclear* family group—whether it's the Mom-and-Pop-with-kids version or a grandparent raising children, or a gay couple with or without kids. We can only be sure of one thing as we move into the next century: Families will change structure again and again as they mature and alter their living patterns. Thus, as we ponder the buildings we call homes that we build to last for a hundred years, we not only have to plan for them to be energy efficient, resource efficient, and healthy, we also have to make them *evolutionary*.

A Healing House must be adaptable and evolutionary so it can change with the family's changing needs.

All manner of things can happen to the people who first buy a home. Take the typical example: a young couple with children, who live there about 18 years and leave. A grandparent comes, becomes ill or cannot use the stairs, and dies. A husband moves his business into the house. Someone is handicapped by an injury. One becomes an artist who needs a studio, or a musician who needs isolated, soundproofed practice space. All manner of things can happen *in any family structure* that necessitate a change in living patterns. Wouldn't it be nice if we could just use the same house, altering it for the use we need at that time, instead of having to sell it and move?

Frank Lloyd Wright also recognized this need when he wrote this passage in *The Natural House* in 1954:

A Usonian house, if built for a young couple, can, without deformity, be expanded later, for the needs of a growing family. . . .The Usonian houses are shaped like polliwogs—a house with a shorter or longer tail. The body of the polliwog is the living room and the adjoining kitchen—or workspace—and the whole Usonian concentration of conveniences. From there it starts out with a tail: in the proper direction, say, one bedroom, two bedrooms, three, four, five, six bedrooms long; provision between each two rooms for a convenient bathroom. We sometimes separate this tail from the living room wing with a loggia—for quiet, etc.; especially grace. The size of the polliwog's tail depends on the number of children and the size of the family budget. If the tail gets too long, it may curve like a centipede. Or you might break it, make it angular. The wing can go on for as many children as you can afford.[2]

His idea that a house could "grow" with its occupants is exactly what we mean when we say that a house must be adaptable and evolutionary. If you do add all those rooms (and our family has some personal experience here!), what do you do with them later? In our own home, three former children's bedrooms have been converted into offices, and two are guest quarters. Another friend had five, fairly compact children's bedrooms, shaped rather like college dormitory rooms, and two family rooms. One of the large family rooms became her husband's architectural office when he decided to quit the big city. One bedroom became a computer room for both of them; and one a room for wood carving, ceramics, and sewing. Another housed an ill uncle. The other two were guest bedrooms.

Another friend who had a smallish older home added a family room, a new kitchen, and two upstairs bedrooms on the back. Of the two existing bedrooms, one became a darkroom/office for her photography business, and the other was turned into a computerized office for her husband's real estate management business. The old kitchen became a new laundry room, and the old dining room, a hallway. And, oddly, as adaptable as the house seemed for them ten years ago, they are now going to be forced to change it again! The old kitchen must become a child's bedroom, and the laundry room is getting moved to the garage. But because their spaces are adaptable, they don't have to sell the house and move in order to access another child's room.

These patterns of changing homes for changing family styles tell a lot about the flexibility that is required in today's families. Sometimes flexibility in a home, or lack thereof, is a reflection of the flexibility of the individuals in the marriage or family. Some people experience more stress than others when changing circumstances force changes in their lifestyle, living environment, or business activities. They have more difficulty rolling with the punches, or, as they say in the '90s, "going with the flow." In my experience, those are the people who have the *least* adaptable houses. They tend to be fairly rigid in their patterns and to have homes whose rooms are more formal and unyielding. These are the very people who *most* need houses that can easily adapt to change, because when something is transformed that is out of your control and you can't bend with it, sometimes you break. If you have an environment that *helps* you bend by relaxing its shape and allowing new forms and uses to evolve within, it is one less thing you have to deal with in a crunch.

A Healing House must accommodate itself to both family group activities and the privacy of individuals, and it must have a separate space for dispute resolution.

A conflict-resolution room, open to light from both sides, with a fountain (not visible in photo) on the north at the entrance, and music (the grand piano) used daily.

© 1997 Holly Kuper

You might think that the above statement would go without saying. However, few people *consciously* address these issues when they plan a home. Psychiatrists and psychologists tell us that, in order for us to remain mentally healthy, we not only need to find ways to reduce stress when it inevitably comes, we also need to be loved, we need to feel safe, and we need to be able to successfully resolve conflicts. Our homes must be built with appropriate spaces to use in filling those needs. They must accommodate both socialization and solitude. A home must both be tolerant of noise and conducive to quiet. It must have places where family members can join together in small groups, and as a whole. And it must have a special area, carefully planned, for dispute resolution.

Families—human or any other kind—are a grouping—flowing, rotating, sometimes spinning, sometimes still mass. They are in every way as constant in their change and motion as the cells of an excited organism on a microscopic slide. Anyone who thinks a family is, by its nature, stable and predictable, either has never raised kids or lives in a bubble—or, I should say, has never lived. Even individuals who live alone—unless they are in a padded cell and cared for in every possible way—experience the vicissitudes of life, the constant surprises and frustrations of living that require that they be flexible. Certain *behaviors* may be predictable, and, thus, can be provided for in every house plan—such as eating and sleeping—*and fighting*. But traditionally, no one has provided a place for dispute resolution, so arguing ends up being done all over the house—messing up the vibrations everywhere. Families have fights. Kids fight. Parents fight. It does not mean they have unhappy families or unhappy marriages. It just means they are alive. It is the nature of living creatures that when they live cooperatively in a group, whether it's a family or a herd or a gaggle of geese, they have disagreements because groups are made up of individuals with different ideas of how things should be. Even single people have moments when they are so angry they want to fight with whomever they are mad at—the phone company, the utility, the bank, the IRS, and so on.

The place where problems are resolved, whether on the phone with the telephone company or sitting down with your arguing, fighting children, has to be prepared so it assists in the resolution and quickly shakes off the conflict afterward. It should *never, never* be a bedroom. It should probably be an active room; that is, one where there is a lot of other action going on when disputes are not being resolved. As a result, the room will be used to vibration changes. Chatter and laughter, piano music, puzzles sitting out for pick-up entertainment, or games to play will dissipate the negative feelings from a family dispute *fast*—especially if there was an equitable decision at the end and nobody left feeling persecuted. In our house, this place is the living room. There is ample room to sit down. Everyone feels they have enough private space not to feel threatened when they present their views, and yet they are close enough to have a satisfying discussion.

One of the smartest moves I *ever* made as a mother (unfortunately, it took me *too many years* to figure this out!) was to make the pronouncement that no fights were allowed anywhere in the house between the end of work or school, and dinnertime. All dispute-resolution discussions, I summarily announced, would be held *after dinner.*

I used to feel completely dragged out by dinner because it always seemed like the house was in a total uproar from four or five o'clock until we ate. The kids were attacking each other over the dumbest little things in the world, and then it would get all blown out of proportion, with the others taking one side or the other. Some evenings it was tantamount to war by the time we sat down to eat. My husband would come in the kitchen while I was up to my elbows in cooking, trying to answer the phone and settle the kids down, and jump on me for some unpaid bill or car that didn't get gassed up or some other of the list of unforgivable sins of wifedom.

Finally, one night, in a burst of inspiration, I looked at him and said, "We are going to have absolutely no discussion of problems of any kind until we have eaten." I could tell he was stunned by my calm, firm words. And I was equally stunned when he said, "Well . . . okay." And he turned and walked away. I rubbed my hands on my apron, congratulated myself, and walked into the upstairs hallway where some brouhaha was going on over somebody's missing whatever, and I made the same pronouncement in my mother-has-made-up-her-mind voice: "No fighting will be allowed until after dinner. At that time, you may bring your disputes into the living room to be discussed, and we will help you resolve them. Until then, please separate and do your individual activities. If you choose to continue fighting, you will have to do it outdoors."

I can't say it was an unqualified success. I remember throwing the boys out into the snow a few times to cool them off. They don't fight long outside when it's ten degrees. They just come back in mumbling about what an old crab I am. But, in general, it really did calm things down during that formerly chaotic period. Sometime later, I realized that what we had all been dealing with was low blood-sugar. Our brains needed food in order to process information rationally. And sure enough, half the disputes disappeared over dinner. We would ask if somebody had an argument they wanted to resolve in the living room. Often one of the kids would say something like, "Naw, it was just stupid, anyway." So true.

But when we did go into the living room to solve disputes, we had very clear rules. One person at a time could talk about their feelings—that is, present their case. No one could interrupt or criticize their method of delivery, and everyone was heard until they felt they had adequately said everything they needed to. Very rarely did we ever have to, as parents, pronounce a verdict. Usually it got settled by just talking it out. A right solution just became apparent. We still use that dispute-resolution format today in dealing with employees who have problems, and we use the same location. It is also the location that houses the grand piano that gets played daily, and it looks out on a fountain to the east, and tree-covered hills and a lake to the west. Problems blow out the windows and are washed away by water. Music and quiet soothe the room again and chase away the tension demons. It feels good.

A Healing House must have spaces inside and out where children can just *be*—and not necessarily just *do*.

A tree, a blue sky, sunshine, and the freedom to just hang out (and, presumably, hang on) equal an afternoon's adventure for Kensie Ross Whitfield, of Dewees Island, NC.

© 1997 John Blais

You may say, "Ah, but I don't have children, and I don't plan to." I would reply that you should remember that your house, if it is built properly, will last a hundred years or more and be lived in by other families. And whatever else happens in a home, for it to function as a Healing House, it must feel good, *particularly to the children.* Again, I choose to quote Frank Lloyd Wright for his uncommon vision and wisdom:

It is more important for the child to live in an appropriate, well-considered home than it is for grownups because the grownups are halfway through and consequently do not have so much to lose or gain from the home atmosphere. The child, however, is just beginning; he has the whole way to go. . . .The Catholics say, "Give me a child up to the age of seven, and who cares who takes the child after that." This is because it is in childhood that impressions are the most indelible. It is particularly important that a child should grow up in building conditions that are harmonious, live in an atmosphere that contributes to serenity and well-being and to the consciousness of those things which are excellent.[3]

As we consider families—their sizes, their makeup, their various structures and needs—isn't most of our focus on the young, the children. Somehow we sense, as Wright did, that that's the true heart of our efforts, our endeavors to produce a Healing House. Yes, our spirits are wounded in the daily battles and need soothing, too. But our children are much more fragile, more malleable, and, yes, more *important* to our families and to our society. Besides, even if we don't have children, is there any iron-clad guarantee in life that we won't end up, at the most unexpected moment, with the care of an orphaned niece or nephew or some other child? Shouldn't our buildings be designed to *consider* the possibility that someday a child may need to find his or her natural, irrepressible, unmistakably unique self while living in a house we design or build? And who knows? That happy child who lives there may turn out to be *you or me!*

◆   ◆   ◆

Neighborhood—
The Larger Place of Belonging

"Thou shalt love thy neighbor as thyself."

— Leviticus 19:18

Sometimes it's a tall order, loving your neighbor as yourself. Then at other times, it's *so* easy. Our family has had both extremes—the truly awful neighbors, and the absolutely delightful ones—fortunately, the latter variety are the ones we have now.

Before I understood that I should check out the neighbors as a preliminary to buying a house, we discovered, only days after moving in, that the neighbor on one side had two sons: one, a very nice, older boy who was in college and came home occasionally; the other, an unemployed, college drop-out. The younger son, whose father had bought him a hot new sports car, revved his motor in the driveway at all hours, then gunned it on the way out, speeding up and down our quiet (formerly!) residential street where children often ran into the street after balls or rode bicycles. When his parents were away, he imported all his drug-using friends and threw big, noisy parties. Finally, just before the family moved out, the police, who had been trying to catch the kid for various drug and traffic offenses, moved in en masse and searched the house. While they were there, he and a friend hid in the attic where they smoked cocaine, apparently *during* the search. A short time later, the fire trucks arrived. A mattress in the attic had caught fire from the cocaine pipe, so the boy called the fire department, then he ran out the back after the police left and before the firemen arrived. He zoomed down the driveway and into the street in his *new* car, shouting proclamations of victory from his cocaine-high as he sped off. To say the least, it caused something of a neighborhood uproar.

If that weren't enough, the father, who spent his time at home yelling at everyone present and bragging to all the neighbors about what a big shot he was, got mad at us because we left our leaves on the lawn in the winter for mulch. He called our answering machine at all hours, leaving life-threatening messages, which we turned over to the police. Needless to say, we and all the other people in our neighborhood were thrilled when they moved away.

Presently, we have the other extreme: two of the nicest neighbors you could ever ask for. If you haven't sat out on your lawn with a neighbor and eaten Popsicles purchased from the neighborhood ice-cream truck with its tinkling kiddie melodies; or watched a midnight lunar eclipse while you shared a pitcher of lemonade, you have missed a treat. My neighbor and I share the joys of having families who empty our refrigerators of vital cooking ingredients without notice, leaving us to borrow from each other. We share freezer and oven space on holidays or during parties, garden supplies as needed, and husbands for male chores when our own is out of town. We laugh together often, sometimes after dark in the driveway, leaning against a car. Such a friendship I would cherish anytime, anyplace, but when it's my next-door-neighbor, it's extra special.

Most of us think of neighborhood as a place where a few houses are placed in some kind of setting that distinguishes them from their surroundings. The dictionary, however, also calls a neighborhood "a community of people who live in a region or area distinct from other areas." The key words here are *community of people.*

Often when we look for housing, we look for a neighborhood *without considering the* people *who live there.* We look at "houses" or "lots" without a thought to the man or woman who will be next door and what they do with their lives. Do they work on their cars, running engines all weekend so you can't use your backyard without exhaust fumes? Do they have teenagers who rev their engines in the driveway at two in the morning or play loud music at all hours? If you are the one with teenagers, are they the kind of people who will be tolerant of kids who are at this difficult age? Or will they be critical and angry when the least little thing goes wrong? What kind of animals do they have? Pit bulls don't make great neighborhood dogs. Horses are okay unless you're allergic or hate horseflies in the summer. The shouts and laughter of little children are wonderful to those who love little kids. But if you don't . . . check it out before moving nearby.

What should you be looking for? Who should your neighbors be? Ideally . . .

Your neighbors should be individuals who recognize the inherent value in all life, who treat others as they themselves would like to be treated, and who understand that all nature is a giant cooperative enterprise of which we humans are part.

If we are all are to fit comfortably into the ecological system, we have to learn to become more cooperative, kind, considerate, generous; and less exploitative of other living things, including, and perhaps *especially,* each other.

Granted, finding neighbors like that may be a *trifle* difficult. I can't exactly picture myself marching down the street of a new area I might like to live in, knocking on the door, and asking, "Excuse me, but are you someone who recognizes the inherent value in all life, who follows the Golden Rule, and who feels a certain kinship with nature?"

However, I might have the courage to knock on the proposed neighbors' doors and tell them I'm thinking of buying the house next to them and ask if there is anything interesting they could tell me about the house and the neighborhood. It's amazing how lovely and open most people are, how they much they like to talk, and how quickly barriers fall. In just a few minutes, I could probably get a pretty good feel for what kind of neighbors they would be.

One can also make some fairly valid observations by looking at other people's yards. More and more people who feel a kinship and responsibility toward nature are realizing the value of landscaping that is native to their area (often called *xeriscaping*), the damage chemicals do to our environment, and the harm we inflict on natural ecology and the food chain when we meddle with some portion of it. If you see the typical suburban "Lawn of the Month," you can just about bet it's chemically supported. If, while chatting with these folks, you compliment them on their yard and hear them reply, "Thanks to . . ." some chemical company name, you'll know. On the other hand, if you see a yard that doesn't need much water, that has plants different from the manicured green grass mat many of us were taught is a perfect front yard, and maybe looks a wee bit "overgrown," you might compliment these people in the same way and find it has triggered a conversation about the benefits of natural landscaping.

Beyond that, just use your powers of observation to notice the pets your prospective neighbors have and the equipment they keep outside. Most of all, pay attention to your own intuitive feelings as you talk with them the first time. Are you truly *comfortable* in their presence; or do they make you a bit edgy, nervous, or anxious? If so, try and figure out why. Maybe it's a bad moment for them. You can usually find out by saying, "I really didn't mean to interrupt anything . . ." Often they will stop you and say, "Oh, you didn't, I was just preparing dinner" or whatever. If they say, "Well, it is a bad time because . . . ," then you will know.

Concentrate on your own gut feelings during the conversation. Once again, balance is required. If you truly love the house next door and the people seem just slightly obnoxious, you may want to buy the house and work out the relationship later. If, on the other hand, you knock on a door and find someone bleeped out of their mind on alcohol or cocaine, you might decide to look elsewhere no matter how much you love the physical structure itself.

Co-Housing: An Idea Whose Time Has Come

Another option to finding a house or lot and investigating the neighbors is *picking your own neighbors.* There is a new housing concept that is sprouting up all around us silently and with the simple elegance of an idea that had to happen. Co-housing, which stands for cooperative housing, is actually nothing more or less than recreating the small-town neighborhood many of us grew up in.

It is coming, I believe, from several natural human instincts that the housing industry has ignored for years. First, more and more people are realizing that the kind of isolation most of our nation's housing fosters is painful *at some level,* conscious or unconscious. Second, many are facing the fact that the great quest for more and bigger is not very satisfying to the soul. They are deliberately downsizing—reducing their possessions and the size of their homes, and, at the same time, their financial obligations, to find peace of mind.

I think the primary drive toward co-housing, however, is the shared community—the "village" concept it embraces. All of us who experienced it have a hundred stories about how a small town—which was really just a single, rather large neighborhood—influenced our upbringing *very directly!*

Watching out for each other's children, helping each other through the tough times, celebrating the good times, and sharing and caring were what small-town life was all about. Then many of us left for various reasons, and we were, indeed, happy about one thing at least: Everybody wouldn't know our business—the downside of small-town neighborliness. Now people are returning—to America's small towns, and to the co-housing concept in larger cities, because they realize that even though people may know more about you than you would prefer, the same people are there for you when you need them in this too-often faceless, impersonal society. As of 1996, there were 30 existing co-housing communities scattered across the American landscape, and 20 or more are in the planning stages. Small towns are thriving and growing all over America as people recognize the values their atmosphere can bring to life—particularly for growing children.

Based on clustered housing unimpeded by through traffic and characterized by the cooperative, eco-spirit of its residents, co-housing was pioneered in Denmark, Sweden, and the Netherlands about 20 years ago. Residents in a co-housing community have their own separate living quarters with all the amenities of their choice, including private kitchens, bathrooms, dining rooms, living rooms, bedrooms, and whatever else the family wants. But there is also shared space—typically a large commercial kitchen and dining room where they take turns preparing food for the whole community several nights a week—a Laundromat, play areas, gardens, and sometimes workshops or photo labs.

© 1997 Wonderland Hill Development

A co-housing development near Lafayette, CO (developed by Wonderland Hill Development, Boulder, CO).

Harmony Village co-housing development, Golden, CO (developed by Wonderland Hill Development, Boulder, CO).

© 1997 Mark Ivins

Famous futurist Faith Popcorn, writing with Liz Marigold in their book, *Clicking: 16 Trends to Future Fit Your Life, Your Work and Your Business,* tells readers how to "click" into recently identified trends to prepare for the world of the future. Obviously a fan of co-housing concepts, she predicts that this practice will become so popular and ubiquitous in the next century that instead of real estate agents, we will have "co-housing counselors" who function like social workers doing family-neighbor matching to create neighborhoods. She describes a meeting with someone living in a co-housing community:

> As . . .one community member put it: "The way we have been living doesn't work. Due to the small size of today's families and the scattering of families, our kids have no chance to experience the joys of a big support system. We rarely see their grandparents, and most of the elderly are treated like pariahs. The whole notion of borrowing a neighbor's ladder or even a cup of sugar has all but disappeared. We're craving some deep, meaningful contact. Co-housing is our solution."[1]

Whether it's co-housing, a tiny village on the Wyoming plains, or an inner-city neighborhood in Chicago, there are enough types of neighborhoods to fit the needs of any of us if we are tenacious enough to search for them. But in addition to the *people* in the neighborhood, there is one more determiner of the quality of a neighborhood we can't forget: the *other natural living things in the environment that will surround us.*

Our Neighbors: More Than Just People

This idea of "neighbor" being only a person is another concept we need to rethink as we grow to understand how all living things are connected. We know that humans throughout history have bonded with the earth in various ways, just as we know that a relationship with "the earth" for these peoples included all living things—natural plants and animals growing around them. Their human neighbors might have been the people living in the next teepee or mud shelter, but those other living things were, in effect, also their "neighbors." In other words, their neighborhood was as integral a part of them as they were part of it. It was just a slightly larger, living circle around the original shelter. Even beyond that circle was their "tribe" or region, much as we live in a town or village, which is then part of a larger county or district. We, as they were, are truly impacted in some way by those living things growing—or, conversely, not growing, in our neighborhoods or our "regions," however they are defined. How our bodies communicate with those other living things in that neighborhood, including human neighbors, must be our concern as we plan our own Healing Houses.

The house that heals our spirits should be in a place that is as close to its original, natural, untouched state as possible.

It almost goes without saying that you couldn't have a healing home on top of a toxic waste dump or next to a noisy power plant or freeway. But *what* should it be next to? How much do you have to compromise? My personal ideal, the visual image I created when we moved to our current house, was an untouched spot with a forest on one side, a green field on another, a lake on still another, with a snow-capped mountain at my back—something out of *The Sound of Music.* Unfortunately, when we looked for a house 14 years ago, I had to be a bit more realistic. Obviously, there was not going to be a mountain at my back in Dallas, Texas, and the lush east Texas forest that used to be here was almost entirely cut down long ago to make way for cotton fields.

However, with our visual goal in our minds like a beacon, we did search for almost a year to find, in the visual landscape here, the *feelings* those things would have given us. As a result, we did manage to acquire some of it. We *did get* hills scattered with trees behind our house, a lake barely visible in the distance, and, believe it or not, a tiny little isolated area of virgin forest across our creek, populated with all sorts of birds and wildlife, including coyotes. Between the hill and the house is a creek and its wide floodplain, which is home most of the year to giant egret and great blue heron. But this beautiful site has a downside. Half of it—the far hill and lake—is part of a golf course, so it is sprayed with chemicals on a regular basis, and we get mechanical noise—usually mowers many mornings beginning at 8 A.M. in the spring, summer, and fall. The chemicals so near were a necessary compromise we accepted in order to get a good inner-city location for easy business travel that still had a "country" feeling. We have been very happy with the neighborhood we picked.

The first thing I say to people who come to my company wanting a custom home is that they need to *visualize what it is they want in their larger surroundings*, as well as in a specific lot, before they begin their search. If they resolutely hold that image before them, they usually come pretty close to getting it, with a little compromising required en route. A virgin forest still exists around Lake Lewisville, for example, but it's a *long drive* if you have to come into Dallas. There are abundant lake lots in any direction from

Dallas, but with them you get recreational-vehicle noise in the summer, along with the moist, cooling breezes. Nothing is perfect unless you have a kazillion dollars and can go buy something out in the wilderness, but the dream you have in your head *does exist* someplace where you can access it if you try, or else it wouldn't be in your head.

Finding the right neighborhood can be more difficult when you've been plopped into a new city or town as the result of a business relocation and have only weeks to decide where to live. Most of us feel fortunate to find a *house* we like, that we feel we could live comfortably in, wherever it is, when we move to a new city. Remembering that, many people have gone about the search in the wrong way. Try starting with the idea that you want a *healthy outdoor environment*; then look for a house, or, if you have time, a lot to build on. If not, then look at what you move into as a temporary solution that will shelter you until you have time to follow your own personal visual image of your "dreamplace."

While you are looking, think about things such as traffic congestion for now and for the next 20 years. Will thousands of cars and trucks be spewing pollution into the air from heavily traveled roadways nearby? Think about the direction that the wind blows. What sounds and fumes will be blown toward you in summer with southeast winds? In winter, with northwest winds? Are there plants producing noxious chemicals in that windstream?

If you like a heavily treed site, how many trees are there in the area and on your proposed lot? How many of them will you be able to save while you're building? Trees ameliorate climate by blocking cold winds and absorbing summer heat. Think about where they are placed in relation to the sun and winds. Whether you want a wide open space for your home or you want to live in a forest, you can have a healthy neighborhood environment if the air is clean and pure, the winds are not contaminated, and it is not near sources of noxious pollution or high noise levels.

There are many, many "neighborhood" options: large acreage with only your house and your animals; large acreage with more than one building and several family groups clustered together—sort of co-housing in the country; small acreages with either of the above; a conventional single-family community; or a multifamily structure of some sort that fits your style. Multifamily high-rises with good security and extensive services managed through cooperative ownership are a choice often made by elderly city dwellers who can afford it. These are just some of the choices available in your search.

Finding the Rhythm of the Land

But whether it's co-housing or five acres in the woods somewhere, it's still a very wise idea to hang around the neighborhood you think you might want to live in. Go there a few evenings, take walks there during the daytime *with your family,* visit the schools, talk to the teachers and principals, sit on the ground of the land you're thinking of buying, and feel the trees. Try to be quiet, and focus for a few minutes on *how you feel when you are in that area* and the vibrations you get, rather than on whether you are going to buy it or build on it or not. Just let the *place* absorb into your skin. If the neighborhood *feels* okay, then look at and try to intensely feel your own prospective lot or land or house. Think about where a house seems to belong on that land—where the land wants it. You will know because there will be a certain, undefinable life rhythm you will sense. Once you have defined your own emotions in that setting, recall the questions I asked earlier: Does the house have the right southern exposure for passive solar? Will it capture spring, summer, and fall breezes? How do my proposed new neighbors act when I introduce myself?

If the answers are positive, you will know that you've found a neighborhood where you can move your heart and soul—as well as your body!

◆　◆　◆

"What we are told as children is that people when they walk on the land leave their breath wherever they go. So wherever we walk, that particular spot on the earth never forgets us, and when we go back to these places, we know that the people who have lived there are in some way still there, and that we can actually partake of their breath and of their spirit."

— Rita Swentzell, Santa Clara Pueblo[2]

◆　◆　◆

The Greatest Circle–
All Living Things
Are Connected

Healing homes encourage their inhabitants to see themselves as responsible members of the larger family of all life.

Machaella Small Wright wrote a book called *Behaving As If the God in All Life Mattered.* It is not a book I would have gone looking for or even picked up in a bookstore. But last year, Gail Lindsay, a talented young architect from Raleigh, North Carolina, and new chair of the American Institute of Architects (AIA) Committee on the Environment, sent me a copy. I was blown away. Wright (no relation to Frank Lloyd) communicates with "nature intelligences." She theorizes that all living things are connected, and that we can all, akin to "Babe" in the Academy Award-winning movie, communicate with each other if we try. During my daily morning meditations, I have thought about what she said. I guess I've been doing a little of that communication myself for a few years without thinking too much about it.

One instance where communication worked pretty well was with our ducks. Our family has adopted a duck "couple"—mates who have nested every May in the bushes under our bedroom window beside our pool for six or seven years. Every year around the end of June, we have five or six ducklings appear in the pool from the eggs "Mama" has been sitting on faithfully for a month. These fluffy, adorable little ducklings are there only for a few hours, whereupon we slide a piece of 4' x 8' plywood onto the shelf at the back so it protrudes out of the water at one end. Mama Duck patiently pushes and quacks them up the ramp, and they exit the backyard through a hole in the fence, left there for this once-a-year journey down to the creek.

We have carefully nurtured and protected the sitting mother, even bringing her corn to eat.

In spite of the warm and fuzzy nature of this annual occurrence, for years my husband got upset when he saw the "duck-parents" because they pooped in the pool. Judging by his erratic behavior toward them, I'm sure the ducks thought he had temporary spells of insanity. One moment he would bring the mother duck corn to eat. The next, he would go outside, waving his arms and shouting to frighten them out of the pool. It didn't work. If he was at one end, they would just calmly swim to the other end. He would run around the pool down toward the end where they were, and they would circle to the other side and swim back, all the while looking over their shoulders at him with wide eyes. They looked for all the world as if they were thinking, *Poor man. He's really gone round the bend this time.*

First view of the new duck family, born in a nest under the author's bedroom window one spring morning.

© 1997 Barbara Harwood

The author's duck friend leads her newborn family out of the Harwood backyard swimming pool on a temporary ramp, used once every spring for the same purpose.

© 1997 Barbara Harwood

I saw him doing this once, and I laughed so hard that I was gasping for air. Eventually, he saw the humor in it all and starting laughing, too. We both ended up sitting on our picnic bench, doubled over with laughter, tears running down our faces. Then the ducks *really* looked puzzled. But I guess my husband felt ridiculous enough that he stopped that "chase" system. Next, he tried running toward them with the pool-skimmer basket in front of him. The ducks would fly out of the pool temporarily and return when he went in the house.

One day I decided to "tell" them what we wanted. I "explained" that we didn't mind them in our yard, but when they pooped in the pool, it diffused throughout the pool water when the Kreepy-Krawly cleaning system sucked it up, and it wasn't too good to swim in. Besides, it stained the bottom. I told them we wouldn't mind them pooping on the lawn because it made good lawn fertilizer. I went through the whole explanation each day for a few days, *politely asking them* to get out of the pool. Each day they dutifully went to the edge and climbed out and sat on the grass. At first, I thought it was just coincidence. Then more and more, I realized they pretty much understood. I sensed that it probably wasn't the *words* I said so much as the *feelings* I projected toward them about what I wanted. I almost think they could pick up the vision—the mental picture I had in my mind showing what I wanted them to do.

The mother duck still lets me get *very* close to her and talk to her without flying away. During the daytime, she and her mate use the pool for an airport strip only. They land, then disembark onto the grass except when they walk to the edge for drinking water. When they see my husband coming, they walk to the far end of the yard.

As I have encouraged this minor little path of communication with her, I have also grown to notice that her quacks sound different for different purposes, as do human voices. One day I was exercising in the pool. She was eating spilled birdseed from the bird feeder under the outdoor redwood couch just a few feet from the side of the pool. I was going to swim, so I walked toward her to move the Kreepy-Krawly over. At the same time, her mate flew over, descending as if he were going to land. He must have been spooked by me in the water, because he abruptly flew up and over the fence, quacking loudly. She came out from under the couch, about a foot from where I was standing in the shallow end, looked in the direction he had gone and quacked him the "what for." You could clearly tell by the tone of her quack that she wasn't happy. I said, "Don't worry, he'll be back. I just scared him." She looked at me *as if she understood exactly what I said and appreciated it,* then waddled down the side of the pool to the grass where she usually sits with him and began grooming herself. When I swam to that end of the pool, she barely acknowledged my presence.

We are now quite comfortable together in our little chats. I told myself, until I read Wright's book, that it's just a "backyard relationship"—that we've grown to know each other, this lady duck and me, because we've both been attached to this place for a while now. We've learned to trust. But maybe, just maybe, this is the "nature intelligence" Wright was talking about. And maybe we really can communicate with other species if we try.

When I was very young, long before I read Wright's book, I had begun communicating with my horses, especially one named Debby, a little pure white, very high-strung Saddlebred. I swore to my dad and my grandfather that she knew exactly what I said. My grandfather scoffed big time, but I *showed* my father how she would change gaits with no hand signals and no foot signals—only spoken commands—when I was bareback, so he believed me. I told myself, once again, that it was "just my relationship with my horse" because I loved her so much and spent so much time on her back roaming the Nebraska plains.

And then there were our wild raccoon friends in Pebble Beach. Some of our children's favorite stories involved teaching Ricky Raccoon and his parents how to eat graham crackers and marshmallows, watching them beg at the dining room windows when we were late putting out the dinner scraps, and, eventually, watching them follow us everywhere when we were packing the house to move away. We all spent *hours* talking to them with graham crackers in our hands. At the end, we *definitely* had a relationship with them and could clearly identify their individual personalities as surely as you could with human friends.

I never had dogs and cats because I'm allergic to them. But I know that people talk to their dogs and cats and swear they understand. So why don't they consciously think about other animals having some sort of communication skills with which they can "connect" with humans. I don't know. Maybe it just took Machaela Small Wright and "Babe" to make us aware of what it seems we instinctively knew all along.

Wright not only communicates with "animal" life, she has also connected with the living spirits within plants. She says these spirits have a name—"nature devas." Most people who are good with houseplants know all about this, although nobody I've met has actually labeled talking to their plants as communicating with nature devas. Years ago I read in some gardening magazine that people who talked to their plants (and played classical music for them) had better, healthier ones, all other things being equal. I'm sure I talked to my plants before, but after that, I was consciously aware of doing it. And, of course, when you talk to a "being," you say things that you say to other humans: "Oooh, you look so pretty today" or "How are you doing? Are you wet enough? Do you need a drink? Is your light okay? Do you want to be turned?"

People always comment on my houseplants. Several people have said I have the biggest ficus they've ever seen. The last time I measured it, it was 16 feet high and 6 feet around, completely filled in with leaves and branches. Also growing in our rather overgrown indoor forest is another ficus, four dieffenbachia, all descended from one 3-inch-high plant that was in a pot with a 4- or 5-inch high selloum philodendrum that I picked out of a basket of plants to be thrown away at a grocery store in 1979. That philodrendrum is now seven feet long, with leaves a foot across in our sunroom, and one of the "children" of the dieffenbachia is two stories tall.

People always ask why I have such success with plants. I used to dismiss that, too, as just having "a green thumb" until I read Wright's book; and having a "green thumb" included all the best gardening advice, such as talking to your plants and playing classical music. Lately, however, I consciously think about what my plants are feeling. I sit with them in my meditation during the winter when it's too cold to go outside, and I just "listen" to their needs. It's quite amazing how clearly they will ask for what they want. They don't ask in words, of course. You just get a sense of what they need—such as plant food or more sunlight. In summer, we move many of the indoor ones outside to join their brethren in our garden. Now and then, indoors or out, I walk around, touch them, "feel" how they are doing, and communicate with them. I haven't even been embarrassed to do this in front of other people because talking to your plants is completely socially acceptable. Machaela Small Wright's version is just another twist.

"It is only with the heart that one can see rightly; what is truly essential is invisible to the eye."

— Antoine de Saint-Exupery

If all life is connected in such a way that, given the effort, we can really communicate, then what relationship does this have to a Healing House? A very intense one, I believe. Plants and animals, which have an energy plane exactly as we do, give off a natural vibration of their own. In the case of plants, they also, very conveniently and in the perfect cycle of natural life, give off oxygen that we breathe. Their energy and their oxygen are *gifts* to us, enhancing our spirits and driving a joyous richness you can literally feel when you are in a state of meditation.

Healing Homes encourage and foster a strong relationship with all other living things, both plant and animal, and leave space in and around them to encourage living things to grow in a healthy chemical-free environment.

An atmosphere in and around our homes, where plant and animal life can live safely without fear of injury or chemical poisoning, is an atmosphere in which *our bodies* can receive the benefits of the energies of our plant and animal "cousins" in the same way we receive energy from our human friends. Their presence can comfort us and bring us joy and beauty; at the same time, we nurture them and give them a place where they feel safe and sheltered.

Nature, when she is free, is filled with joy. It is that joy you feel when you sit quietly with her. It is her energy you feel when you allow her into and around the spaces you carve out as shelter.

Once we understand our relationship with all living things, we, as creatures of alleged intelligence, assume the responsibility for caring for that larger scope of *all* life, not just human life, on this planet. And if we are responsible for *all life*, that means one another as human beings—not just our husbands, wives, children, aunts, and uncles, but all human life, even those people who live in ways that we disapprove of. The privilege of being alive *should* create in us the desire to act responsibly toward *all life* with whom we share this miraculous small planet.

The Zen philosophy:

> *Ultimate gratitude toward all things past.*
> *Ultimate service to all things present.*
> *Ultimate responsibility to all things future.*

◆   ◆   ◆

PART III

Awareness As the First Step to Self-Renewal

"That the sky is brighter than the earth means little unless the earth itself is appreciated and enjoyed."

— Helen Keller

The Earth and Sky—
Our Renewal Resources

A Healing House must acknowledge, in its design, the vital, innate connection between our bodies and the earth and sky.

A young woman who had just moved into our affordable subdivision called "Esperanza del Sol" stopped me as I was leaving the model home one Saturday afternoon.

"Could you please show me *exactly* where my fence can go," she said. "I'm not sure, and I've gotten some bids for a fence. I'm anxious to get it up. I guess I'm basically an outdoor girl. I miss my clothesline." I was stunned. When she said, "I miss my . . . ," I expected the next words to be *dog* or *sitting outside* or *lunch in the backyard* or almost anything but *clothesline*.

Then I laughed in complete sympathy. "I know exactly what you mean. I missed mine *desperately* when I didn't have one."

My daughter-in-law and I have discussed that very thing—*how good it feels to hang out your clothes.* We've both tried to figure out why, but we both started hanging our clothes outside for the same reason. It seemed completely ridiculous to pay money to blow hot air into a dryer for an hour when it's hot enough outside to dry your clothes in half an hour, and it costs nothing.

Then, out of our original motivation came something unexpected: a soothing feeling of satisfaction that went beyond the ease of folding clothes off a clothesline, beyond the sweet smell of clothes and bedding dried outside. I'm not sure I can specifically define it even yet.

Is it the sunlight? That probably has something to do with it. Is it the smells and sounds of outdoors? Yes, surely that's a factor, too. But perhaps it is something more profound, something we hear about in this old Indian legend:

The young warrior came to the old chief and asked him the meaning of life. "Come with me," the old chief said. They walked and walked from sun-up to midday, when they came to a rock hanging from a cliff that looked like the prow of a sailing ship. The old chief sat on the side of the hill under the great ship's prow, facing a tall standing stone halfway down the hill. "Sit at my back and wait. Do not speak," the old chief said. So the young warrior waited and watched. Soon he saw a great light in the sky. At first, he thought it was a reflection off a white storm cloud moving across the western sky. Then he saw that it was only a great white light. It moved above the old chief and centered over him, pouring down on him as water is poured from a buckskin pouch. Then he saw a great light under the earth beneath his feet. It grew larger and larger, until it, too, was centered under the old chief. Soon the great light from the sky met the great light from the earth in the center of the old chief. He had become a connection between earth and sky.

As the young warrior watched, the old chief's arms stretched out. Light flowed down them and out from his hands, and the young warrior saw, flowing past through the great light between his hands, people he knew: a Shaman healing the sick, a young man watering his horse, an old dying woman being comforted by a young girl, all surrounded by the clear rainbow colors of love. He saw many more images before night fell. Then the young warrior spoke, his own voice filled with awe. "O great chief, what wonders I have seen with my own eyes." As the lights slowly vanished, the old chief stood and turned to face him. "This, my son, is the meaning of life." And he held out his hand to guide the young man back home. Light still shone from the old chief's hand.

If the meaning of life is to make this great connection between the earth beneath our feet and the sky over our heads, perhaps when we stand or sit on the earth with nothing but the sky over us, and our mind is in that quiet alpha brainwave state you come to when you are hanging up clothes, that great connection between earth and sky is made within us. It fills us with light even if we don't see it as clearly as the young warrior did. Hanging up clothes becomes, in other words, something of a meditative state, an openness to what George Lucas calls "The Force."

A Chicken Coop or a Healing Connection?

If we are to receive "healing" for our bodies and souls while we are in our homes, then we have to provide *appropriate spaces* inside them and around them to maintain that connection between earth and sky. There are ways to do that. Thought must first be given to how the home is placed on the earth, its orientation. Then the materials between our bodies and the earth, and between our heads and the sky must be considered. Last but not least, provision must be made for meditative spaces in the home, whatever form they take. Among the types of "meditative" spaces (even though they have not necessarily labeled them as such) chosen by our homebuyers have been an aviary; a small, separate south-facing room with a floor connected to the earth; a window looking outside at a beautiful pond and garden; and a garden space in a sunroom. One family literally raised their living area to the second story, where they touched and saw the treetops reaching toward the sky all day long. Their meditation space was in the living room. Their sleeping spaces were at tree-trunk, garden-space level.

There are design elements in buildings that raise us toward the sky subconsciously—clerestory windows, skylights, cooling towers, and naturally lit stairwells, for example. All these lift us, literally and figuratively, as we feel the light flowing from them onto us, and as we lift ourselves toward them, either mentally or physically.

Connections to the earth can also be subtly integrated. A concrete slab with rock and gravel underneath and natural material on top—printed concrete itself, a wood or clay tile flooring, or a natural fiber rug—maintains the connection with the earth you can feel when you sit on the floor. But the very best form of integration is an inner courtyard with a natural earth floor and an open sky above. If the weather where you live is too harsh, a transparent covering can be placed over the courtyard, making it an enclosed atrium. Plants and flowing water can be added to enhance your ability to easily make that connection of earth and sky through your body more quickly and easily.

All those design factors negate what I call the "chicken coop syndrome." I first labeled it when I spent a few days at the Department of Energy (DOE) doing research in 1980. I felt like I'd been sent to the dungeon—the dark hole of the universe: endless concrete corridors, windowless rooms with dingy gray furniture, and, for the most part, sad-faced, bored, miserable people working in them. I know that people now working in that building probably think I'm exaggerating. However, keep in mind, I'm only talking about how it *felt to me*. I couldn't wait to get out. I've experienced similar feelings while doing research in a library basement, visiting a windowless space in a hospital, and being in an interior cabin in a cruise ship. But where I really felt it most strongly was, believe it or not, in a chicken coop.

I visited a chicken farm in a small Texas town a few years ago, and I could actually feel the spirits of those chickens crying out to me. They were lined up side to side in long metal troughs the exact width of their bodies, unable to move anything but their heads, which could reach down to another parallel trough to peck their food It was dastardly. Not that I have any great love for chickens! When I was quite small, my grandparents would send me out to the chicken house to spread the feed. The chickens, aggressive, ornery, flighty little critters, would peck your legs if you didn't move fast enough to suit them. When I decided to stop eating meat a few years ago, I made an exception for chickens. I decided that they *deserve* to be eaten. But, nonetheless, when I went to that chicken ranch and felt what was happening to them, I was revolted. They are living creatures, and there's no reason why they should be mistreated while they are alive. They don't deserve to be cooped up in a small, almost dark, space where they can't get out and move about on the earth beneath the sky. They don't deserve to sit there all day without being able to do anything but eat. They don't deserve to have their spirits crying out for openness, light, and relief! This is *not* sending out good vibes into the universe, or into the food we eat!

Now transfer that "chicken coop syndrome" to average office workers today. Do *they* deserve to be cooped up in a small, artificially lit space where they can't get out and move about outdoors occasionally? Do they deserve to have to sit all day without being able to do anything but push buttons on a computer or telephone and eat at their desks? What happens when their spirits cry silently for openness, light, and relief? Do they say something, or do they just accept it as the "way our building is" or the "way our cubicles are"? Do they risk losing their jobs over that frustrating, cooped-up, fenced in feeling? No, probably not. So what happens? They bury that natural instinct, that natural drive to feel the earth and sky. At the very least, it probably is disruptive of creativity, digestion, and circulation. At the very worst, it probably makes us sick.

Recently in "Dilbert," the satirical comic strip on corporate America, one character decided to start smoking so he could have "outdoor" breaks of 10 or 15 minutes, four times a day. He wanted to get *outside*. And when it hits Dilbert, you can be sure more people than just the creator of that cartoon strip and I have thought about escaping from a chicken-coop office!

Now transfer that syndrome to housing, particularly multifamily housing for low-income families. In some cities, we expect them to live in bunkerlike high-rise buildings of concrete, with lots of small, windowless rooms. There are no parks or open spaces nearby where children and their parents can safely play or spend time relaxing outdoors. There are few windows "because people throw things out of them." What does this lack of space and light, this lack of contact with the earth and sky, do for these families—particularly for their children? For one thing, it makes them angry—even if they're not consciously aware of what they're mad at. It makes them rebel against the system that puts them where they are, in circumstances they didn't ask for and over which they have no control.

The Green Classroom

Carla Marshall, one of the most remarkable women I've ever met, runs a small enterprise on the south side of Austin, Texas, called the "Green Classroom." Carla has created an ecology classroom out of an old house and its gardens across the street from an inner-city school. She takes kids from the poorest families and gives them back their connection with the earth and sky, and she has had some *remarkable* results in changing young lives. She recalled one day in late 1996:

> I think the most exciting example of what this kind of environment can do was a young boy who was in fifth grade and had never talked. He expressed his anger by refusing to communicate. The more he resisted, the more the teachers insisted. His teacher told him she was absolutely going to force him to speak. Well, of course, his *treasure*—his silence—became more valuable every time he kept it away from *them*. So the more people insisted he talk, the more precious his silence was to him. When the principal was so desperate he was ready to remove him from the school because he wouldn't talk, he called me. I agreed immediately to take the boy here full-time. I told the principal I would make him my "special, silent assistant."

Carla welcomed the ten-year-old boy by telling him she didn't care if he *ever* talked or not. She worked with him in the garden for a few days, then she took him inside and gave him some magazines and two empty scrapbooks. The front of one said, "Things I Like," and the front of the other one said "Things I Don't Like." She explained that in order to find out what he liked and didn't like, she needed him to cut pictures out of the magazines and put them in the right book. And she said he could do his garden "work" or work on the scrapbooks, whichever felt best, whenever he wanted-ed, but those were his duties, and they must be worked on sometime during each day.

A corner of the Green Classroom in Austin, Texas, features a wall of cementitious material shaped over a chain-link fence. The cement-form-art, done by the children who attend the Classroom with the assistance of neighborhood senior citizens, also formed a fountain and several planters in the wall.

© 1997 Carla Marshall

A child from a neighboring school who visits the Green Classroom twice a week for one hour, gets in touch with nature.

© 1997 Carla Marshall

At first, when the other schoolchildren arrived each day, he stayed inside. Gradually he inched closer to the other children. First he stuck his head out the door, then he walked out onto the porch, then to the end of the sidewalk.

Carla recalled, "I was careful never to put him in a position where he was forced to talk, but when he seemed comfortable outside with the other children, I would say, 'Joey, show them how we do this or that.'" As time passed, Joey helped Carla with the basic routine involved with teaching all the other kids, such as fetching, showing someone how to plant a flower, or where something was. But he still didn't talk. When he showed Carla the scrapbooks, she saw that the one labeled "Things I Like" was full of pictures of the natural environment: gardens, flowers, the sky, birds, and animals. The other one, "Things I Don't Like," had pictures of busy cities, big machines, angry people fighting with each other, and guns.

"I knew he would talk eventually," Carla said. "I just had to wait long enough."

The breakthrough came one day when Carla walked inside and saw the boy playing with two of the little plastic wrestlers children call "transformers."

"When he saw me," Carla said, "he quickly thrust them under the table. I said, 'It's okay. You can play with them. You don't have to hide them.' A few minutes later, I was on the phone with my back to him and I heard him speaking *aloud* for the first time. He was talking for the toys, but he was speaking aloud. I didn't acknowledge it at all because I didn't want to make it a big deal. I thought if it was just natural for him, he might do it again."

The next words she heard from Joey came several days later. "He went in the bathroom, which has a real loud fan, so he thought we couldn't hear outside, and he started singing 'James Bond Junior' in this goofy, nasal Texas twang. I found out later that this was the music from a kids' TV program, but I didn't care what it was. I was very excited because it meant he was *happy enough to sing!*"

The vegetable garden at the Green Classroom. Students ages 6 to 10 sell the vegetables that they grow.

© 1997 Carla Marshall

Most of Joey's time was still spent outdoors in the garden, and sometime later, he spoke a word or two while he was working outside with clay, shaping it, creating objects and destroying them. "I think the art we do was therapeutic for him, too," Carla said. "Besides the clay work, we drew pictures together. He liked to draw houses. One day, the house he drew had a number on it: 1722. I asked him if that was his house. He shook his head no. But he drew it over and over, day after day. Then he drew a little boy in a teeny, tiny room with things very precisely in the same place every time— the bed, the lamp, the window. I asked if that was his room, if that was him.

Finally, I got him to say, almost in a whisper, 'Yes.'"

Carla built on that gradually. "I got him to answer one-word questions inside the classroom. Then outside, I would ask, "Do you know where the shovel is?" and he would say, "The shed.""

Right in the middle of Carla's crucial work with him, his mother moved him away because they were evicted from their house. Carla's not sure what impact that had on him, but she does know that three weeks later, he was back. "We had some rebuilding to do, but I was able to continue working with him until the end of fifth grade, the highest grade in this school. Later, I did check on him at the middle school, and he was doing very well. He's still in Special Education because there was so much he lost, but he is doing well and talking."

Joey, indirectly, gave Carla one more surprise. "One day, two little girls came by. One of them said, 'Are you Miss Marshall? I'm Joey's cousin, and he said you were the only teacher who was ever nice to him.'"

A psychologist might say it was strictly the one-on-one attention from a kind, compassionate, and very smart teacher that brought Joey around. Someone else might say it was only the "green" classroom. I believe it was both. Carla Marshall, talented as she is, would not have had the same effect in a windowless, basement room. It took both a healing teacher and a healing environment. What a lesson for our nation's school designers! A French theologian, almost a thousand years ago, said it better than I ever could:

"You will find something more in woods than in books. Trees and stones will teach you that which you can never learn from masters."
— Saint Bernard[1]

The Green Classroom is an idea that needs to be duplicated nationwide in every school, every classroom there is. I know there is a movement to go "back to the basics," and I'm all for it *if it's done right.* The right way is not to put a child in a chicken-coop environment and make him/her memorize reading, writing, and arithmetic all day and then spit it back in a test. We no longer need to follow Henry Ford's model of education, which trained workers for factories to be precise, on time, loyal, faithful, and not too analytical. We need to teach them science and math *as a working tool of the modern world, and we need to do it in a nurturing environment.*

Carla Marshall *first sanctions the children's innate need to feel connected to the earth.* Then, and only then, does she proceed with teaching. She teaches the youngest children their numbers and to tell time with a "garden" clock that they hop around on the ground. She teaches older children science and math using, for example, the effects of how much rainwater falls on a roof that is a certain size, where that flow goes, how it increases, what volume of earth it takes with it, and what pollution it picks up or discards as it flows. The children also sell the vegetables they raise themselves at a local natural-foods grocery called Whole Foods. They figure out their gross and net, and they share the profits based on the co-op principle that kids who work the most hours get the most money.

As Carla has learned with Joey and the rest of her children, we must act, in some way, on our connection to the earth and sky before we can heal ourselves. Most children, she said, have never had that opportunity, and often it is missing from their parents' lives as well. Sometimes they will say, "My grandmother has a garden," but usually they are quite removed from the grandparents.

"It is so ridiculous for us, as educators, to say to a 12-year-old, 'Love the environment. Get out there and protect it,' when they have never felt that connection with it," Carla said. "I hear a lot from the kids about protecting the rainforest. But it's clear they haven't realized there is something right here, in their own backyards, to protect and nurture. It's the ground under their feet and the clear, blue, unpolluted sky."

As Carla said, very simply: *"You can't love the earth if you haven't touched it."*

If it is vitally important that we recognize this for ourselves and that we work to maintain that vital, life-giving, health-inducing connection in our living, learning, and working environments; then it is even more important for our children, from whom we have borrowed this beautiful, small planet.

◆   ◆   ◆

"My words are tied in one with the great mountains, with the great rocks,
with the great trees, in one with my body and my heart.
All of you see me, one with this world."
— Yokuts prayer

"I saw a hand-rolled dumpling of Heaven-and-earth:
I gulped it down, and easily it went."
— Dim Sum Zen

◆   ◆   ◆

Light–
The Illumination of Spirit

"Another time I saw a child coming toward me, holding a lighted torch in his hand. 'Where have you brought the light from?' I asked him. He immediately blew it out, and said to me, 'O Hasan, tell me where it is gone, and I will tell you whence I fetched it.'"

— Ancient Asian myth

L ight mobilizes our happy, inner child. It jump-starts our mornings, and displays the joys of our days and nights. It reflects off the faces of those we love and shines back in our eyes.

According to ancient mythology from many cultures, including the Inuit of the Pacific Northwest, *light* was the first thing created by the Holy Ancient One. This probably tells us a great deal more about how important light, the *first* on the list of creation priorities, is to our survival than it does about how the earth was really created.

> Men say that the world was made by Raven. He is a man with a raven's beak. When the ground came up from the water, it was drawn up by Raven. He speared down into it, brought up the land, and fixed it into place. The first land was a plot of ground hardly bigger than a house. There was a family in a house there: a man, his wife, and their little son. This boy was Raven. One day, he saw a sort of bladder hanging over his parents' bed. He begged his father for it again and again, but his father always said no, until finally he gave in. While playing, Raven broke the bladder, and light appeared. "We had better have night, too," said the father, "not just daylight all the time." So he grabbed the bladder before the little boy could damage it further. And that is how day and night began.
>
> — Inuit creation story

Healing homes must have a tie, through maximum daylighting, to the natural flow of days and nights.

Because we also evolved in that light environment, it is impossible to overstate how important natural light still is to the health of living things. We know from elementary school science that most life on this planet depends on light for survival, using a process called photosynthesis to create nourishment from water and earth.

People who have spent time underground in caves for long periods as a test of natural human cycles tell, when they return, of their craving for daylight. We all get a little stir-crazy when day after day it remains cloudy, dreary, and cold. How many times have you heard someone's edgy, frustrated voice saying, "Oh, if I could only see some sunshine again!"?

The success of natural daylighting strategies are now beginning to be documented so we can actually prove their beneficial effects on the human psyche. Believe it or not, those benefits even include a reduction in *tooth decay!* Incredible as it sounds, a two-year study of five schools in the state of Alberta, Canada, which compared the health of elementary school children in classrooms with conventional lighting, to children the same age in natural daylighted classrooms, found the full-spectrum light of daylighting had many benefits:[1]

- Growth: children in daylighted rooms grew 3/4 inches more in two years.

- Tooth decay: children in daylighted rooms had nine times less tooth decay.

- Attendance: students in full-spectrum classrooms had 3.5 fewer days absent per year.

- Quiet: daylighted libraries had significantly less noise, either a cause or a result of the students' increased concentration levels.

- Mood: daylighted classrooms induced more positive moods in students and caused them to perform better scholastically.

Daylighting also reduces utility costs by the amount that would have been spent on electric lighting, which is an estimated 40 percent of the average building load. Another 10-plus percent of the building load comes from cooling equipment to eliminate the unwanted heat emitted by light bulbs. That's *more than half* of the monthly utility costs *due to artificial lighting,* if you include the additional cooling load. So utility cost savings become a *bonus* that can be added to what we might have assumed was the logical outcome of measuring whether human beings do better in natural light. As the report said in its conclusion: "Natural light, far from being neutral with respect to effects on children, has *significant nonvisual* effects." Although this was probably referring to the psychological effects, it also meant that those reductions in the school's operating expenditures would release extra dollars that could be spent directly on the education of children.

The exterior of the Selma Middle School, Selma, NC (design by Innovative Design, Raleigh, NC), showing light monitors on the roof.

"Daylit" class-room at the Durant Middle School, Raleigh, NC (design by Innovative Design, Raleigh, NC).

To verify those tests and to get data on their own daylighted, passive solar designs, architectural partners Michael Nicklas and Gary Bailey of Innovative Design in Raleigh, North Carolina, did their own study of grades six, seven, and eight in three innovative schools their firm designed versus the same grade levels in traditionally lighted schools. To avoid bias based on the particular neighborhood where a school was located, the duo studied students of this grade group *nationwide* (which, unknown to them, may have included some daylighted schools with natural light as well) versus their three daylighted schools. They found a 5 percent relative improvement after the first year on standardized California Achievement Tests (reading, language, and math—tests given nationwide to each student) in the daylighted schools. Over a three-year period, the improvement in the three daylighted schools increased to 14 percent over traditional schools. Tracking stopped after three years because students dispersed to other high schools. The Nicklas-Bailey study assumed some improvement of students would accrue from just *moving* into a new school building whether it was daylighted or not, so they measured their daylighted schools against one other new, nondaylighted school in the area. The surprise result was that, in fact, test scores *dropped* 4 percent in a new nondaylighted school.

Since daylighting has been proven to help kids learn, it's such a simple thing to implement in the design phase of any building, and it saves money for the school district (approximately $500,000 over ten years in the average middle school), I believe daylighting should be *mandatory* in the design of every new school in America. And if it is proven to work in our schools, why shouldn't every American home be designed with maximum daylighting as well as passive solar access? It has been folk-wisdom for a long time that all of us need as much natural light in a building as we can get.

Some buildings are as important for their daylighted designs as they are for the function they serve. A good example is the Isabella Stewart Gardner Museum in Boston. I have never felt as peaceful and relaxed in a museum as I did when I sat on the stone benches in the *glass-topped* main atrium in the Gardner, looking at the beautiful interior gardens and listening to the fountains. In spite of a raging March snowstorm outside, I felt like I was on a beautiful, tranquil island in the Mediterranean. I had a *very* hard time leaving. Unfortunately, the kind of architecture that brings the outdoors, indoors, *with its own natural daylighting,* is all too rare in America.

Seasonal Affective Disorder

Many of us, by now, have heard of Seasonal Affective Disorder (SAD). It is basically winter depression due to lack of daylight, and it has been proven in hundreds of studies done all over the world. Every study showed "more mental and somatic depressive symptoms in winter than in summer," and more than half the 543 subject respondents in foreign studies said they experienced seasonal changes as a problem in direct relationship to those reported in the U.S. at similar latitudes.[2]

(A rather humorous footnote to one of the studies done in Italy reported "a high prevalence of summer seasonal suffering in Capri, which, the authors said, "may be caused by social factors." Anybody who has been to Capri in the summer would understand that it's just STCD—"Summer Tourist Congestion Disorder"—also common in places such as Carmel, California; and Disneyland.)

SAD *is absolutely connected to the amount of daylight an individual gets.*[3] It varies from nonseasonal depression in its seasonal variation and in the tendency of sufferers to eat and sleep more. Most evidence, according to Tim Dalgleish at the RC Applied Psychology Unit, Cambridge, England, shows that SAD is biological in origin and linked to disorders in either melatonin secretion, circadian rhythms, light sensitivity, or neurotransmission (increased or decreased neurotransmitter chemicals in the brain—such as seratonin—which transfer messages across brain synapses so we can think and react better and faster).[4] Exposure times from 15 minutes to 2 hours to a light level equivalent to natural sunlight (2,500 lux) is usually prescribed for treatment. Most patients showed significant improvement or elimination of symptoms within one week, or further improvement in the second week.[5]

Interestingly enough, other problems in addition to depression are caused by a seasonal lack of natural light. In a five-year research project to determine whether nursing errors, specifically in patient medications, were related to seasonal daylight, the University of Alaska Institute for Circumpolar Health Studies in Anchorage found that an astonishing 58 percent of all medication errors occurred during the first quarter of the year when days are shortest. Medication errors were 1.95 times more likely in December, January, February, and March than September. "The best statistical prediction was for errors associated with levels of darkness two months earlier," the study said. "There may be not only an impairment of work performance among hospital nursing staff that reaches a peak in late winter, but, more importantly, medication errors appear to follow a pattern that is closely associated with the natural cycle of daylight and darkness."[6]

Windows, Wonders, Willows, and Whippoorwills

No matter how we get the natural sunlight we need, it is clear that some of us are more sensitive to the need for it than others. What we are able to see through our windows combines with, and perhaps is as important as, the sun we feel and the light we get. But how many of us think what a wonder it must have been when someone, long ago, replaced a hole in the wall covered with a piece of cloth, a shutter of wood, or a chip of mica rock, with glass. Imagine the thrill of looking through it for the first time!

My Windows

These are my two windows; one
Lets in morning and the sun,
Lets in tranquillity and noon,
Lets in all magic and the moon.

One, looking on my garden, shows
Me miracles; a sudden rose,
A poppy's flame, a tulip's cup
A lily's chalice lifted up.

Wonder-windows! who could guess
The secret of their loveliness?
Beyond transfigured sky and cloud
My two windows show me God.
— Sister M. Madeleva[7]

Now windows have moved from a single layer of glass—sometimes not totally transparent—to very sophisticated coatings on glass that increase our comfort by keeping out cold air, decrease sun penetration in summer to keep us cool, or increase it in winter to keep us warm..

Without getting into a lot of fancy explanations about things such as "emissivity," which is the "e" in low-E, just remember that low-E glass has a thin coating of metal oxides on it that can do tricky things like keep ultraviolet light out so your furniture won't fade, and reflect heat back in during winter or out during summer. There is Southern Low-E for the south, and Northern Low-E for the north. Some have an argon gas between panes that does a little bit to increase the insulation protection of the window, but primarily it is used for sound-transmission reductions. If you live near an airport or freeway, argon reduces noise levels.

Ask your window supplier or builder which is better for you. Then check in the National Fenestration Rating Council (NFRC) Certified Products Directory, which lists every window approved by them. This is a reliable group, and this guidebook was born out of a committee I chaired when we saw a need to be able to compare "apples for apples" in window specifications. Your window dealer should have one and be able to show you the important statistics, such as energy efficiency and wind infiltration numbers, on windows you are interested in.

We have found that the most cost-effective, best-performing windows are those with CertainTeed's Thermaflect™ silver and metal oxide glazing. CertainTeed's two-layer coating doesn't add tint or haze to your view, and it is less expensive than the other, more prominently advertised windows. We use these in all the custom homes we build.

Artificial Lighting: A Costly, Unhealthy Daytime Habit

With the abundance of electric power in this country, we have come, architecturally, to rely on artificial lighting for most of our buildings, unlike Europe, where using "solar power" in its "light" form to illuminate buildings is a common architectural technique. When you consider that one square foot sunlight passing through clear glass can illuminate 200 sqare feet—assuming it were evenly distributed—it seems ludicrous, almost spendthrift, not to take advantage of it. Granted, there are problems regulating it. Windows created to fully light a building on a cloudy day would admit overpowering brightness on a sunny day. On the other hand, windows designed for sunny days wouldn't provide enough light for cloudy days. But there are strategies that can easily be used to control interior lighting under varying conditions, and wonderful examples of buildings that have been able to do that, such as the Norm Thompson, Inc., headquarters in Hillsboro, Oregon.

The Norm Thompson Building

Rather than use a house for our example, I will use the Norm Thompson building specifically, because one of the major concerns in overall shape, compass orientation, and interior layout of these headquarters was daylighting. Other concerns were saving the surrounding natural environment and reducing energy costs as much as was cost effective. The list of requirements for a Healing Home would include all of those considerations and many more, perhaps in a different order, depending on many factors (see Chapters 13 and 14 and the Technical Appendix).

However, since we are now dealing only with daylighting as an individual issue, I selected this building—basically a 90-foot-long rectangle set on an east/west axis. The south side, graced with balconies and terraces, lends a placid view of a natural wetland. The floor plans minimize walls and partitions to let daylight reach interior work spaces (as well as to reduce the amount of material used).

> Daylighting accomplishes several things at once for Norm Thompson. It provides the highest-quality light for the company's catalogue designers to work with, makes the working environment a more beautiful and pleasing place to be, and greatly reduces energy use.[8]

The difficulty of controlling the intensity of natural light under sunny conditions while you get enough on cloudy days is best handled by using indirect and diffuse light in interior spaces, rather than direct rays, which cause glare. North light in the building is either indirect or only enters work spaces in the early morning and late evening during summer months. Designers controlled summer glare and unwanted heat gain on the south face with external light shelves (4' outside the building, and 4' inside) that reflect light from the windows deep into the interior. East and west light is more difficult to control because of the low angle of morning sun on the east and evening sun on the west, so Sienna Architecture of Portland designers placed most windows on the north and south sides (27 percent and 30 percent), and fewer (22 percent each) on the east and west ends, which also have light shelves, but have added mini-blinds to cut out early-morning and late-afternoon sun that is not shaded by the shelves. All windows are clear low-E glass that provide maximum light transmission for catalog designers.

The building's lighting system is fully integrated with its daylighting design, using fully dimmable fluorescent lamps suspended in rows from the ceiling. Controls with sensors dim the lights in response to daylight levels. As a bonus, the daylighting design and reduced artificial lighting *reduced the size of cooling equipment* needed for the building by about 1/3, from 152 tons to 105 tons, immediately *saving* $30,000. Even though the building cost $4/sq. ft. *more* to build initially (about $170,000) so the annual "rent" is $13,000 more than in a conventionally constructed building, Norm Thompson, Inc., can subtract that from the annual dollar savings on utility costs of about $22,000 and *still have $9,000 of savings a year* from the day they moved in. And last but not least, writer Burke Miller said that the Sienna design group has created a "healthy and beautiful place to do business."[9]

Electronically operated, these clerestory windows provide daylight, passive solar heat in winter, and natural wind ventilation in transition seasons. Unwanted summer heat is kept out by roof overhangs.

The "light shelves" we described above can also be used in residences to assist natural light, although they are costly. A less expensive alternative is clerestory windows. The Westbrook custom home my company built in 1996 in Fairview, Texas, has high clerestory windows to admit light to the back tier of the house, in addition to bringing passive solar heat to the interior in winter. Electrically operated, the windows can be opened to release summer heat, while light still enters the space or when natural ventilation is desired instead of air conditioning. The home, designed for maximum daylighting, as well as energy and resource efficiency, is a rectangle on an east/west axis, with most of its windows are on the south so the sun can heat the house throughout the winter. Unwanted summer heat is kept out by 30" overhangs and blinds that open from both the top and bottom, allowing in light without heat.

The Natural Resources Defense Council Building

Because most of us, even though we want to *live* in a Healing House, spend almost all of our winter daytime hours in a business setting where light and indoor air quality definitely affect our health and well-being, we can't leave this subject without mentioning the famous Natural Resources Defense Council (NRDC) building. When NRDC decided in 1988 to move

into a 25,000-sq.-ft. space in an old loft, they rethought all the office traditions that predominate in New York City, particularly the windowless office
spaces with harsh fluorescent lighting. Their architects used a huge skylight
to open up a three-story atrium to sunshine and daylight. Instead of saving
corners for executive offices, they were left open to illuminate corridors and
open work areas. Inner walls of offices are lit by clerestory windows.

© 1997 Otto Baitz

The National Resources Defense Council Building.

Their employees not only rave about how wonderful their offices feel
to work in, but NRDC is also saving big bucks on energy costs. They are
using only 0.55 watts per sq. ft., compared with 2 watts or more in conventionally lit offices. The additional cost of lighting was repaid in three years
by electricity savings. The building design will feed the spirits of those who
work there for as long as the building lasts, because daylighting not only
makes people *feel better* and want to come to work more often, it also saves
on lighting electricity costs. For a nonprofit organization, every dollar
counts, so coming to work there, for employees, is what Tom Landry,
famous ex-coach of the Dallas Cowboys, used to call "walking the talk."

Productivity and Daylighting?

There's yet another wonderful benefit to daylighting that has delighted all of its proponents because it might finally focus the attention of the business world on energy efficiency! When you read about it in the *Wall Street Journal,* you can be sure it's hit the big time. In addition to the healing and energy-saving benefits of daylighting, businesses have found that there are *productivity* increases. Although no studies have been done on *productivity* in homes (probably because they haven't found researchers with enough stamina to follow mothers around for weeks with their typical 18-hour days), it follows that *we can be more creative and have more energy in our daylighted homes as well.* According to a 1995 *Wall Street Journal* article:

> In 1987, Nederlandsche Middenstandsbank opened a new headquarters in Amsterdam that bank officials hoped would be "organic, which integrated art, natural materials, sunlight, plants, energy conservation, low noise and water." Instead of a monolithic tower, the 538,000 sq.-ft. building is broken up into 10 slanting towers, laid out in an S-curve with gardens and courtyards over parking and service areas. No desk is more than 23 feet from a window, and interior louvers in the top third of windows bounce daylight onto office ceilings. These and other measures to conserve energy paid for themselves in just three months. Meanwhile, absenteeism among NMB employees has dropped 15%."[10]

A classic healing office environment, the Nederlandsche Middenstandsbank, which opened in 1987, has water flowing down banisters for employees to play in and listen to as they go up and down the stairs.

© 1997 Bill Browning, RMI

But What About Healing?

In addition to making people feel better and making them more productive, there is also actual evidence of the *healing* effects of daylighting on adults. The same *Wall Street Journal* article said:

> Researchers have found other benefits to daylighting. Roger Ulrich of Texas A&M University studied gall bladder surgery patients housed on both sides of a corridor at a nursing unit. On one side, the rooms looked out at a brick wall, on the other at tree-dotted lawns. The patients with the tree view had fewer postoperative hospital stays and fewer negative evaluations from nurses. They also took fewer pain relievers and had fewer minor postsurgical complications.[11]

© 1997 The ENSAR Group

Way Station exterior.

© 1997 The ENSAR Group

The daylit interior of the Way Station, combined with passive solar heating and other energy-efficiency innovations, has saved the facility $38,000 a year in energy costs (Architect: The Ensar Group).

The Way Station, Inc., a very energy-efficient, daylighted building, was built *specifically to fulfill a healing mission* in Frederick, Maryland. Residents think of the environment of their house as a "clubhouse" where "members" with long-term mental illnesses voluntarily come for clinical treatment and rehabilitation. The ENSAR Group of Boulder, Colorado, the building's designers, began with the idea of achieving minimum energy requirements cost effectively. Their analysis showed that the *biggest savings* would result from daylighting and passive solar gain (free heat from the sun shining in windows). As Greg Franta, world-renowned architect and founder of ENSAR Group, said, "A building designed holistically, looking at all systems at once to maximize energy efficiency and resource efficiency, also gives you daylighting and passive solar gain."

The Manager of the Way Station said recently, in describing his holistically designed, new facility, "It is a wonderfully healthy environment. If you ask the members what they like most, you'll find it's a lot of subtle things that simply add up." Perhaps it's the exposed natural wood beams, or the trees growing in the atrium, or the warmth and smell of the greenhouse. Or maybe it's the feeling of lots of open space, or the way the natural light changes as the sun moves across the sky and in and out of the clouds." The building was designed to use 75 percent less artificial light than most buildings its size. The rest was natural daylighting.

Writer Burke Miller, in summarizing the benefits of the construction and design methods used in the Way Station, says it teaches us three important lessons. First, we can design buildings that rely on solar energy and energy efficiency to greatly reduce the environmental impact of energy use; second, this type of construction saves money year after year. And third...

> The third lesson is immensely important but often overlooked. We can create buildings that contribute to environmental well-being and personal well-being at the same time. The real beauty of Way Station's headquarters is that it is truly a healing place. As mounting social and environmental challenges clamor for solutions, this remarkable state-of-the art building is a shining example of what climate-responsive and people-responsive design can do.[12]

More about Light

Strange as it may seem, perhaps the light we *see* is not the only light we need for human health. Picture yourself holding a baton that twirlers use when they march in front of high school bands. Hold it in front of you with your thumb and two fingers, balanced about evenly with a little bit less than half of it to the left, and a bit more than half to the right. Now pretend that this baton is the spectrum of *all* electromagnetic wavelengths. *Visible light is only the space of your fingertips.* Visible light comes either from natural (the sun and moon) or artificial sources. The two most common artificial sources are incandescent light, which comes from a filament, heated until it glows; and fluorescent light created by gas substances being hit by ultraviolet radiation until they glow.

Every other light wavelength on this long spectrum is invisible to us. To the left of your hand, first, is ultraviolet radiation, then, far left, are x-rays, including gamma rays. To the right of your hand, nearest it, is infrared radiation; and beyond that is the band of radio waves, first microwaves, then radio and television broadcasting wavelengths. We can only "see" some of these wavelengths by using special human tricks, one of which I first became acquainted with as a child looking at my foot through those old x-ray viewers the stores used to check the fit of new shoes.

When x-rays pass through certain gases and ionize them, they cause phosphorescence, which is captured in the chemical changes on photographic plates. Thus, we can see broken bones and other internal body images, or where the bones of our feet fit inside the shoes we are trying on. (The beginning of x-ray technology is an interesting study in "accidental" invention. Wilhelm Roentgen was actually setting up an experiment with *light* in his laboratory when, to his amazement, he saw the bones of his own hand on the photographic plate.)

Infrared radiation is electromagnetic waves, produced by temperature rises, that can be captured on special film, letting us know, for example, where heat loss is coming from in our homes. Satellites use infrared photography to spot problems around the world—from rust on corn crops in Iowa, to nuclear explosions in Siberia. If humans could see infrared with our eyes, our body outlines would probably look quite different to each other. First, we would have colored auras. Second, our outlines would be blurry—as if we melded into all the space around us and with all things in our environment. It would show us more clearly that we are really part of all that is outside ourselves, and that the artificial boundaries humans have made for themselves are not as important as we've made them out to be. And last, but not least, we'd all be the same colors—in varying densities and intensities—because we'd be the color of heat. Skin color, which so often divides us artificially, would be an issue no more.

I also wonder whether this is the source of all the ancient traditions about auras. Could earlier humans—or even evolutionary ancestors beyond that—use infrared vision at will? Do some animals still have it? Do children still have some of it? If so, where does it go? These are all questions for which I have no answers. Someone, someday, will.

Meanwhile, colors, the product of the natural dispersion of the different wavelengths of *visible light*, that small space at your fingertips in the center of the baton I described above, do seem to have an impact on the way people feel. When all the different wavelengths of visible light fall on the eye at the same time, white light is what you see.

Here's an interesting piece of trivia for you: You thought the three primary colors were red, yellow, and blue, didn't you? Well, they're not. They are the *artist's* primary colors. Nature's primary colors are red, blue, and *green*. Those are colors that cannot be made by combining other colored lights, but if the light of each is mixed equally, they give off white light. By mixing those three lights in the right proportions, every other color in the spectrum can be produced, even though each is a tiny portion of the visible light wavelength. That mixing happens, for example, when sunlight hits raindrops suspended in air. It's called a rainbow!

Reflections on the Interior: Colors and Lighting

Light interior colors, in addition to the psychological benefits of increasing natural light, reduce the need for artificial light. When I say "light colors," though, I don't always mean white, which most people feel is too harsh for relaxing, resting, or sleeping. Often pastels do well: blues and greens for resting areas; the peach and pink shades for dining rooms and places where you need others to feel comfortable and communicative; and whites and yellows where you need bright light, such as kitchens and laundry areas.

Pale peach, I have observed, has something of a magical ability to make people feel happy, relaxed, and comfortable. I have it in my office and all the rooms of our model homes. Our dining room is a slightly darker shade of peach, which is a nice background for art, and when lights are dimmed, it seems to make people feel a lot like talking, so we have wonderful dinnertime conversations.

When You Must Use Artificial Light . . .

We all know that daylighting and light colors only go so far. There is night, and there are closets. Luckily, there are now many *good* alternatives to Thomas Edison's hot, high-energy-use incandescent bulbs. Fluorescent light has been a more energy-efficient and longer-lasting alternative for some time, but there were problems with it. The long, awkward tubes wouldn't fit everyplace, and the light was too white and harsh for most household uses. Now there is an alternative that *belongs* in a Healing House.

A Healing House uses as little electricity as possible; therefore, compact fluorescent lights are used instead of incandescent wherever possible, and lighting design is such that the least amount of wattage creates the most light.

The best and earliest supplier of smaller fluorescent lights, called "compact" fluorescent, was Philips Lighting Company. For about two years, they have had their "IQ Lighting Series"—five "intelligent" bulbs. These bulbs employ innovative microchip technology to perform a variety of tasks never before possible with light bulbs alone. The IQ series, five selections called Auto-Off, Dimmer, Back-up, Timer, and the NiteLite Plus bulbs, is all compact fluorescent.

The Auto-Off bulb shuts itself off after 30 minutes (the teenage run-in-and-out-of-the-house-and-leave-on-a-light-everywhere-you-touch bulb). The Dimmer is a real bonus, because the lack of them has been one of the major drawbacks to using compact fluorescent lighting for specific areas where dimming is needed—as in dining rooms. The Philips Dimmer provides four levels of light without having to install a dimmer switch or use a special light fixture.

The Back-Up is made with two separate filaments to provide "back-up" when the main filament burns out, although the average compact fluorescent typically lasts between 7,000 and 10,000 hours, or an estimated five to seven years, so I'm not sure this is a great bargain. However, I have to admit, if you're sitting there threading a needle or fixing something at the very moment when the light burned out, you'd probably be very glad you had a back-up without making a trip to the pantry or the hardware store.

The Timer bulb, as you might have guessed, turns itself on at a time set by the user and then goes off in six hours. The NiteLite Plus operates like a 60-watt bulb, but at the flick of a switch it can be dimmed down to a nightlight.

This Philips line of "Earth White" compact fluorescent lamps produces soft white light comparable to standard incandescent in color and intensity, yet they consume only one-fourth the electricity! They also have "Softone Pastels"—peach, pink, and blue—which add a hint of color to the soft white bulbs for decorating choices and moods. When you buy these, know that the softness or harshness of the light is determined by numbers. Lights numbered below 36 grow progressively softer as the numbers grow smaller. Lights above 36 are harsh and grow more so as numbers increase.

Do Fans and Fixtures Fit Fluorescent?

Ceiling fixtures that will fit compact fluorescent bulbs, and ceiling fans with compact fluorescent lights are also available, although not in as wide a variety of designs as incandescent. If you find a ceiling fan you like, but the globe is too small to fit a compact fluorescent, look at jerry-rigging it yourself by changing to a larger globe (I paid $5 for one at Payless Cashways, added a compact fluorescent and put it on the ceiling fan, and voilà—a compact fluorescent ceiling fan)!

For your bathrooms, Broan makes a compact fluorescent bath/fan light that comes with a 13-watt double twin tube cf bulb that produces a light output equivalent to a 60-watt incandescent bulb and should last 13 years! With an average usage of two hours per day, this fixture reduces electricity usage by about 34 kWh of electricity per year, saving from $35 to $50 over the life of the bulb (at $.08/kWh).[13]

Nontrivial Compact Fluorescent Trivia

Here's a fun comparison with which you can impress your friends, courtesy of Ned Nisson, famed founder of Energy Design Update:

- A typical compact fluorescent bulb costs $15 and lasts 10,000 hours.

- A regular incandescent costs $.50, but it lasts only 750 hours.

- The same 10,000 hours of operation will require thirteen 75-watt incandescent bulbs that will use 750 kWh of electricity.

- During the same 10,000 hours, a single 18-watt compact fluorescent, *with equal light output,* will use only 130 KwH.

- At $.08/kWh electric rates, the cost on your utility bill will be $60 for the incandescents and $10.40 for the compact fluorescent.

- So you *save* $45 by spending $15—a 300 percent return on investment for a compact fluorescent bulb.[14]

Piping Light into Your Healing House

If you just want to *enhance* daylighting in some rooms rather than adding artificial light for daytime purposes, another simple and remarkably effective device for "piping" daylight in is called, of course, a "SunPipe." It is a 13-inch diameter hollow aluminum tube with a highly reflective plastic film laminated onto the interior surface. Daylight enters through a clear acrylic dome on the top of the tube and is channeled by a reflective surface to a white acrylic diffusing dome at the bottom. The lower dome looks just like a ceiling light fixture.[15]

No More White-Light Horror

If you wonder how all these compact fluorescent lights will *feel* in your house, an interesting experiment was done in Rochester, New York, to test customer acceptance of a home entirely designed with fluorescents, compact fluorescents, and halogen low-wattage lighting.

Two side-by-side townhouses were put on display during a "Homearama 1994" home show. Both were designer decorated with the same base prices of $119,000. But one builder installed a standard lighting package. In the other, Rensselaer Polytechnic Institute's Lighting Research Center (LRC) had installed a custom energy-efficient lighting package. The results surprised even them. Of the 706 people who looked at the two homes, *79 percent liked the appearance of the energy-efficient lighting as much or more than the traditional lighting.* Of those, 97 percent said they would be willing to pay more (half said they would be willing to spend upwards of $825 more) for the efficient lighting. An interesting sidelight to that test was that the efficiently lit home sold immediately, and residents were very happy with it. The other one was still on the market a year later.

Doing a Lighting Fix on Your Own House

Obviously, you can buy compact fluorescents for yourself and put them in your existing house. In case you're wondering how much it will *really* save you, the Florida Solar Energy Center (FSEC) decided to find out by doing a whole-house evaluation. They measured a standard 1,341 sq.-ft. house in South Miami until they had isolated the lighting load (separated it from other things such as TV, VCR, hair dryers, etc). Then they retrofitted every light bulb or control they could—27 in all. *The connected household lighting load dropped immediately from 2.5 to 1.1 kW—a reduction of 56 percent!* The cost of the entire retrofit was $405 retail (no labor included because it's an easy do-it-yourself project). Over time, the lighting load was reduced by 61 percent, which works out to 2,500 kWh per year, or about $200 at $.08/kWh. So the payback period is about two years.[16]

And there's another bonus. You can feel proud because you've contributed a little to cleaning up the air. Each time you replace a common incandescent bulb with an energy-efficient compact fluorescent, you will save 157 kilowatt hours per year. That equates to 300 pounds of carbon dioxide, 1.4 pounds of sulfur dioxide, and .9 pounds of nitrogen oxides. Other forms of pollution can also be reduced, depending on the source of electricity, such as boiler ash, scrubber waste, acidic drainage, waste from coal mining, and radioactive waste from nuclear power plants.[17]

And, remember, every little bit helps!

◆   ◆   ◆

"No one makes a greater mistake than she who does nothing
because she can only do a little."

— Edmund Burke

◆   ◆   ◆

Silence–
The Womb of Creativity

SILENCE

Silence was the open door
through which the world was born
through which all sounds that
were ever to be
came.

Silence nurtured life in its exquisite
richness
with only the wild sounds of a new
planet breaking through
ice cracking, volcanoes exploding,
thunderous storms, rain falling
the crash of a meteor.

Then life itself
brought from silence
birthed
eventually
unrepentant chaos and noise
from the first squeal of a frog
on land
to the roar of a dinosaur
thence to man with his engines
and machines
His burning of the sun's stores in
the earth

The crashing and clattering of
wondrous new technologies
The driving force of his long grasp
His search to find . . . what is it . . .

He can't.
He reaches.
He struggles.
It isn't there.
What was it he wanted?
Oh my god, he buries his head in his
hands,
What was it? What is it? Where has it
gone?

Wherefore art you now, silence?
I pray for your solace.
I search endlessly for your balm.
Have you closed the door?
Do you remove yourself
after you have given birth?

— Patricia Marie Kraus

Most of us crave silent moments. Sometimes silence seems to be the rarest, most distant, and often most expensive, commodity on earth. We labor each day amidst ringing telephones and faxes, clicking keyboards, clattering printers, and roaring machines. When we arrive home, we long for nothing so much as quiet. Then our families, much as we love them, greet us with noise—shouting kids, wives with the day's tales to tell, barking dogs, more ringing telephones. We are happy to see them, and they us, but the silence we long for has been vanquished to a storage closet in the farthest reaches of our house.

As we are busy dealing with all that, we stop for a second now and then to think about how nice—*and how quiet*—it will be when the work is done and the children are in bed. Finally, we tiptoe out and close the door to their room one last time, stand outside and take one long, deep breath, listening to . . . the silence. If we are conscious of it at that point, what we hear, in the childless silence, is the noise our house makes. We hear the refrigerator motor go on or ice drop into the basket from the automatic icemaker. In a second or two, the furnace clicks on, and the blower whines.

Seconds later, we are aware that someone has turned on a shoot-em-up movie or, even worse, the longest running body-bag series on TV—the evening news. Somehow that sound draws us to it. We watch and listen, body tensed, waiting for . . . until our subconscious whispers to us, through the din, that we have to be up at six in the morning to go back to work. We look at our watch. Bedtime. Somehow, there was no time for silence. And it's always the same. Yesterday, today, and tomorrow.

If you have no time for silence in your life, you can have no healing.

Granted, there is no such thing as *complete* silence. Even when you sit in the forest miles away from another human being, there is no silence. A bird sings. A twig falls. A small animal scrambles through the underbrush. But those are sounds of wondrous stealth. There lies the nurturing silence in which the deep breaths of our life are born and reborn. True silence, as in a vacuum, were we ever to experience it, would pound in our ears, demanding our attention. The solitude of a silent forest, or a wide, lonely plain, gives us the gift of hearing the *delicate* sound of a mockingbird twittering in the tree beside me, so clear, so welcome, so cheerful. Where else could you hear a tiny lizard run across a rock or an acorn fall from a tree?

"Silence teases us with the silver vapors of its emptiness.
It is the enigmatic womb of creativity,
falling over us like a soothing curtain of calm,
opening our souls to a realm beyond."

— Patricia Marie Kraus

If we have no silence, no place of peace, not only can we not center our-selves each day, but we also severely limit our own creativity. The chaos and din of modern cubicle offices leave no place for that deep kind of calm that is required for true, original thought to develop. Our homes, with elab-orate sound systems and large-screen TVs in every bedroom, give us no respite. These tools of connection are sitting there, staring us down, so we turn them on, instead of spending that 30 minutes in silence with our thoughts. When we jog, we take earphones so we have constant noise, music, and talk. We *think* we are living life at its best in this gadget-ridden world, so we have abandoned our body's, our soul's, and our mind's best friend: silence.

"There is a sacred place within each of us—a secret, silent place of
stillness—between health and healing, between healing and moving on.
It is at this place, this velvety place of quiet, that gates open
and transformation emerges."

— Jody Seay

I, myself, had not stopped to analyze my body's need for silence until I began meditating. I knew I always loved the profound silence of the out-doors—camping, hiking, riding horses alone, whose only familiar sounds were my horse's hooves on the gravel road, the wind in my ears, the occa-sional screech of a hawk or the flutter of a pheasant escaping from under my horse's galloping feet. I thought this pleasure in silence came because I grew up on the Nebraska prairie where all spaces are truly wide and open—where it is so quiet you can hear a thunderstorm a hundred miles away.

During the years of my childhood, before cable, there was no television in western Nebraska. There was no local radio station until I was in high school. Denver radio was always crackling with interference, so it was lis-tened to sparingly and with great concentration. Thus, the sounds that filled our home were few. Cars occasionally passed by. The washing machine was in the basement. Laundry was either hung up down there or on the outside clothesline. There was no automatic dryer and no dishwasher except me, my brother, and my father. The iron was silent. So was the oven. Footsteps and voices were the only sounds other than my piano, which I played several hours each day.

It may sound idyllic, but to me as a kid, as it would to many kids now, there were a couple of problems with that silence. I hadn't yet learned to distinguish healthful, restorative silence from tense, unpleasant, destructive silence. And second, I perceived that supposedly idyllic life as just plain boring. I couldn't wait to escape to the excitement of the big city: Los Angeles, New York—someplace where the *action* was. When I practiced the piano as a kid, I would daydream that, if I left the door open, some music producer would drive by on Highway 30, just two blocks away, and somehow be drawn to where I was playing. He would hear me, rhapsodize over my incredible talent, and sweep me away to New York, to Juilliard or Eastman, and on to exciting fame and fortune. Of course it never happened. But my humble piano music, springing to life in the ubiquitous silence of that little town, nurtured the kind of alpha brainwave creativity that spawned those fantasies and many more, perhaps forming the web of creativity that one carries into adulthood.

The primary thing, however, that kept silence in our house, our town, from being idyllic, was not boredom. It was the *wrong kind of silence*—the silence spawned by the terrible tension between my parents. As a kid, I *felt* it—like an elephant in the living room that nobody talked about. When that kind of tense, uncomfortable silence that makes you hold your breath in fear prevails in a household, it is, to say the least, *not* a situation conducive to healing or creativity! You seek escape. I ran to the silent solitude of the farm and rode my horses, or I hid in my downstairs room and played Beethoven or Tchaikovsky. And it wasn't until I began meditating as an adult that I was able to differentiate between the two kinds of silence: frozen, anxious silence; and the free, welcoming silence of nature, born of breathing deeply of pure air and listening to the voices of nature.

Too many of us today have experienced those tense, uncomfortable silences, so, out of fear, we reject *all silence* and fill our lives with noise and chaos. Rabbi Sheldon Zimmerman put it very well:[1]

> Silence does not mean nothingness. Now I know we're scared of silence—we don't like to be silent. My God, we can't stand it, what are we going to do, there's no noise! People have to put on radios and televisions because we are frightened by silence. Try it someday, a minute of silence, and when you can do a minute, try two. Let life enter and refresh and touch. Be lifted by just the heart's beating, by the soul's murmuring, just by the rhythm of life. Let that happen to you sometime. No big, big

bang—just a quiet silence. You know where God speaks best? In the sound of a thin silence, absolute silence, that just embraces all of us. Not in the earthquake or in the thunder or in the wind, but in the still, quiet voice, the sound of silence.

I repeat: *If you have no time and place of silence in your life, you can have no healing*. Therefore...

A Healing House must have a place for solitude and silence.

That place can be outside the building if you live in a climate conducive to sitting outdoors all year round. But if you're in a mixed climate, as most of the United States is, you will need a place indoors as well. Maybe you'll need more than one place. And it is very simple to create these places. Walls can be soundproofed with building materials. Floor plans can be created so there is a private space off the master bedroom where you can hang plants and put a small rug or chair for yourself. But most of all, if a house is built properly, it will have virtually silent systems operating it. People who live in homes we have built say things such as, "It's so quiet in here. You can't hear the cars or even airplanes outside" (Louise Bridges). "We love the quiet. You never hear the cooling system go on or the fans operate. All we hear is the wind in the trees off the porch" (Elena Westbrook). "It's so peaceful inside—like you walk into this little calm space in the middle of the noisy world" (Gail Johnson-Williams).

Healing homes have as few noisy mechanical systems in them as possible, and those that are there need only be used very sparingly.

The first component of *quiet* in a Healing House, the silence of passive solar heating, requires proper initial placement of the house on the lot or site. Houses designed with passive solar orientation, appropriate thermal mass, and appropriate exterior envelope insulation and sealing need very little extra heat in winter, so they are *mechanically* very quiet. The house is heated by the sun, passively. Passive solar heat is the kind of heat you find in your car when you park it in the sun on a very cold day.

Our family lived in a Northfield, Illinois, home designed by Frank Lloyd Wright and his student William Deknatel. It sat low to the ground with windows wrapping around its angular formation to catch the winter sun. Properly engineered overhangs (ours were four feet, with approximately one inch per degree of latitude) kept out unwanted summer sun. Floors were of terrazzo, so when the winter sun shone on them, they were warmed all during the day. At night, that heat from the floor was released into the interior of the house. The bright, reflective whiteness of the winter snows increased the sun penetration. It was an incredibly quiet, very peaceful home. Our family, including my plants, loved it.

© 1997 Barbara Harwood

The Harwood house, Northfield, Illinois, with windows that follow the sun's path and four-foot overhangs to keep summer sun out.

And, as I described in the Preface, our neighbors also came to more fully appreciate the reality, simplicity, and effectiveness of passive solar that Sunday morning in 1980 when the chill factor was a record 80 below zero, the winds blew down power lines, and the neighborhood's electricity went out. Even gas furnaces couldn't operate because the fans were electric, and power was out everywhere. But our passive solar house was toasty by 10 A.M., as it always was when the sun was shining, so everyone in our neighborhood gathered there to stay warm. That day, they became aware of that great gift of passive solar design bequeathed our family by Wright's inventive genius. I was also consciously aware of the silence it gave our home—no motors and fans going on and off constantly, just sun shining in.

You can reduce the operating time of a heating system, and, thus, the noise it makes, even further in winter by protecting your home from cold winter winds that come from the northwest. During initial planning stages, particularly in colder climes where maximum passive solar heat is desirable, it is extremely beneficial to "back houses up" to a hillside facing south. The hill protects from north winds, and the sun shines in from the south. If you can't back your house into a south-facing hill, you can do the next best thing: Build a berm (a little artificial hillock) on the north, partially earth-shelter the north walls, and plant evergreen trees on it. Homesteading farmers like my grandfather who planted "windbreaks" of trees north of their houses knew what they were doing!

Active solar hot water systems operated by gravity and convection are silent and very useful in reducing water heating bills. Graywater drip systems, produced in conjunction with septic systems, eliminate both the sound of sprinklers going on and off, as well as the wasting of water to green your site.

Windows that can be opened and combined with ceiling fans for circulating fresh air are another silent operating advantage for a home. Many people know by now that if you keep windows open and fans operating certain months of the year, you have no need for mechanical heating and cooling. This is true in climates such as Texas and all across the South during spring and fall, in the North during summer, and in the desert Southwest during winter. And you get the added benefit of hearing the birds sing!

Planning where those windows will be placed to optimize natural breezes at desired times of the year is just as important as planning for passive solar heating. Nature's gentle summer breezes come from the southeast. (Now when you see porches wrapped around the southeast corner of Southern homes, you'll know why.) Summer storms come from the Southwest in our area, from other directions in other areas of the country.

The more natural ventilation you can use, the quieter your house will be, unless you live in a high-rise building on a busy street in a place such as New York City. Then the noise of cars and people all night, garbage trucks at four in the morning clattering over the manholes and slamming trash cans up and down, and ambulance sirens at *any hour* is *worse* when you open the windows. So, if you live there, a quiet, high-efficiency system in a well-insulated and sealed building is better suited to creating a place of respite. Windows, in that case, are for leaning out of, Venetian style, and watching the world go by!

Thick Exterior Walls and Ceilings for Maximum Quiet

The most important factor in creating a quiet house is the way you treat the building exterior itself. If the walls aren't insulated and sealed enough, you won't have a quiet house unless you live in the middle of a forest. If you do, even though you don't need to make your house quieter, you probably need to use less energy to heat and cool it. And by now, I'm sure you've gathered that a *silent home* is also a very energy-efficient home, so it has much lower utility bills than a conventional home built in America today.

But if you do live in that forest, you probably also know that listening to nature's sweetest, softest sounds is restorative to the soul. Here are some beautiful thoughts from William Wordsworth on this subject:

Tintern Abbey

And this prayer I make.
Knowing that Nature never did betray
The heart that loved her; 'tis her privilege,
Through all the years of this our life, to lead
From joy to joy: for she can so inform
The mind that is within us, so impress
With quietness and beauty, and so feed
With lofty thoughts, that neither evil tongues
Rash judgments, nor the sneers of selfish men,
Nor greetings where no kindness is, nor all
The dreary intercourse of daily life
Shall e'er prevail against us, or disturb
Our cheerful faith, that all which we behold
Is full of blessings. Therefore let the moon
Shine on thee in thy solitary walk;
And let the misty mountain-winds be free
To blow against thee: and, in after years
When these wild ecstasies shall be matured
Into sober pleasure; when thy mind
Shall be a mansion for all lovely forms,
Thy memory shall be as a dwelling place
For all the sweet sounds and harmonies.

It is those kinds of sounds in and around our healing homes that create the kind of solace required for us to learn about ourselves, to reflect on what we do, to make appropriate decisions, and to function at our maximum levels of creativity on a daily basis.

A Healing House provides for the eternal music of the spheres.

The sounds that were there when human life began are the sounds of nurture; the gurgling of waters, the flow of waterfalls, the wind in treetops, the rustling of grasses, and the quiet call of an owl. Most likely after an early human first blew breath through a reed growing beside a stream, music was born from the reed flute, drums of animal skins, and various types of string harps—quiet music that blended with the natural sounds but which expressed the creativity of the human playing it. These were songs that captured the soundtrack of human experience. Noah Adams, host of National Public Radio's "All Things Considered," recounts, in his book, *Piano Lessons,* the thoughts of the famed poet-philosopher and dean of the Yale School of Medicine, who won a National Book Award for his essays on science and nature:

> Dr. Lewis Thomas, a writer whose work I'd long admired . . . believed that music is "the effort we make to explain to ourselves how our brains work." And he was convinced that music is at nature's center. In his book, *The Lives of a Cell,* Dr. Thomas imagined an orchestra of earthworm instrumentalists, and crickets and the voices of whales. "If we had better hearing," he wrote, "and could discern the descants of sea birds, the rhythmic timpani of schools of mollusks, or even the distant harmonics of midges hanging over meadows in the sun, the combined sound might lift us off our feet."[2]

Luckily for us, those kinds of expressive, relaxing sounds are finally being reborn in music. My personal favorite relaxation tape is called "Interlude . . .Ocean Waves." The intermittent roar of a wave is gently caressed by a single flute. Others are "Interlude . . . Mountain Stream," "After the Rain," and all piano music by Michael Jones. These tapes provide me with a reconnection to the natural sounds, so they trigger the emotions, the relaxation I felt when I first heard those sounds. When one relaxes with those memories, medical studies show, heart rate and blood pressure drop, beneficial hormones are produced in the brain—which triggers the immune system to function more effectively—and alpha brainwaves begin to tune up, increasing creativity.

Whether or not you already live in a Healing House, begin to use that kind of music to heal yourself. Then add to those the sounds, a small indoor fountain or pool of water, and when you can, turn off all the mechanical systems in your house. Unplug your phone, turn on that music and the fountain, and sit back, preferably in an old rocking chair, and let the world slide away.

When the music ends, *feel* the silence flowing over you like water from the fountain. Feel it wash away all the tension, the worry, the anxieties—as you become one with the silence, the beginning of all life.

◆   ◆   ◆

O Great Spirit, help me always . . .
to remember the peace that may be found in silence.

— Cherokee prayer[3]

◆   ◆   ◆

Water—
Gift from the
Earth and Sky

The spirit sat still and silent in the center of the swirling waters. Her long, light hair flowed upward into the aquamarine currents, fishes gliding through their tresses. As she absorbed more and more deeply the warm, comforting waters, she felt herself begin to move, gliding slowly through the dim passages, guided by a force coming from deep beneath her in the dark, coal-black waters; pulled upward by a light, a penetrating flash of glittering diamonds, sparkling and dancing off the silvery backs of her friends, the sea creatures swimming with her. She rose higher and higher, reaching for . . .

We all came from the waters. We may return to dust and ashes first, but eventually, we return to water. Our bodies are 92 percent water— actually a saline solution of approximately two teaspoons of salt for every quart of water. Without food, we can last for quite a while. Without pure water to drink, we can only last a matter of hours. Yet we often forget how important water is to the survival of humanity, and the impact it has on our development. We look at the giant oceans covering the earth and forget to worry about drinking water for humans and animals, both of whom continue to grow in population on a planet with limited freshwater resources. Before we go further with water, you must understand that a Healing House is not just healing to the physical, mental, and spiritual well-being of its occupants. It is also healing to the planet. Therefore:

A Healing House makes the most economical possible use of all water resources available to it. Its occupants continually remind themselves that this water is a gift from the earth and sky.

Being mindful is one of the most urgent lessons taught us by the great spiritual leaders, and it is the lesson that is desperately needed by our Mother Earth at the moment. Most of us use the *gift* of fresh, potable water as if it were always going to be available in endless quantities. We take it as much for granted as the earth spinning around to meet the rising sun every morning. Even as we drain and chemically pollute the huge, underground lakes, called aquifers, that provide our best Midwestern areas with agricultural water, we mindlessly continue to mine them for growing water-intensive crops in areas where dryland crops should be.

Developers cover desert areas with manmade structures and import water from rivers far away, counting on nature to *never* return to its natural cycle of long droughts alternating with wet cycles. Hoards of people move to desert areas, completely unmindful of the scarcity of water, only aware that there is employment and housing available in an area with warm, dry weather.

We pour chemicals onto the earth to green lawns and golf courses, to kill insects and weeds and as waste from household activities such as painting and cleaning, without thinking that it runs through the earth and into the water table that provides most of our drinking water.

We turn on the tap in our homes, run our washing machines and dishwashers, fill our swimming pools, water our lawns, and wash our cars without thinking about the path that water takes to get to us, and where it goes when it leaves. Dr. Syed Qasim, professor at the University of Texas at Arlington, says *average* water use is as follows:

- Dallas, Texas—161 gallons per capita per day (gpcd)
- Houston—250 gpcd
- Los Angeles—181 gpcd
- Japan—77 gpcd
- Switzerland—107 gpcd
- India—14 gpcd

Sadly, much of this water is used to carry away waste for toilet flushing, showers, and washing machines. Compare these numbers to 30 gpcd used by the Westbrook family, for whom our company built a Healing House in 1996. They said this level of use is no hardship at all because they have a graywater system and rainwater collection in place.

How many of us understand *how many energy resources it takes to get fresh water to our houses?* How many of us are truly thoughtful about the amount of water we use in a day?

So What Can We Do?

As we become aware of water as a precious gift and want to make the best use of it, there are multiple systems available to us for maximizing water use—water-conserving fixtures and appliances, and various graywater reuse systems and rainwater collection systems. However, almost nobody is using them, as builders rarely advise clients that they are available. In areas where there is *already* a water problem, that makes no sense at all.

What Is a Graywater System?

"Graywater" is simply water that has been used for washing clothes or bathing—bathroom sink water, bathtub and shower water, and washing machine water. A single bathtub of "graywater" can irrigate 300 square yards of landscape, and the phosphates in the soap are good food for green, growing things. The balance of household wastewater, from toilet flushes, dishwashers, and kitchen sinks that may contain grease, is called "Blackwater."[1] This cannot be used for landscaping unless it is more thoroughly treated, usually by combinations of green plants and sand filters. We do not address those kinds of systems here, but Ben and Jerry's plant in Waterbury, Vermont, for example, has used such a system for years to treat waste from ice cream production. They are usually proud to send information about it if contacted, or if you're in the neighborhood, they are open daily for tours so you can see a remarkable, natural water treatment system—*and* get free ice cream![2]

Graywater Systems for a Healing House

Graywater systems can range from the simplest individual home systems, to complex citywide or subdivision-wide endeavors, now being used in some areas of Australia. One of the best I have run into is a simple, little graywater system invented by David Omick of Proveto Fe Y Esperanza, a very low-income housing provider along the border in Alamo, Texas. He ran polyvinyl chloride (PVC) pipe from the washing machine drain out into the backyard 42 feet into an oblong depression about 40 feet in circumference. In the center of the depression, 12 to 16 inches deep at its center, he placed an empty swimming pool supply bucket in which he had made six identical 1/2-inch holes, spaced equally apart around the bucket. Then he ran PVC pipe out from those holes in a wagon-wheel pattern to six drain points a little more than halfway to the edges of the oblong depression. Then he poured a small amount of concrete, sloping into the bottom of the bucket to force water that ran into it from the washer to run *out* the PVC pipes around its circumference. (The concrete also weighted the bucket down so it wouldn't float up in case of torrential rains, which happen occasionally in this south Texas desert.) Then, he and the family who lived there filled the depression with a mixture of mulch and dirt, and planted fruit trees on it.

Close-up of the mulch pit system, which needs no maintenance other than the periodic addition of mulch. Kitchen-sink water or dishwater cannot be used because of grease that would clog pipes, but washing machine, bathroom sink, and shower and tub water all work well.

This simple mulch pit system delivers water from the washing machine in a 900 sq. ft. house below grade into a deep layer of mulch, where any organic matter in the water is broken down naturally. The mulch pit should be about 12" deep, with the excavated soil forming a berm around the perimeter. The diameter of the pit is dependent on permeability of the soil and volume of water to be processed. This can range from about 20 sq. ft. per 100 gallons in sandy soil to 120 sq. ft. of pit in clay soil per 100 gallons.

© 1997 Barbara Harwood

© 1997 Barbara Harwood

"The largest mangoes anybody had ever seen" grew on the South Texas mulch pit. Sadly, though, the hundreds of bananas it produced were normal size!

One little washing machine in a 900-sq.-ft. house has produced the biggest mangoes and avocados ever grown on the border—*with no additional water, food, or fertilizing chemicals added.* Those fruits probably give us a clue about what kind of fruits and vegetables were produced naturally by rainwater in ancient times. And, unbelievably, this little system cost a total of $25 to construct![3] As my grandfather would have said, "Now, that's usin' your head!"

"We perform the Snake Dance for rain to fall to water the earth, that planted things may ripen and grow large, that the male element of the Above, the Yei, may impregnate the female earth virgin, Naasun."
— Hopi man, 16th century[4]

Preserving Water, the Flow in All Life

Some desert cities, such as San Antonio, Texas, have recognized their potential for disastrous water shortages and are trying water-conservation programs, including a larger-scale graywater system, although not for residential use. San Antonio, like hundreds of other cities and towns throughout the dry Midwest and Southwest, is built over an aquifer, or underground freshwater lake, which is their main water source. In August, 1996, the Edwards Aquifer, 175 miles long and covering 3,600 square miles—which supplies water to 1.5 million people in San Antonio—was 30 feet below its average water level for summer months because of three years of below-average rainfall and nine months of serious drought.

Everywhere in arid, desert climates, rainfall amounts run in unpredictable cycles of very wet and very dry years. The great question for residents of that area is: What will happen to the Edwards Aquifer in a time of prolonged drought? The last serious dry cycle in 1956 dried up both of the two largest springs in the southwest U.S., the Comal and the San Marcos, which furnish most of the water for the Guadalupe River, which, in turn, supplies water to many down-spring towns. That year, the amount of water pumped from the aquifer was only 321,000 acre-feet.

As the town fathers and mothers began studying water issues in San Antonio in 1989, they realized that the city was *already* pumping at an annual level of *542,000 acre-feet per year* (and it has *grown* 6.8 percent since then). So they began thinking about how to reduce water use to prepare for the next inevitable dry cycle, as cities all over the West, which have rapid population growth—such as Phoenix, Las Vegas, and Los Angeles— *should be doing much more vigorously.*

Among a wide variety of programs already in place in San Antonio, which could be mimicked in other dry-climate cities, are a toilet rebate program to replace wasteful old fixtures with the new low-flow models, leak detection programs, "Plumbers to People" low-income plumbing repair assistance programs, community-wide education programs, and watersaver landscaping rebates.

However, the most innovative program for a large city, and perhaps the beginning of what will hopefully become a nationwide graywater recycling plan, will be fully implemented in San Antonio in three years. The San Antonio Water System (SAWS) will build two pipelines that will loop back from the central wastewater treatment plant, where they will pick up partially treated wastewater, to the center of Bexar County, where industrial use is heaviest. Customers will be able to tap into this graywater source at a much reduced rate for use in their industrial processes, and *it will save an incredible 20 percent of the current demand for aquifer water.*

In Australia, a few subdivisions have been built with graywater systems available to all residents. Two sets of pipes are built into the homes—one that takes blackwater into the traditional sewage treatment system, and one that takes graywater from the house and connects it to drip systems for exterior irrigation.

An Assistant City Manager (ACM) in Austin, Texas, a city that has been very innovative in creation of "green" systems of all kinds to preserve the environment, said there will be considerable resistance to systematized graywater programs in cities because of the extra cost of two sets of piping—*until there is a water crisis.* Sadly, he is echoing common sentiment that betrays what we seem to think is the "normal" way to plan in America—post-crisis. After past water crises, we have responded to supply inadequacies by development—building dams and reservoirs, or cutting long, often ugly gashes called aqueducts across the landscape to transport water from water-rich areas to water-starved ones. But those options are fast disappearing, because the best storage sites are already in use, and there isn't that much *excess* water to be stored anyway.

I'm sure the Austin ACM is right that there will be tremendous resistance to in-house piping for graywater discharge; however, the sad thing is that when there is finally a real drought and people need water immediately, there will be *one set of water pipes and one set of sewer pipes* throughout whole cities. Making changes at that point in existing homes and subdivisions probably won't be cost effective, so I believe we should be planning for that situation *now by putting in simple systems that allow us to use graywater for exterior irrigation.*

A Regulatory Barrier to Simple Graywater Systems

There is one more problem in addition to retrenching old attitudes about sewer systems: We are going to have to change some health codes so that soapy water is not considered too contaminated to put on plants. My company is doing graywater in our custom homes as part of the on-site sewage treatment system in areas where septic systems are normally used. Water is treated underground in a mini-sewage treatment plant, *and chlorine is added.* Then it is piped out onto the landscaping. The sad thing remains the state health code requirement that it be *chlorinated.* A better method would just use bathwater, and sink and laundry water *without doing anything to it,* as the south Texas system does. Our underground water tables don't really need more chlorine. However, that type of graywater system for recycling of water on-site, combined with rainwater collection, is probably as water-conserving as a builder or homeowner can be until current health regulations are updated.

Rainwater: The Great Gift We Ignore

"The Apache seem to be very strong when somebody dies, very strong about death. There is a reason for that. When somebody dies, when you hear thunder way over there—so that you just hardly hear it— that means that the white cloud is taking him to another world. They travel for many days, and then sometimes on the fourth day, it rains. When that rain drops on you, they are touching you."

— Philip Cassadore, Apache[5]

There is nothing revolutionary about rainwater collection. My grandparents collected and stored it in cisterns, just as it had been done for millennia around the world. Rainwater is used extensively today in Australia, Bermuda, the U.S. Virgin Islands, and Hawaii. According to *Environmental Building News* (*EBN*), even skyscrapers in Hong Kong are collecting and using rainwater.[6]

Rainwater collection, sometimes called rainwater harvesting, is probably something we can do fairly easily now in some places in this country because of a homegrown pioneer named Charles Gibson. Last fall, at the Green Builder Conference in Austin, Texas, a city now known nationally as the hub of the new rainwater-collection movement, he described how he first began rainwater collection.

Several years ago, Austin had limited water use for landscaping due to drought conditions. Because I loved my garden too much to let it die, I put old-fashioned rain barrels under my gutters and collected water. During a period of drought, one barrel filled so quickly that I got another and another and another. Finally, I was watering my entire small acreage with rainwater, *my water bills had dropped significantly, and my plants were healthier than ever.* So I began to ask questions about why everybody didn't do it. By this time, I had two 6,000-gallon tanks that were always full, even in dry years. With them, I took care of my grass, my big garden, a 35,000-gallon swimming pool, and a water garden. Over three drought years with a 30" rain deficit in Austin, my tanks never went below 75%. Last year, when it was *so dry,* my tanks never went below 96%. Sometimes I've had a tremendous surplus, and I know now it would take seven very dry years for me to run out.

Back in '88, I decided to convert totally to rainwater for drinking and household use. However, the County Health Department told me I couldn't because rainwater wasn't "clean" enough to drink. So I did some research. I went to the water treatment plant and traced the water we drink back to its source. Guess what? It's rainwater. Rainwater that washes off my roof and all your roofs, runs down my driveway picking up a little grease and transmission fluid and windshield wash fluid which leaked out of my car or has been spilled while I was working on it. Then it goes to the gutters on the streets where it picks up condoms, beer cans, plastic cups, paper, and leaves. Then it flows into the sewer and goes into a treatment plant where we add poisonous chemicals to it so we can . . . yeah right, ***drink it.*** And they tell me that rainwater *straight off my roof* isn't healthy enough for me to drink.[7]

To make a long story short, he got an exclusion from the health department so he could use his own rainwater for drinking, washing, and bathing, and now he uses no city water at all in the little burg of Dripping Springs (yeah, believe it or not, that's the name of his town!) in Travis County, Texas. And even more amazing, Travis County has gone from a place where no bank would lend money on a house that depended on "an Act of God" for water, to a county that will provide "back-up" and "start-up" water if someone is building during the dry season and needs a first water charge for its rainwater collection tanks. Recently, a major savings and loan in Austin, which was about to finance a home a few miles outside that city, *actually recommended that the homeowner install rainwater collection* instead of going to the expense of running city water several miles to the building site.

Gibson had a caveat that we will talk more about in the next section of this chapter on Healing House Landscaping. He said, "If you love St. Augustine grass, you will *never* have enough water to keep it going in full sun from a rainwater collection system in this climate." But then, nobody with good sense plants a Kentucky grass in southern Texas, anyway, and especially nobody with the sensitivity to create a Healing House!

© 1997 Peter L. Pfeiffer, A.I.A.

The two 7,500-gallon rainwater collection tanks at the passive solar Texas Specialties Clinic in Lufkin, TX. Water is used for grounds irrigation and a pond and waterfall at the front entry (Architects: Barley and Pfeiffer, Austin, TX).

© 1997 Connie Moberley, Imagiz Photography

A semi-underground 26,000-gallon poured-in-place concrete rainwater collection cistern that supplies all domestic and landscaping water needs for this 2,200-sq.-ft. passive solar home in the Texas hill country. Cost of the cistern was $12,000. Not once in three years has the household run out of water. When water is needed, a pump is turned on, and water comes up from the cistern through a sediment filter and then an ultraviolet filter. This simple process has delivered water tested to be four times as clean as Austin city water and ten times less hard. (Architects: Barley and Pfeiffer, Austin, TX).

© 1997 Peter L. Pfeiffer, A.I.A.

A well-concealed rainwater collection tank below the back patio at a Benbrook, TX, residence. The 25,000-gallon tank is hidden behind the decorative rock (Architects: Barley and Pfeiffer, Austin, TX).

What If I Need to Drink It?

Gibson used completely untreated rainwater—which passed the state health test every year—until 1992 when his wife had a baby. At that time, he spent $400 to buy and install the most common rainwater purification system, an ultraviolet light that lasts for three years or more (regardless of use) and can purify about 70 gallons a day for cooking and drinking (and mixing baby formula!).[8]

Lady Bird Johnson's pride and joy is the Texas Wildflower Center outside Johnson City. Integrated into the building, as an architectural element, is a 70,000-gallon rainwater collection tank with 17,000 sq. ft. of galvanized steel roofing as part of their irrigation system.[9]

In the Caribbean's U.S. Virgin Islands, you cannot get a building permit *unless you have a rainwater collection system* designed into your land and building plan, and we have installed rainwater systems in several of our custom homes—and our own house—in the Dallas area.

So we've come full circle. My grandparents collected rainwater in a cistern in the country when I was little and used it to augment the windmill pump in the yard. My grandchildren in Texas will see their grandparents collecting rainwater and remember its clean, pure, sweet taste (and how wonderful it is to wash your hair in!), as I do. According to *EBN*, Dr. Dennis Lye, a microbiologist with the U.S. Environmental Protection Agency (EPA) in Cincinnati, professor at Northern Kentucky University, and currently president of the American Rainwater Catchment Systems Association, surveyed state public agencies a few years ago. He found that there are roughly a quarter-million rainwater harvesting systems in America. Lye told *EBN* that there are about 40,000 rainwater harvesting systems in northern Kentucky, southern Ohio, and West Virginia, mostly on the homes of lower-income, older people.[10]

Beyond that, there is hope, because of an affordable, rugged new device called UV Waterworks developed at the Lawrence Berkeley National Laboratory (a DOE lab), that rainwater can be used for poor people the world over. This tiny unit runs on 40 watts of power in a ten-hour day, costs less than five cents a day to operate, and puts out four gallons a minute, or ten tons in a ten-hour day, of purified water—sufficient for 1,000 people.[11] And the cost is a mere $525! One of the problems with using unpurified water in Third World countries is that villagers have had to cut down the few trees left for firewood to boil the water. Just as bad, the burden of foraging for firewood fell on women and children, who typically carried up to 50 pounds of it in a load, back and forth from what was left of the forest to the villages. With this alternative, developed with DOE funding (good things for your tax dollars!), far more villagers or slum dwellers can be provided with water at far less cost to the environment—with respect to both trees and the carbon dioxide emitted from burning them—and rainwater can be used instead of draining valuable aquifers.

Rainwater Harvesting from a Healing House Roof

The three-person Westbrook family, for whom we built a custom home with a rainwater collection system, averages from 1,700 to 3,000 gallons per month, about average for families collecting rainwater, according to Garrett Pollard, who teaches the first formal course in the nation on rainwater collection at Austin Community College. The Westbrook system has a 1,500-gallon black opaque (to keep algae from growing) HDPE tank (which cost about $700) sitting on the natural Austin Chalk rock behind their house. From runoff from their Galvalume roof, the tank filled completely during a four-day rainy period immediately after they moved in. Their rainwater will be used to water all their indoor and outdoor plants and wash their cars. Mrs. Westbrook said that visitors have been stunned by how clear that untreated rainwater is. Solar electric cells (photovoltaic cells) operate the pump for the tank. For more information on what will be required to do a rainwater harvesting system on your own house, see the Appendix to Chapter 12.

The Westbrooks' 1,500-gallon high-density polyethylene rainwater collection tank.

Conserving Water: Let It Begin with Me

Here are some ways to conserve water in your own home, or a Healing House that you build:

- Install low-flow devices on all sinks and showerheads. There are varieties now that you can barely differentiate (by the feel of the water) from the full-flow ones.

- Install low-flow toilets.

- Buy water-efficient dishwashers and clothes washers.

- Fix any leaks in your home's plumbing, and repair a toilet that makes a short flushing noise even when it is not being flushed. The noise means there is a leak.

- Reduce your water use. The three-person Westbrook family, for whom we built a custom home with a rainwater collection system, averages from 1,700 to 3,000 gallons per month, or 30 gpcd, with what Elena Westbrook describes as "no problem or inconvenience at all." Comparative use in the nearby town of Plano, Texas, ranges from 4,500 to 15,000 gallons per month for a family of four. Look at your own water use, and think about how you can use less.

- Use Oxygen Purification systems instead of chlorination in swimming pools, spas, and for any business uses over which you have control, such as physical therapy facilities and city water facilities (swimming pools). It will stop skin and eye irritations, bleaching of swimwear and hair, and make it easier to breathe in an enclosed pool areas where chlorine gases evaporate into the air. And it will remove chlorine from the natural flow of water back to the creeks, rivers, and water table from which it came.

Water is life.
We are the people who live by the water,
Pray by these waters,
Travel by these waters.
We are related to those who live in the water.
To poison the waters is to show disrespect for creation.
To honor and protect the waters is our responsibility
as people of the land.

— Winona LaDuke

(Translated from the Anishinabe by Marlene Stately[12])

Water Conserving Landscape: Xeriscape

An integral part of living lightly on the earth is learning to adapt our-selves to its natural surroundings, not constantly feeling it necessary to alter *them* to suit *us*. There are natural plants that have perfectly adapted them-selves to our individual climates over eons. If we drive out beyond our cities into areas that are untouched by development or agriculture, we can see what those plants are. *Those* are the kinds of plants we should be using in our gardens and yards. This landscaping, which involves only plants that have evolved naturally in an area, is often called "xeriscaping" (pronounced "zeer-uh-scaping"). The term is also often used to refer to low-water-use plants. Nature will provide all the water they need except in severe drought conditions, and they are usually self-maintaining. Except for pulling weeds, your garden will be self-sustaining.

Typical suburban green lawns are high-water-use (as much as 50 per-cent or more of the typical household's water use), high-chemical-use, and high maintenance. Air pollution generated from a half-hour's use of a typi-cal lawn mower can be the same as driving 200 miles in a recent-model car! And, most of the time, those lawns give a homeowner more aggravation than pleasure. Just ask anybody who has to weed-kill, mow, and fertilize one every weekend so their yard will be up to snuff in the neighborhood. God forbid your perfect green lawn should get *weeds*! Why, the neighbor-hood homeowner's association may censure you, send you a letter saying you're degrading property values, and bar *your* children from playing with *their* children. We, in America, take our green lawns very seriously—too seriously. Just look at the professional lawn fertilizer trucks stopped in front of all the houses from March to November, soaking us in toxic chemicals so we can have socially acceptable green carpets from our doors to our front sidewalks!

How much better, and more interesting, are the front yards in Victoria, Vancouver Island, British Columbia. No grass. Only flowers of all vari-eties—annuals, perennials, wildflowers, and weedflowers mixed in. In Texas, some of the most beautiful areas around homes are sprinkled with wildflowers, which might, after they have finished blooming, look like weeds to some. But they are green cover—they require no watering or maintenance. Lady Bird Johnson got it right when she started promoting them during her tenure as First Lady as replacements for grass in all the Texas highway medians.

The front atrium at the author's home—left wild and natural. The live oak tree (left rear), and the mulberry tree (near left), were planted by squirrels. Four occupied birdhouses line the walls. Birds are fed in the little red barn.

Wild Growth—Weeds or Relatives?

Why don't we like this unkempt look—the natural growth of wild plants climbing over each other, pushing up their sprouts in odd places, surviving in spite of us? Perhaps, suggests writer Baker Morrow in *Designer/Builder* magazine, because they are most like us: They adapt as necessary for survival.

Siberian elms, trees-of-heaven, salt cedars, and mulberries were dragged around the world with us from one continent to another and were at first admired for the way they adapted themselves to our purposes. They became street trees, park trees, lawn trees, and handsome specimen plantings, quick providers of shade and wind deflectors, in our western frontier settlements. We soon discovered they would grow along eroded ditchbanks, or along the baselines of walls or in our old fields, all very much without our help or approval. Therein lies the key to their reclassification as pests. They have easily occupied, in only a handful of years, open space that had been ours. Their adaptability made them undesirable, because it implied much the same things that bears, lions and wolves had always stood for: a competitive independence that was always present as a threat or an affront to the human race.[13]

However, these same weeds and fast-growing trees give us great service, in spite of our rude treatment of them. They quickly cover mudslide areas, riverbanks, and wind-blown fields to inhibit erosion. In our area of north Texas, black locusts, mesquite trees, hackberries, and mulberries provide food for birds, as well as ground cover and shade. Wild plants also provide food for other small creatures, such as honeybees—nature's great pollinators. Our virtuous attempts to wipe out "weeds" and wild places have caused more than half the wild honeybee colonies in the United States to be lost in the last 50 years, with 25 percent lost in the last 5 years alone. It is rarely considered that honeybee pollinator activity is 60 to 100 times more valuable than the honey the bees produce. In fact, they are called "flying $50 bills" by blueberry farmers who count on them to *each* pollinate 15 to 19 liters of blueberries in their life. Yet modern agricultural practices are, in many cases, actually limiting productivity of crops—reducing pollination—by wiping out wild areas, or "nectar corridors" that provide food sources to migrating pollinators. (In other cases, the high levels of pesticides used on crops such as cotton to prevent *other* insect infestations are also accidentally killing honeybees.)[14]

Wild plants, called weeds, and wild trees also bloom often. When I was a child, I thought sunflowers were weeds. My parents said so, and Dad routinely mowed down acres of them from the edges of his wheat and safflower fields. Today, however, sunflowers are valued for their seeds and oil, and I use one as my company logo! Stubborn, hardy plants that bloom and bloom endlessly without any watering, feeding, or encouragement from us, all they need for survival is sunlight and whatever rain and soil minerals are there. And they have the additional benefit of providing "nectar corridors," nesting places for honeybees.

A beautiful xeriscaped environment in Arizona.

© 1997 Barbara Harwood

Even more recently, my husband and I had cut back a thriving weed vine that insistently climbed over our back fence, fully occupying it like an invading army within a month. We cut it back, threw it over the fence, and hacked away, while it spread speedily and quietly, practically enveloping us in its tendrils as we stood there with our scissors. Then one summer a couple of years ago, we were gone for a month. It took over with no one to interfere. When we came back, our fence was covered with tiny purple morning glories. Our "weed" was the most beautiful fence cover we've ever had, when we finally left it alone long enough for it to demonstrate its beautiful lavender bounty.

More and more, we're learning to let the natural take over. We planted a little Asian jasmine under an ash tree where grass wouldn't grow at all, and every time it rained, soil washed down into our driveway. In just two years, the Asian jasmine is six inches thick all around the base of the tree, and it has spread to another semi-barren area in which we vainly tried to grow grass. My husband just looked at it, and said, "Hey, baby, it's all yours. I'm sick of mowing the lawn, anyway." If we live there long enough, it will make its way all around the house, and more power to it. Xeriscape is for us, whatever the neighbors think And indeed:

Xeriscaping is the best type of landscaping for a Healing House because it is the most resource efficient, the longest lasting, and is completely compatible with the earth.

It's becoming quite popular to eliminate chemical assistance and use natural products. You couldn't locate them anywhere but the bottom of somebody's chicken coop five years ago, but now they are prominently advertised by garden shops. The first step to detaching from your lush green water-sucking, chemical-eating-monster lawn is to use chicken "doo-doo" fertilizer. The smell will make you decide you don't *really* need to fertilize as much. The second step is to pull weeds instead of using chemicals. Right away, you'll see the advantages of planting something else, such as wildflowers or a permanent ground cover.

If you want to know what grows best in your area, first try a local garden shop or nursery that specializes in native plants, or call around to find a specialist in wildflower gardening. If you can't find one that way, call your local university extension service. They probably have brochures on native plants, trees, and birds.

An Electric Lawn Mower: The Environmentally Friendly Choice

If you *must* have a lawn, or if you've inherited one that it will take you a while to transition out of, at least do one thing: Take your gasoline-powered mower out to the curb and put a For Sale sign on it tomorrow. Then buy an electric *mulching* lawn mower.

Our Black & Decker "Green Machine," a cordless convertible mulching mower, cuts up to a quarter acre (or 90 minutes of run time) on a single charge. Recharging the 12-volt battery up to 75 percent capacity takes three hours. Full recharge takes 20. It double-chops the cut grass and returns it to the soil where it belongs, not clogging up our already overburdened landfills.

And, maybe best of all, besides being able to innocently preach a little environmental sermon to our neighbors every time they ask what that thing is we're mowing with, there is an end to the pollution. Our remaining grass was a constant source of Saturday-morning contention around here. When my husband was mowing the lawn, our outdoor areas were either unavailable while he was doing it, or we were gasping for air from the fumes. The last time he mowed, before I did what I'm recommending that you do—that is, took it to the curb when he wasn't here and sold it to the first person who offered $20!—he ran a friend and her kids *out of our swimming pool from the horrible air pollution the lawn mower caused.* After that swarm of angry, screaming women and kids attacked him over it, he was probably secretly glad to be rid of the gas-powered mower, too. Especially since I *bought* him a new one.

Oh, and one more thing: It's so quiet you won't believe it. No more roar, just a hum. You can even hear the birds over the sound of an electric lawn mower. Imagine that!

Very few manufacturers are offering electric lawn mowers, all in the range of $250 to $400, depending on the accouterments you need. Toro makes a cordless electric mower that recharges in two to three days, and a corded one, $100 plus cheaper, at $250.

Protecting the Site of a New Home

If you're building a new home, start from scratch by doing it right. Plant the right ground cover and trees, or better yet, leave alone what is already there. We strive to disturb the natural site as little as possible by making subcontractors use *only* designated areas for entering the site and parking. If there are small plants in areas that have to be disturbed—to make way for a driveway or the building site itself, we transplant them someplace else or save them in a temporary planting place until the building is finished. Let your contractor know *from your first meeting* that you want the site's natural growth preserved, and then hold him/her responsible.

Most of East Texas was covered with woods like this before the trees were cut down to clear land for cotton fields. Today, many desirable building sites exist within these remaining forest areas, which builders should protect as assiduously as possible.

© 1997 Barbara Harwood

Saving the trees on a site requires effort. First, lay out the building to protect existing trees. Then, remember that the entire "drip line" of the tree must be protected from soil compaction, piling dirt, or material-waste piles. Fence off the drip line area around the tree with highly visible orange plastic fencing. *Don't change the grade in the protected area.* Be particularly sensitive to trees that have lived their whole lives in a dense forestlike environment or woodland. They may be extremely vulnerable to disturbances of any kind, sunlight, or dehydration. Water them frequently during dry periods, and, if possible, get to such a site in winter, and prune the deciduous trees to acclimate them to more sunlight. Or, have an arborist wrap the trunks to reduce high summer sun levels.

Use terracing or retaining walls to maintain grades as close to the original as possible on sloping sites, and leave as much natural vegetation—particularly trees—on the slopes as possible to retard erosion.

Think about planting trees in strategic places to shade your building: evergreens on the north for wind breaks; and deciduous trees on the south, east, and west for summer sun protection. The leaf loss on deciduous trees in winter allows passive solar gain through south, east, and west windows in winter, but keeps out the hot summer sun.

Healing Homes use landscaping and natural materials to eliminate urban heat islands.

As part of the exterior design of a Healing House, you need to either shield paving with tree cover, or eliminate it altogether. If you must have paving, consider using pervious paving.

Beginning with the worst case: If, for some reason, you are required to have paving, use a landscape architect or planner to determine which trees are fast-growing shade, and which are slower growing for longer lifetimes of shading. Alternate them around all paved areas (and buildings) to help reduce what is called the "urban heat island effect." This effect, characteristic of areas with large areas of paving to absorb heat through exposed concrete and asphalt, can increase the overall temperature of a city area about ten degrees over the nearby countryside. This, in turn, causes much more cooling energy to be expended in that city for air conditioning, which, in turn, dumps the heat outdoors, irritating the sun gods all the more, so the temperature goes yet higher . . . and so on and so on. The city of Houston, for example, dumps enough heat outdoors from air conditioners every summer to heat *seven Astrodomes full of water!*

Trees, combined with light-colored walls and roofs, and reduced amounts of concrete or asphalt, can significantly reduce the heat on your site, and, if implemented by whole communities or cities, could cut overall average temperatures in the summer by as much as ten degrees. As architect Bill McDonough likes to say, "Asphalt is a word that assigns blame."

This is especially true on the site for a Healing House. Therefore, Healing Houses use stone for walkways and have gravel driveways instead of concrete or asphalt. Gravel has the added benefit of being a free burglar alarm. The right kind of xeriscaping can do more for crime prevention than you might think. Chinese holly bushes, with their razor-bladelike leaves, *always* prevent unwanted entrance when planted under windows, especially after they've had time to grow thick and wide.

An option if paving is required is "pervious" paving. It is a discontinuous mixture of coarse aggregate; hydraulic cement; and other cementitious materials, admixtures, and water, which allows water and air to pass through the pavement. It provides a "void content" (a fancy way of saying there are holes in it) of from 15 to 25 percent. Through those voids, water can filter to the ground, helping to retain stormwater and allowing slower percolation of water back into underground aquifers. If you choose pervious pavement, be sure to find someone who knows how to test subsoils to see what kind of subbase is required.

An inexpensive trellis cover made from 2" x 4" posts and old bamboo branches in Point Reyes, CA. Natural materials can make beautiful garden amenities in xeriscaping environments.

What Can You Do to Enhance Xeriscaping?

Outdoor bird baths and fountains, arrangements of rocks, little seating areas, and patios with natural branch or plant covers all make important places in our xeriscaped gardens. The wonderful guide to home and interior decor design called *The Western Guide to Feng Shui,* by Terah Kathryn Collins,[15] says fountains should be near the front door, in your "career" area. I find that ours, just outside the dining room and living room windows in the front, is very soothing to watch and listen to as we eat meals or when we're just sitting in the living room talking. Our outdoor bird bath in the backyard is a summer splashing delight, especially with our 90-degree-plus temperatures for three months. That, combined with the two bird feeders, one in front of our house and one in back, and the variety and number of trees, draws beautiful birds and their ubiquitous songs (and squirrels who insist on sharing their food and water!) to us all year. And there's a bonus to attracting those wild creatures in your xeriscaping. They plant trees for you! We haven't planted a tree since we moved in, and so far we have three new elms, two new hackberries, one new ash, one new live oak, and two new mulberries—all for free!

◆   ◆   ◆

"For all at last returns to the sea—to Oceanus, the ocean river,
like the ever-flowing stream of time, the beginning and the end."
— Rachel Carson

◆   ◆   ◆

PART IV

◆   ◆   ◆

Adapting the Physical Realm to the Spiritual– How Do We Change the Way We Build Houses?

Shouldn't builders in America today be building the *best quality homes* they can for the money the buyer has? Of course. And I venture to say that most builders believe they do. There are exceptions, but then every industry has its greed and ineptitude. But *are* builders *really* doing the best they can, or are they deceived into believing they can't improve what they do because it will too negatively impact construction cost and, therefore, undermine affordability? I believe the answer is that most builders can do much better.

The first thing builders and architects have to do is learn that when implemented properly, *the initial design of the house can include,* at no extra cost, *elements that reduce the heating and cooling load, increase comfort levels, and improve natural daylighting.* It is at the design stage that many green building principles are applied: using land plans and building designs that are at appropriate human scale and that have the least disruptive impact on the earth, and incorporating art, natural materials, sunlight, and green plants.

In the next two chapters, I am going to give you the very short course on the *Principles for Designing a Healing Home* and explain them briefly. Many details on exactly how to do so must be left out because each house is unique; each climate and house site is different. However, with this information, you will have a checklist for yourself so that when you discuss the issue with builders or architects, you will know what to ask for and understand the answers you get. For more detailed information, you can use the not-too-technical Technical Appendix to these chapters, attend one of the author's seminars, or go to any of the excellent national conferences held throughout the country—including those held by the Energy Efficient Building Association (EEBA), Affordable Comfort, the Northeast Solar Energy Society (NESEA), or the American Solar Energy Society (ASES).

Design Is More Than Half of a Healing House

"The goal of life is living in agreement with nature."
— Zeno, ancient philosopher (335–263 B.C.)[1]

THE FIRST HEALING HOUSE DESIGN PRINCIPLE: PASSIVE SOLAR DESIGN.

The first, and, as far as I'm concerned, quintessential element to creating a Healing House is *passive solar design.* There are *two kinds* of solar in the common lexicon: passive and active. When people think "solar," many think of "active solar" and picture ugly panels on the roof that reportedly didn't work back in the early '80s. *That is not the kind of solar I'm talking about now.* Active solar, which works just fine, will be described in Chapter 17.

Passive solar is the kind of heat you find in your car when it's parked in the sun on a very cold day. Your car is a "passive solar collector"—that is, it gets heat from the sun *without doing anything active.* Like a passive person who just lets things happen to him or her, your car just sits where you parked it, while the sun shines in and heats it. The unfortunate thing about cars is that they are also passive solar collectors in summertime—just what you don't want. However, *proper building design allows passive solar heat into the house in winter and keeps it out in summer.*[13A]

This passive solar house with a Victorian feeling was designed and built by South Mountain Co., Inc., Chilmark, MA.

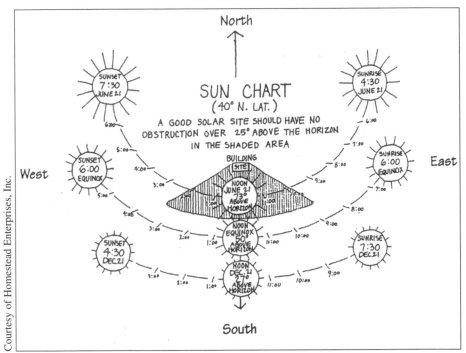

A sun chart can be used to determine a site's solar resource throughout the year. This illustration depicts a sun chart that pertains to those sites located near 40 degrees north latitude. The designer can place a transparent copy of the chart over an appropriate site plan to determine the sun's path and the quality of the solar access.

How do we get this *free solar heat in winter* and keep it out in summer? First, by placing the windows in the right place. *Most windows should be on the south side* (between 0 and 30 degrees of due south), with a few on the north and east; and in northern climates, a few on the west. In hot climates, ideally there should be *no windows on the west*. Because the sun is at a low angle in winter, it enters the windows and, during the coldest part of winter, brings heat as far into the house a the floor plan and window sizing will allow. During the summer, the sun is at a higher angle, so *properly engineered overhangs* keep it from coming in the windows.

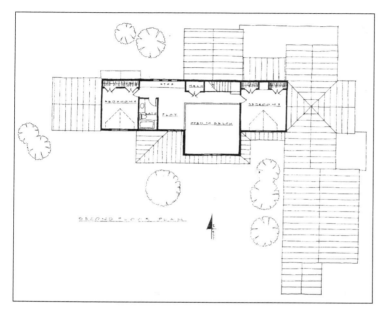

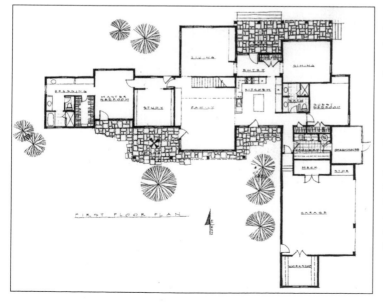

The Miller house, built by the author's company, Enviro Custom Homes, in Fairview, TX. Site constraints required the garage to be on the southeast to block an unwanted view and utilize the only treeless spot on the site. The plan is a perfect example of passive solar and natural wind ventilation design within specific site constraints (Architect: Patricia Magadini, Dallas, TX).

The next part of passive solar design follows the same principles. Because collecting the sun's rays is desirable in any climate where heating is required in winter, and, in fact, *would provide a large percentage of winter heating to most homes,* it makes sense to create a building in which the most rooms get sun penetration. A home whose long axis is east-west can have the most *south windows and the proper width overhangs,* as you can see from the floor plan of the Miller house we built in Fairview, Texas. Its narrow span from north to south not only allows the most sun to penetrate the living spaces in winter, it also allows the small north windows, along with "openable" south and east windows, to pull natural breezes through the house in spring, summer, and fall, using natural wind ventilation to reduce air-conditioning costs. The garage, placed on the site to break an unwanted view to the southeast, was also on an area that had no trees, shown below, allowing maximum tree preservation on the remainder of the site.

© 1997 Richard Harwood

Site of the Miller's garage.

THE SECOND HEALING HOUSE DESIGN PRINCIPLE: NATURAL WIND VENTILATION DESIGN.

An integral part of passive design—*just letting the house reduce our energy costs while it sits there and does nothing*—requires our knowledge of how winter winds penetrate our house, as well as how cooling breezes flow through in summer. As most of us know from watching the weather on the evening news, the jet stream—which might be thought of, for better or worse, as our national weather source—flows from west to east. In winter, ''s definitely "for worse." Those icy Arctic storms (we in Texas call them the "Siberian Express") blow down through Canada and strike us from the northwest. So *proper design will shield our homes from the northwest winds in winter.* Garages, evergreen trees, small earth berms, or earth backfilled against the house (called partial "earth-sheltering") can offer that protection.

Although winds vary somewhat between different regions, in general, summer storms come from the southwest, so the rising cool winds before and after a summer thunderstorm can cool a house rapidly. Pleasant summer breezes arise in the southeast, which is why all the old homes in the South had porches wrapped around the south and east. *Windows that open on the southwest and southeast and encourage air flow through the house to openable north and east windows (assisted by ceiling fans) can reduce spring, summer, and fall cooling costs significantly.*[13B]

THE THIRD HEALING HOUSE DESIGN PRINCIPLE: DESIGNING IN PROPER THERMAL MASS.

Don't let the term *thermal mass* throw you. It's simple. Just think of an iron frying pan. When you put it on the stove, it takes a long time to heat up, because it takes a long time for the increased temperature to penetrate and heat the heavy iron, or "mass" of the pan. When you take it off the fire, it takes a long time to cool down because it has a high degree of *thermal mass*—that is, its mass holds temperatures well.

Now, for contrast, think about aluminum foil. If you put the foil on a hot burner, it heats up instantly, then cools down to room temperature the second you take it off, because it has almost no thermal mass.

What do frying pans have to do with Healing Houses? It may surprise you to know that there are places in the world where people have done nothing in the way of energy efficiency but passive solar and wind design for thousands of years, and they have lived quite comfortably without auxiliary heating and cooling *because their houses have a high degree of thermal mass.* This means that their houses hold and stabilize temperatures inside.

A wonderful example in our own backyards is the impressive cliff dwellings of the Anasazi, where each of nine identifiable towns in the cliffs contain hundreds of rooms capable of housing thousands of people. These communal dwellings, built on the south face of cliffs, were solar heated in winter, yet cut into the cliff in such a way that they were protected from overhead summer sun. The hill protected them from the north winds in winter, and the mass of the earthen houses held the heat from the winter sun well at night. It also retained the cool temperatures from the mountain at its back in summer.[13C]

In modern houses that are passive solar and very energy efficient, the addition of mass helps ameliorate temperature swings caused when the sun heats up the house during the daytime, and nighttime air cools it down. The mass holds the sun's heat—stores it—then releases it slowly during the night so you get free solar heating both day and night.

The ceramic tile floor under the south-facing windows provides thermal mass in the author's Esperanza del Sol (Hope of the Sun) development (Architect: Betsy Pettit).

© 1997 Holly Kuper

One popular and simple way to get more thermal mass in a house is to use a concrete or ceramic tile floor under the south-facing windows. If the house has a poured concrete slab, using a portion of the slab as a finish floor gives mass and also reduces the cost of floor coverings.

Another fairly inexpensive way to create thermal mass is using double drywall on the inside of the house. Because only about one inch of a mass wall of concrete works to absorb heat, and two layers of drywall are about one inch thick, it functions the same way as that one inch of concrete (releasing heat at night), and is much cheaper. However, thermal mass in a house is usually created in the design and construction of the entire walls and ceilings of a home, as in courtyard-style adobe homes that are open to the south, found in the southern U.S. and Mexico.[13D]

Indian Tribal Headquarters

A wonderful example of many of the systems I have described to you thus far is the Wampanoag Indian Tribe headquarters in Martha's Vineyard, Massachusetts, which you can see in the photograph on the next page. With the north wall set into a south-facing hillside, only one story is above grade

on the north, but both stories can still face the south sun. The siting and orientation shield the building from harsh winter winds and cold, and give it
maximum passive solar exposure. The sun provides a significant portion of
both the building's heating and lighting needs, saving the tribe about $7,600
a year. You will understand, when you read this description of it by writer
Burke Miller, why Healing Houses must have these components:

> Tribal members felt it was essential to honor what is to them a sacred
> and powerful site, and to use low impact, environmentally sustainable tech-
> nologies. In addition to its maximum passive solar and wind design, the
> building used many recycled products, including carpet made from recy-
> cled plastic bottles, insulation made from container waste, and tile made
> from recycled glass. It has a waterless composting toilet and graywater sys-
> tem which includes extensive plantings in deep-soil beds to convert all
> human waste and wastewater to resources used within the building.
>
> The Wampanoag tribal headquarters has a soul. People can feel it
> when they enter. The building seems to speak of home, family, and har-
> mony with the earth. It reflects the spirit that still lives in this small group
> of Native American people who have inhabited Martha's Vineyard for
> many hundreds of years.[2]

*Both stories open up
to south sun in this
Wampanoag tribal
headquarters in
Massachusetts, but
because it's set into
a south-facing hill,
the north is shielded
from cold winter
winds (Architecture:
ARC Design Group).*

*The sun in the south-
facing windows has saved
$7,600 a year in this trib-
al headquarters, which its
Native American owners
have described as "hav-
ing a soul" (Architecture:
ARC Design Group).*

Passive Cooling Techniques

A *passive cooling technique* that we have found to be very effective in our own home is a *radiant barrier*. This foil material acts like an umbrella over your house, radiating the sun's rays back outside and preventing heat build-up in the materials and insulation of your attic. When we installed it in our house, it reduced our summer cooling bills by 50 percent immediately. However, I always add the caveat here that our last teenager left for college at the same time it was installed, so not all of the credit should go to the radiant barrier![13E]

© 1997 Barbara Harwood

Radiant barrier in the author's attic.

Room Arrangement and Comfort Levels

If you're thinking of changing the use of some rooms—perhaps because the *feng shui* in your house isn't right, or you have outgrown a use—remember to consider that east light is wonderful for breakfast areas and morning duties, and west light is wonderful for sunsets and evening beauty in the winter, but west windows may need covering in summer—perhaps with the addition of a covered patio if you wish to leave them open for daylighting all year—or with interior coverings if the rooms are expendable in the late hours of a summer day.

Minimal First Steps

At the very least, the first step we can take to reduce heating and cooling costs for ourselves—and to lower pollution levels on our planet at the same time—is to demand a passive solar and natural wind ventilation design for ourselves if we are building; or increase our passive solar and wind ventilation exposure in our current home as much as possible whether we are remodeling or not.

I believe that every builder and remodeler in America has a responsibility to their customers and to the future of this planet to understand these principles and, insofar as is possible, to follow them.

THE FOURTH HEALING HOUSE DESIGN PRINCIPLE: THE RIGHT LEVEL OF INSULATION IS NECESSARY TO KEEP YOU WARM.

Think about your own two-layer skin with its epidermis and its dermis. What keeps you warm? For one thing, the fat layer between your skin and your internal organs and systems. It insulates your body in the same way a blanket of insulation shields a house from temperature changes.

A Healing House should have a blanket of insulation around the exterior envelope, the thickness of which is calculated to give maximum cost-effective benefit for its specific climate region.

(Insulation levels and sealing gaskets are specified in the "wall section" of an architect's design, so they have to be part of the initial design to be drawn—"prescribed" for the builder—correctly.) Insulation is measured in "R" values, or "resistance" to temperature change. The higher the "R," the more insulated a house is. In the Dallas area, a "mixed climate region," where we need both heating and cooling in roughly equal proportions, we use R25 walls and R38 ceilings (or R26 ceilings with a radiant barrier). In the North, more insulation is needed; in southern parts of California, Florida, Alabama, Mississippi, Texas, New Mexico, and Arizona, less can be appropriate.

The first layer of insulation should be outside the studs of the wall. It is called "insulated sheathing."[13F]

The insulated sheathing on the outside of this home is the home's overcoat.

Insulation Blanket

The second part of the insulation blanket in a "stick-built," framed, on-site house is the material inside the walls and above the ceiling. Here, there are three main choices and a couple of less common newer ones, all of which work to accomplish the goal of insulating your house. Some do it better than others. The most common materials are fiberglass, cellulose, and rockwool, sometimes called mineral wool. Newer, but increasing in popularity, are recycled cotton, and a sprayed-on material called icynene. We have used fiberglass, cellulose, and icynene. Our preference is for cellulose, because it is made of recycled newspaper and cardboard and seals the wall better than fiberglass. Wet-spray cellulose is excellent *but cannot be used in homes for chemically sensitive people.* Dry cellulose and icynene are good for both. (For details of each of these, see Appendix 13G.)

Excess icynene being cleaned away after installation.

© 1997 Barbara Harwood

© 1997 Barbara Harwood

Cellulose insulation is made from recycled newspapers and cardboard. Dry cellulose can often be tolerated by chemically sensitive people.

THE FIFTH HEALING HOUSE DESIGN PRINCIPLE:
PROPER SEALING OF THE EXTERIOR BUILDING SKIN

If you cut up a blanket in pieces and laid it across your body, it wouldn't keep you very warm because the cracks between the pieces would let in cold air. A house is the same. Sticking insulation in between the studs in a house is many builders' idea of how you insulate a house, and it's no different than using a cut-up blanket to warm your body. To finish the job, you must, first, have a continuous cover of insulation on the outside wall. Then, you have to *seal all the cracks or holes in that wall where cold air can come in (or go out in summer).*

We do this by using rubber gasketing under the first piece of wood on the concrete slab or wood subfloor (called the bottom plate or the sill plate). No matter how level you try to make the concrete of the slab, there will always be some "waviness" in it. When you place the first piece of flat wood (called a sill plate) on the slab, there are little air gaps under the sill plate. When warm air rises, cold air is sucked in through those tiny spaces. That's why your feet get cold in winter in almost any house in America.

© 1997 Richard Harwood

Double rubber gasketing protects your house from air infiltration at floor level.

After we install the gasketing, we caulk the inner edge of the sill plate as added infiltration protection (foot-warmth insurance).We also caulk and seal every crack and opening in the inner wall where plumbing and electrical installations have created holes, and we use rubber gasketing around window and door openings.

To Wrap or Not to Wrap?

People often ask me about housewrap materials for sealing the exterior walls. I say it's a real good news/bad news situation. The good news is that laboratory tests show effectiveness at reducing air leakage through outside walls in almost all walls, no matter how they are constructed, although the measure of effectiveness does depend on the wall to which they are added. They share the wind load on the vapor barrier in climates that require vapor barriers.

The bad news is that no matter how effective they are, they save so few BTUs (dollars) that, for their cost of about $500 per 2,000-sq.-ft. house, they probably have too long a payback to be useful.[3] The bottom line for our company is that we don't use them. We choose to solve air leakage problems in different ways, and most notably, when possible, we use structural insulated panels. This will be discussed with building materials in Chapter 14.

However, in making the decision yourself, look at what the building code requires. If tar paper is required by code, housewraps are a good alternative. Tar paper, commonly called Thermoply (made of cardboard and tar paper) is not a healthy material and is made in three-foot rolls. Housewraps are made in nine-foot rolls, so they are easier to put on.

THE SIXTH HEATING HOUSE DESIGN PRINCIPLE: HEATING, VENTILATING AND AIR CONDITIONING (HVAC) EQUIPMENT SHOULD BE AS EFFICIENT AS POSSIBLE, IF USED, AND MUST BE SIZED CORRECTLY FOR YOUR ENERGY-EFFICIENT, PASSIVE SOLAR HOME.

As part of the design phase for a building or remodeling, the *size* as well as the kind of heating and cooling system you want should be carefully considered. Sizing your heating and cooling system properly sounds so easy and logical that you would assume that *every HVAC contractor in America* would be doing it, right? Wrong. Almost every HVAC subcontractor battles with me over the sizing. It has been common practice in the industry to oversize for *so long* that getting them to stop is like trying to stop the earth from turning. The joke in the electric utility industry for years was that, to figure out how big the heating and cooling system in a house should be, a builder or HVAC contractor would just stand on the opposite curb and hold up his fingers. If the space between his thumb and index finger when he held them up to measure the house from across the street was two inches, he needed two tons (one ton equals 12,000 BTUs). If it was three inches, three tons, and so forth. For a long time, that's about how scientific it was.

Then it went a little beyond that to minimal calculations that included only basic insulation. Later, the industry began actually looking at levels of insulation, but didn't include infiltration—that is, air leakage. Now they include infiltration, but almost none take into account passive solar and a very tightly sealed and well-insulated building envelope.

To build a Healing House, you will have to find a builder who understands all the elements we have discussed in this book. That builder should use an HVAC subcontractor who is capable of using one of the computer programs that help calculate all the energy-efficient, passive solar elements of such a building when determining the correct sizing of the heating and cooling system. Proper sizing of mechanically controlled ventilation for days when it's too polluted or to hot/cold outside to open windows is also crucial during the planning stage.

Oversizing of heating and cooling equipment is costly to you in two ways. First, you pay more than you need to for the equipment. Saving one ton of HVAC equipment can *save you a thousand dollars or more* in the initial cost of building your home. Second, you'll pay much more than you need to for monthly utility bills for as long as you live in the house because the system will never run at steady-state efficiency (when it runs more "steadily" instead of short cycling on and off). Steady-state is far more cost efficient and comfortable because heating or cooling is evenly introduced into the space. When equipment is too large, it heats/cools the space very quickly, then cycles on and off, on and off, repeatedly.

If you're in a house now where the heating/cooling system goes on and off frequently, when it needs replacing, make sure the contractor *does not automatically use the size of the existing units as his guide.* He should recalculate exactly how much equipment your house needs to function at its optimal level.

In an energy-efficient house, the temperature will hold constant for a long time. If the HVAC units are sized right, they won't have to run much, and when they do, they will do so in a steady, and—if chosen properly— quiet manner.[13H]

Open Fireplaces: Romantic Energy Losers

Open fireplace dampers, which, of course, must be open when you have a fire burning, are big energy losers unless you have the type with sealed glass doors on the front and a sealed combustion unit As romantic as an open fire is when we sit in front of it with a lover, as warm and comforting as it is for a child watching the dancing flames, an open fireplace is terribly impractical in a Healing House. First, it costs you in monthly energy bills. A French study showed that an open fireplace in a well-insulated house can raise overall heating energy consumption by 30 percent. And second, open fireplaces can introduce a lot of combustion pollutants into the air. This smells up your rugs and furniture and doesn't do your personal breathing apparatus any good either.

A better choice is a sealed combustion fireplace or wood stove with a fan-driven recirculating system that draws combustion air from outside the house and blows it, and the combustion gases, back outside. This type takes room air, independent of combustion, circulates it outside the firebox, and returns it, heated, into the room.

In a very tight, passive solar home, it is often all the heating source that is needed. Caution should be exercised in deciding on a wood-burning source to heat your house. Wood is not a limitless resource in most parts of the world, and it does cause air pollution when it burns. However, good wood stoves are now available that are EPA certified, and because of the very efficient way they burn wood, they may be more environmentally sound and emit less CO_2 than other alternatives.

Mechanical Ventilation: A Necessity in a Very Tight, Energy-Efficient House

In the *passive* section above, we talked about natural wind ventilation design. In tight houses, controlled mechanical ventilation is also required as part of the HVAC system to exhaust stale, moist indoor air and introduce outdoor air. A builder of a Healing House can prevent most toxic materials from being used during the building process, but many pollutants are brought into homes after they are built that are beyond the builder's control, including excess moisture from cooking and bathing, pets with their moisture factors and odors, aerosol sprays with perfumes, household cleaners, hobby supplies, and cigarette smoke. Even fireplace smoke in a nonsealed wood-burning fireplace must be ventilated for air in a living space to remain "breathable."

In smaller homes, the ventilation system can be relatively simple. For example, Quiet Vent fans in the bathrooms and kitchen can be "hot-wired" to operate continually in some climate zones. In larger homes, or homes with allergic or MCS residents, a whole house air-cleaning system may be preferred. However, in most homes, a simple heat and humidity recovery ventilator is all that is needed.[131]

THE SEVENTH HEALING HOUSE DESIGN PRINCIPLE: GIVE PREFERENCE TO NATURAL OR COMBINATION RECYCLED MATERIALS FOR ROOFING, AND NEVER, NEVER USE WOOD.

Shake Roofs

The type of roofing you will use is also part of the *design* process. Without going into too much detail, I will simply say: *Under no conditions should a Healing House ever have a wood shake shingle roof.* They have a serious flame-spread problem, even though they are lovely to look at and made of natural, organic materials that we usually prefer.

A better choice from a fire-prevention standpoint when a less expensive roof material is needed is asphalt shingles in a light wood color. For environmental reasons, I prefer not to use products that contain oil-derivatives such as asphalt, but in some cases—affordable housing, for example—it must be used because all the more environmentally friendly conventional alternatives are too expensive.

© 1997 Barbara Harwood

This galvalume roof is used for rainwater collection, and is highly reflective and long-lasting.

We prefer metal roofing because it can be used for rainwater collection, and it is highly reflective in natural metal or light colors (although not as reflective as white paint). It costs about three times as much as asphalt shingles, but if you factor in the water you don't have to buy because of your rainwater collection system (see Chapter 12), it helps cushion the cost. In addition, it has four to five times the life of other roofing materials. Metal roofs come in standing seam or metal shingles, which can look very much like asphalt or concrete shingles. Other good materials, also more costly (about four times as much as asphalt), are clay and concrete tile, or one of the natural materials such as slate. These are heavy, so load-bearing walls and roof rafters must be properly sized; however, they are beautiful, particularly in Spanish-style buildings, and rainwater can be collected off them almost as well as off standing seam metal They come in a wide variety of styles, finishes, and colors, and are very long-lasting.

© 1997 Owens-Corning

New "Mira Vista" shake lookalike shingles, made from natural clay and slate-bonded with resins and fiberglass, provide homeowners with a fireproof, natural material alternative.

Last, but not least, are the new combination materials, well worth considering in a Healing House. There is no testing information on rainwater collection use for these materials, but they *appear to me* to be adequate. First, there is a composite material shingle by Owens-Corning, made to simulate cedar shakes without the upkeep, the cost, or the fire-spread danger. Called "Mira Vista Shake Shingles," they are formed from natural clay and slate materials bonded with resins and fiberglass under extreme pressure. Mira Vista Shakes offer natural colors and will not warp, discolor, or rot. Another, called Heartwood, by Monier, is a very dense material, color-blended to look exactly like wood. American Cemwood also produces three lightweight, class "A" fire-rated products made through a patented manufacturing process that uses a composite of Portland cement and wood fiber.

THE EIGHTH HEALING HOUSE DESIGN PRINCIPLE: USE AS MANY RECYCLED PRODUCTS AS POSSIBLE, AND RECYCLE EXCESS BUILDING MATERIALS ON-SITE.

One of the most exciting developments of recent years is the production of fabrics for both upholstery and carpets made from recycled plastic soda bottles. It's *so wonderful* to be able to say to a child walking around with a plastic soda bottle, "If you save that for recycling, someday it will be made into a carpet you can walk on!" We use this kind of carpet, made by Image Carpet Mills (800-241-7597). It costs very little more than the lowest-priced, so-called FHA-grade carpets, looks and feels better, wears like iron, and because it's made of plastic, resists stains extremely well. Several of our custom home buyers *prefer it* to fancier wool or berber carpets, which are so popular now for their durability and stain resistance. We have heard, from one of our potential customers, that she had a puppy who was able to so severely damage her new Berber carpet by chewing and clawing holes in it that the entire carpet had to be replaced—not something that could happen with the recycled plastic carpet.

Nor could this happen, for that matter, with another product—the new modular carpet tiles, made by three companies who are all leaders in carpet recycling:, Milliken, Collins & Aikman, and Interface. These tiles, traditionally used in commercial applications, are tough, stain resistant, and, unfortunately, more expensive than residential carpeting. However, they are all made from recycled or partially recycled materials.

The carpet industry in this country is *huge*. People think nothing of throwing housefuls of perfectly good carpet into a landfill because they are "redecorating." Carpets, in fact, make up about 2 percent of the volume of our landfills, from 3.5 to 4 billion pounds, according to *Environmental Building News (EBN)*.[4] Carpet tile may reduce the need for carpet replacement, because when an area is damaged or discolored, the area can simple be pulled up and new tiles inserted. In addition, the adhesive used to place them is less harmful for allergic persons than most carpet adhesives.

Other companies, including the four largest carpeting manufacturers, DuPont, Monsanto, Allied-Signal, and BASF, have begun to realize the bonanza available in the huge volumes of carpet that are trashed every year, and have started recycling programs of their own. DuPont has developed a collection program called its Partnership for Carpet Reclamation, through which all old carpet removed by their dealers is reprocessed. According to *EBN*, a large part of that program's expansion is being driven by a new commitment from Ford to purchase a nylon resin with 25 percent recycled content to make air-cleaner housing for all its domestic autos—another bit of good news for those of us who care about the environment. About a third of the DuPont recycled carpet is shredded and mechanically separated by resin type for this use.

Whatever resources we can glean from recycled materials reduces the need for virgin materials. More and more products are being made from recycled materials. I have mentioned many throughout the book, but for those hundreds of others I have missed, or to get more information on the ones I have listed, get the catalog of available recycled building products from the Center for Resourceful Building Technology.[5]

THE NINTH HEALING HOUSE DESIGN PRINCIPLE: USE THE MOST EFFICIENT APPLIANCES AVAILABLE IN THE SMALLEST SIZE USEFUL FOR YOU.

Due to DOE regulations, it is much easier now to select the most energy-efficient appliances for your home than it was five or ten years ago. Just do a little research when you shop by *carefully* reading the labels and by demanding that the salesperson working with you knows answers to the questions you ask. If you get evasion when you ask tough questions, ask for a supervisor.

There is, however, one area that has been neglected in the energy-efficient appliance revolution. That is clothes washing. As *EBN* said recently, "1997 might well be remembered as the beginning of the end for the good old top-loading vertical-axis washing machine." Frigidaire and Amana recently unveiled their new redesigned horizontal-axis machines, sometimes called "front-loading," but most commonly now referred to as "H-axis," and on March 20th in New York City, *EBN* said, "With much fanfare, Maytag announced its new Neptune high-efficiency, horizontal-axis washer."[6]

Several European manufacturers also sell their machines in the U.S. (including Kariba of Italy, recently bought by Bendix), whose combination H-axis washer/dryers our company has used for four years in our model homes. The Bendix-Kariba washer/dryer saves 6,000 gallons of water a year for a family of four, uses less detergent, and half or less of the electricity of other washers and dryers. The two functions combined into one machine and started with the push of one button are spectacularly easy to use for the physically challenged. No more lifting of heavy, wet clothes to move them into a dryer. The price of the combination unit is about the same as buying two conventional top-loaders.

These small units are also big space savers, particularly the combination washer/dryer units, and they hold more than you would think because there is no agitator taking up space in the center of the drum.

◆   ◆   ◆

MCS Times 2, Chemical Brew & IAQ

"The teepee is much better to live in; always clean, warm in winter, cool in summer, easy to move. The white man builds big house, cost much money, like big cage, shut out sun, can never move; always sick . . . Indians and animals know better how to live . . . nobody can be in good health if he does not have all the time fresh air, sunshine and good water. . . ."
— Chief Flying Hawk, Oglala Sioux, nephew of Sitting Bull[1]

THE TENTH HEALING HOUSE DESIGN PRINCIPLE: IN A HEALING HOUSE, EACH COMPONENT IS INTEGRAL TO EVERY OTHER COMPONENT. NOTHING CAN BE SEPARATED OUT AS UNIMPORTANT, FOR EACH AFFECTS INDIVIDUALS WHO LIVE THERE, WHETHER THEY HAVE MULTIPLE CHEMICAL SENSITIVITIES (MCS) OR NOT.

Every material with which you build—that is, everything you add to the building, such as cabinets or a heating system—affects whether or not the house is nurturing or distressing to your mind, body, and spirit. Many people have chemical sensitivities they know nothing about. Many people have psychic sensitivities they have never recognized. There are "hidden" factors that influence us every day. In our company, when we build people a Healing House, we try to help people avoid using anything that might be a problem. Just as plants require certain basic life-giving elements: sunlight, air, and water to thrive, so do humans require the same basic uncontaminated things—sunlight in the right amounts, and water and air, that nourish and cleanse our bodies rather than harming them.

To create a Healing House, builders must deal with Materials, Components, and Systems (MCS-1), while at the same time dealing with Indoor Air Quality (IAQ).

MCS 1: MATERIALS, COMPONENTS, AND SYSTEMS

There are many *types* of buildings. These are the most common in America:

— **Frame homes:** Sometimes called "stick-built" homes, in which the slab or basement is poured, then wood or metal studs and framing are put in place to build the frame. Various types of insulation, walls, and roofs are used with frame construction.

— **SIPS homes:** Built with Structural Insulated Panels (SIPS), sometimes called foam core panels. Here, the wall system is made of oriented strand board (OSB) on the outside of foam insulation, which is built in pieces in a factory and craned in place onto the foundation. Various types of roofs and exterior wall finishes can be used with SIPS.

© 1997 Richard Harwood

Structural insulated panels being unloaded by crane from the delivery truck and placed on foundation. The panels, made by Korwall, have 5/8" OSB board sandwiching and 6" of expanded polystyrene.

— **Foam-form concrete building system homes:** Two parallel layers of a foam (usually either expanded or extruded polystyrene) are connected with a metal and/or plastic web, and concrete is poured inside this foam form. Many types of exterior and interior finish systems can be used with foam-form concrete buildings.

A foam-form concrete building system wall being installed.

— **Adobe homes:** Some form of mass material used for a thick wall, such as sun-dried adobe bricks, concrete blocks, clay-fired bricks, or rammed earth in some form as the exterior structure, with either the same material—metal or wood—for interior walls.[2]

There are others *less* common, but their proponents are no less passionate about them than the purveyors of building systems that are *more* common. I can't possibly list all of them, because it seems that a new one pops up every week. However, these are the most well known of the alternative building types:

— **Steel Framing**—Another alternative framing material some builders are using is steel and at least one Green Builder program recommends it *for interior walls only because it is made of partially recycled metals.* Even though it has partially recycled content in most cases, we don't use it because of its conductivity and sound conduction, and because it is a thermal disaster on exterior walls with heat conductivity of 400 times that of wood. This is a particularly important issue in the colder climates, a lesser one in the southern areas. "With 16" on center framing, you are essentially throwing away half your cavity insulation due to the thermal bridging caused by the studs," efficiency expert Ned Nisson wrote.[3]

Oliver Drerup, a Canadian builder who founded the famous Canadian R2000 program, says steel is fine as long as it has exterior sheathing completely covering it. He finds it necessary for homes he builds for the chemically sensitive, who often can't tolerate any wall systems other than inert steel.

— **"Cob,"** or coursed mud and straw, is simple, labor intensive, and, as one wit put it, "Dirt cheap." Cob houses in England are still standing from Elizabethan times, including the birthplace of Sir Walter Raleigh. Cob is ideally suited for free-form walls, since the undulating shape gives them increased rigidity and strength over a traditional rectangle. The English system requires an 18"-wide foundation and 18" to 24" high stemwall of stone or masonry to keep it off the ground.[4] I have seen similar houses in Point Reyes, California, made of a coblike material called "Permaculture." It has the same enchanting ability to shape and form a house like you would craft a clay pot.

© 1997 Barbara Harwood

A "permaculture" house in California made of "cob," a straw-clay mix, which can be shaped into interesting forms as walls are constructed

— **Straw bale houses** have made a comeback in the last ten years. There are some that are over 100 years old still standing in Nebraska, and Real Goods just built their retail outlet on Highway 101 south of Ukiah, in Hopland, California, of straw bale. (Straw is the waste from the harvest of grains such as wheat and barley, as differentiated from hay, also baled, which is a type of grass grown for feed.) Straw bale walls, from 24" to 36" wide, sprayed with gunite, a cementitious slurry, and stuccoed, have an insulation value of R50 and stand up to windstorms just fine, contrary to rumors spread by the Three Little Pigs. Often, "cob" is used to shape doorway or window openings in a straw bale building. It makes extraordinary good sense in an area with a lot of waste straw, such as Mexico, where straw bale offers an inexpensive alternative to brick construction.[5]

© 1997 Real Goods Trading Corp., Ukiah, CA

The large new Real Goods headquarters in Hopland, CA, is a straw bale building. (Building design by Sim Van der Ryn of the Ecological Design Institute, Sausalito, CA.)

The "truth window," a wall cut-out to show the walls of rice straw bale, gunite, and pise (pneumatically impacted stabilized earth); a mixture of clay, soil, and water sprayed on with a gunite gun, at the new Real Goods store in Hopland, CA.

© 1997 Real Goods Trading Corp., Ukiah, CA

— **Rammed Earth:** As David Easton, rammed-earth proponent and builder in Napa, California, said at a recent Green Building conference, "Rammed earth makes sense because it is, in essence, natural soil cement." He explained it this way: When we manufacture regular concrete, we take a soil-gravel mix, and rinse out all the good soil. We mix the remaining gravel with cement and add lime, or lime and flyash to create a building material. Instead of going through all that, Easton said, "With rammed earth, we just leave the soil in and use it for monolithic wall construction."

© 1997 Cynthia Wright

A rammed-earth home in California, a monolithic wall construction of what builder David Easton calls "soil cement."

— **Greenforms:** Developed by Pliny Fisk III of the Center for Maximum Potential Building Systems in Austin, Texas, recycled rebar is used as a building skeleton that can be bolted together and taken apart for building flexibility. Walls and roofs can be in-filled with locally available materials such as straw bale, earth blocks, industrialized by-products, and cement-sawdust combinations, which Fisk is researching.[6]

(For much more detail on construction methods with all these materials, see Appendix 14A.)

© 1997 Pliny Fisk, III

This "Greenforms" house utilizes nine different wall types within the rebar framing. The front-entry "pillars" are rainwater collection barrels, and the ponds, filled with plants and flowers, are the home's wastewater treatment system (Architect: Pliny Fisk, III).

Indigenous Materials

> *THE ELEVENTH HEALING HOUSE DESIGN PRINCIPLE: HEALING HOMES MAKE USE OF AS MANY INDIGENOUS MATERIALS AS POSSIBLE IN THEIR CONSTRUCTION BECAUSE THEY ARE MATERIALS THAT ARE NATIVE TO THE REGION. THEY ARE, THEREFORE, "RESOURCE EFFICIENT," ASSISTING US IN PRESERVING THE EARTH'S PRECIOUS RESOURCES.*

Indigenous materials are those that naturally exist *within the environment where your home will be*. Adobe block made from the earth beneath your feet is an *indigenous* building material. Straw bales cut from wheat fields next door to the building site are *indigenous* building materials. Mesquite trees cut from the building site and used for floors in the building are *indigenous* materials. Anytime you can use indigenous materials for buildings, you are being *resource efficient;* that is, you are preventing materials from being trucked in for hundreds or thousands of miles, using fuel to transport it that dirties the environment and is economically unsound (imported oil is about half the trade deficit).

© 1997 Randi Baird

This bus shelter, built entirely of indigenous, on-site materials, outside the Wampanoag Tribal Headquarters in Martha's Vineyard, MA, was designed and constructed by South Mountain Co., Inc., Chilmark, MA.

IAQ—INDOOR AIR QUALITY

Perhaps the most common question I get from people *outside* the energy-efficiency community is: "Won't there be a problem with indoor air quality because you've made these houses too tight?" They have subscribed to the uniquely American myth that a house that *leaks* fresh air gives you better air quality. As propaganda designed to thwart increases in energy efficiency, this myth is second only, in its level of dishonesty, to the one that says you can't "afford" to increase energy-efficiency measures in your house.

Obviously, every home needs a certain percentage of fresh air. The national engineering standard is 0.3 air changes per hour, which means about one-third of the air in your house should be changed every hour. In a very leaky house, say, a log cabin in pioneer times, you got something like a total air change every ten minutes from leaks (and if it was windy, every *two* minutes), so the only place you were totally warm in winter was under a pile of quilts. If you stood in front of a roaring fire, only half of you was warm; the other half was getting windburn from the air rushing through the leaks.

I'm sure those pioneers were happy to get into a log cabin and out of an even leakier covered wagon, but if they'd had the technology, they would have preferred to *control* the ventilation, which is what we do in a Healing House. Controlled ventilation with a heat and humidity air exchanger (called "enthalpy type"), such as the AirXchange we described in Chapter

13, allows a home to retain as much as 80 percent of the heat or cooling energy in air before it is exchanged for outside air. This gives the occupant control over the quantity of fresh air in the home. In a leaky house, nature has control, and you have the utility bills to prove it.

However, for certain people, even an enthalpy air exchanger is not enough to control the quality of the air they breathe, so they must have electronic air cleaners added to the heat and humidity air-exchange systems. These people are unusually sensitive to the chemicals that pervade our homes: fumes from dry cleaning fluids used on our clothes, formaldehyde from building materials and fabrics, household cleaners, and even printer's ink. These people need more fresh air, or they need it to be filtered—and, most importantly, they need to control the materials that enter their homes. Even people without Multiple Chemical Sensitivity (MCS, as it is called) can benefit from reducing these chemicals in their homes. We will discuss types of those in the next section on MCS. For now, let's talk about the materials and chemicals you should and should not use to keep the air quality in your Healing House at as high a level as possible *even if you do not have MCS.*

And, interestingly enough, most of the indoor air-quality problems we hear about do *not* occur in houses. They are found in commercial buildings, offices, hotels, and hospitals. Even though this book is primarily about housing, let me tell you the story of one woman as an illustration of how indoor air contamination can affect our health in such subtle ways that we barely notice until we are truly ill, and then we have a hard time linking the contamination to the illness.

Detailing a Devastating Discovery

Even though she loved her job, a woman who had worked as an attorney for many years in a very responsible position was sick enough to stay home quite often with chronic colds, coughing, sinus infections, headaches, laryngitis, and bronchitis. She had just assumed that was "the way my body was." Then, in one of those little coincidences life offers us, she decided to take a leave of absence to spend time with her dying mother in a distant state. She was gone several months, living in her old home. After two months, she noticed that she hadn't had any colds. After three months, she noticed that her energy level was significantly improved, in spite of the tragic circumstances under which she toiled daily, helping her mother through her final days.

By the time of her mother's funeral, she told me, she was in better health than she had been in years. "I was excited to get back home to my friends and my job, which I really do love. I didn't know exactly why I felt so much better, but I knew, in spite of my sadness over the loss of my mother, that I would feel more positive about everything since I had improved so much physically."

So she went back to work. A month later, she had a cold that lingered and lingered, first into laryngitis, then bronchitis, then a sinus infection. She was on antibiotics for three weeks. Slowly, that infection left, then another one appeared in a month. One evening at a party my daughter was having, she mentioned she'd had a sinus infection for which she had been on antibiotics *for over a year!* When I questioned her, she told me about being symptom free while she was in her old home. I suggested that this long-lasting sinus infection might be more than a sinus infection—it might be a sensitivity to something in the environment at home or where she worked. I sent her some data on IAQ and MCS. She began checking. Her home was fairly new, three or four years old. She sensed it was not the problem. So, she began snooping around for information about her workplace. After several complaints and questions she issued tenaciously to every available individual and agency, a formal indoor air examination of the 50-year-old office building where she worked was performed.

It had fungal and bacterial concentrations at "severe levels" in the HVAC system, from which most of the highly contaminated samples were taken. One of the researchers told her, "At certain levels of fungus and bacteria, nobody is bothered. Above that level, allergy-prone or sensitive individuals are affected, and at levels even higher, more and more people will have problems." Because she was more sensitive than others, she was the canary in the coal mine for her fellow workers, some of whom, she found during her research forays, were also having similar problems.

In addition, a coroner worked in the basement of her building doing autopsies. Outside his office was a tank of formalin (formaldehyde mixed with methanol), and the Welshman used that toxic mixture two or three times a week in his lab to, as he told her, "keep the buggers from rotting off before I'm finished." The problem was, vapors from the formalin used on the "buggers" were being spread throughout the building by the HVAC system and through evaporation. Levels of formaldehyde were *three times the acceptable maximum limits.* In addition, the examiners said, cigarette smoking in the building added another significant amount of formaldehyde.

County officials closed down the building, moving employees to temporary space, while mitigation efforts were under way. They hired specialists to clean and disinfect the HVAC system, interior walls, ceilings and other vertical surfaces with ozone before installing permanent air monitors. They implemented a nonsmoking rule for both employees and visitors, and installed formaldehyde destruction devices and air treatment systems in the area where the formalin was used. Three months later, everyone moved back in.

I heard through my daughter that not only is this woman feeling better—and therefore happier—but everyone in the building is thanking her for her persistence. In the process, she said, she has become aware of her own sensitivities and how to avoid problem chemicals. She has discovered she can no longer go near formaldehyde, so she has technically become "chemically sensitive." She has also become sensitized to new fabrics, some new clothes, fabric stores, upholstered furniture, new cars, and new cabinets. She is now pushing to get toxins of all types removed from the building where she works and her own home, including chemicals used by the janitorial service, and the pesticides used annually.

The officials for whom she worked "wouldn't have done anything about this if it hadn't been somebody like me who complained—a person who had been there for a long time in a highly responsible position. They were used to me, and they knew I wasn't some weirdo, although one of them did tell me later that another top-level official had suggested sometime during my effort that I might be going 'batty.'"

Building Materials: Increasing Your IAQ

Your own common sense tells you that the fewer air pollutants you use inside a building when it is built, the better the air quality will be, and the less chance you will have or a problem sneaking up on you later, as hers did. There is a long list of offenders, but let's begin with the most common offenders in new buildings, including homes—volatile organic compounds (VOCs).

THE TWELFTH HEALING HOUSE DESIGN PRINCIPLE:
A HEALING HOUSE USES AS FEW MATERIALS WITH
UREA-FORMALDEHYDE OR OTHER VOCs IN THEM AS
POSSIBLE, AND ATTEMPTS TO SEAL OFF THOSE
THAT MUST BE USED.

All building materials and most consumer products release into the air, or "offgas," the chemicals from which they are made, some in quite high concentrations immediately after their manufacture, and, often, at lower levels for years later. Those materials that off-gas the worst should be avoided in building materials. The one we watch for most closely as builders of healing homes is *urea-formaldehyde*, perhaps the most common and problematic VOC used in building materials, and a potent mucous membrane irritant. This is the chemical that burns your nose when you walk into a fabric store, because most new fabrics are treated with it for color and texture retention. It off-gasses from new furniture and in new cars. VOCs are responsible for the "new car smell" car manufacturers actually market in their ads—without telling you that the air quality in new cars has so many offgassing chemicals that if it were a building, it would have an acute case of "Sick Building Syndrome."

Formaldehyde is the acidic, slightly irritating smell of many newly installed carpets, glues, and wall fabrics. Upwards of *five billion pounds* of the chemical are manufactured in this country alone every year, and about half are used for materials that go onto or into buildings, such as particle board, plywood, cabinets, and fiberglass insulation. It is also in thousands of consumer products, such as paper towels, grocery bags, waxes, oils and polishes, napkins, facial tissues, and disposable diapers. And believe it or not, as if tobacco smoke weren't already bad enough, it's in that, too.

The problem with the chemical comes primarily when it is trapped inside a space where living things need to breathe, particularly any living beings who are sensitive to it. I became hypersensitized to it in my college premed curriculum. I was getting bad headaches in zoology labs my freshman year, and I actually began to suspect formaldehyde as the cause, but I was in major denial because I desperately wanted to become a pediatrician. Finally, I actually became physically debilitated by the intensity of the headaches, which made me dizzy and nauseous and eventually created visual problems. A doctor told me that the chemical was causing dilation of blood vessels in the brain (which in turn caused the headaches), and he said if I didn't get away from it, I could have serious health problems—such as a broken blood vessel in the brain called an aneurysm. I switched to a journalism major the next day, and the headaches went away. However, those years of exposure did make me hypersensitive to formaldehyde.

So, needless to say, when someone tells me they get headaches from the smell in new homes, I'm completely sympathetic. After doing a little research on building materials a few years ago when a customer came to us with Multiple Chemical Sensitivities (MCS), I began to realize that *nobody*, MCS or not, needed to be breathing this stuff. At that point, my company started consciously eliminating as many VOCs from our homes as possible.

If you remember, early in this chapter, I recommended using SIPS, structural insulated panel systems, which are made with Oriented Strand Board (OSB). OSB is constructed with formaldehyde glues, but they are *phenyl-formaldehydes,* which off-gas much less than urea-formaldehydes. They are not perfect, and they *cannot be used by people with true MCS*, but they are tolerated by the average person without any noticeable ill effects.

Other Volatile Organic Compounds (VOCs) to Be Avoided

Volatile Organic Chemicals are carbon-based compounds that volatize (evaporate) at room temperature. It is alarming to consider that an EPA study of indoor air quality in 1988 *found more than 500 chemicals in the air inside government buildings that were visited by thousands of Americans every year.* It further stated that there were *more pesticides* and other chemicals found *indoors* than outdoors. Another 1989 EPA study warned that one major cause of "Sick Building Syndrome" was building materials, particularly VOCs. We may know that the dangerous chemicals listed below are *individually* harmful to us, but imagine what happens when they are all together in the same air and we breathe several hundred at once. Is this stacking the deck against ourselves? Probably, since it's not likely that one would cancel out the other like a little sugar cancels out too much salt in a recipe! The best solution is this:

People in a Healing House make it a personal habit to be aware of everything in their environment and to avoid building into or bringing into their home those products containing harmful chemicals.

Paint VOCs

The first Volatile Organic Compound that *builders* can avoid, in addition to urea-formaldehyde, is probably also one of the most annoying to people moving in immediately after a home is completed: paint. Its smell gives many people headaches. Now it is possible to buy paints that are virtually VOC free. We had an exhibit at a home show of two kinds of paint—one regular paint, and one low-VOC paint. People could tell a significant difference in our informal "smell" test, and a comment was made that the low VOC paint smelled like a milkshake.

Chemical Contamination: Keeping It Out

Even though the chemical that causes the "paint smell" is now easy to avoid, many other toxic chemicals containing VOCs are not so easy to stay away from *because nobody ever tells us what they are or talks about how damaging they are to us*—especially not the chemical industry, which benefits from their sale.

Here is a possible checklist for you. Most people reading this book are already "label-checkers," but if you're not, start reading labels and don't let long words intimidate you. Take this list with you, and *don't buy products with the following chemicals in them.* I recognize that one of the problems you will have when building a house is that there are a lot of products that have "hidden" chemicals. (A useful, everyday example of this "hidden chemical" syndrome is monosodium glutamate [MSG], hidden in many foods under the words *natural flavorings*). However, the most hidden chemicals in buildings that affect the quality of the air we breathe are on the list below:

- Methylene chloride (paints, strippers, aerosols)
- Dichlorvos (DDVP) (pesticides)
- 2, 4-D (herbicides)
- Hydroxides and lye products (drain cleaners, toilet cleaners)
- Trichloroethylene (cleaners, polishes, waxes)
- Paradichlorobenzene (PDB) (moth balls, nail polish)
- Naphtalene (solvents, moth repellents, toilet bowl deodorizers)
- Benzene (volatile chemical in gasoline)
- Perchlorethylene (dry cleaning solutions)
- Formaldehyde
- Toluene (cleaning solutions)

(For more details on each of these, what materials they are found in, and what substitutes are available, see Appendix 14B.)

The rest of the chemicals are those that people bring home...

Organochlorines

People residing in a Healing House make a stringent effort to eliminate the use of organochlorines.

The organochlorines are another group of unfriendly fellows, some of which were found at Love Canal. They are not likely to be found in building materials themselves, but some are by-products of industrial products used in buildings or brought in by residents after a home is built. Some are simply dangerous to the environment around our Healing Houses, the air, water, and the ground, and, therefore, are harmful to us and our fellow creatures.

Organochlorines, which are stubbornly persistent and last hundreds of years, include famous chemicals such as DDT, Heptaclor, CFCs, PCBs, chlordane, and dioxin, which is so potent that one barrel full of it could kill every person in our nation. They are basically all some chemical combination of hydrocarbons and chlorine, so they are hazardous from the moment they are manufactured, and they don't break down in the environment for decades. Because they can't be metabolized and excreted, they accumulate in the fatty tissues of our bodies, undermining the endocrine system and hormones that control many of the body's autonomic functions, including our immune systems.

These chemicals function in our bodies as hormone mimickers, sending the wrong molecular messages to the systems on which our bodies depend for survival. Hundreds of millions of pounds of these chemicals are released into our air and water each year. Because they are present for many, many years once they are in existence, they pose significant potential harm to future generations. Earth's fragile life-support systems are being bathed in thousands of these synthetic chemicals, constantly released into the environment by conventional industrial processes and careless use of chemicals. This toxic chemical soup creates biological treachery.

Author Paul Hawken says:

> If you need any proof of the ubiquity of organochlorines, know that, with every breath, you exhale between ten and twenty types of these compounds into the air . . . . The most disturbing suggestion of the research in this area is that because organochlorines clearly react with and disrupt sexual hormones, both androgens and estrogens, they can alter the function of the brain, and thus affect behavior, thought and intelligence.[7]

The chemical names of these ten noxious neighbors are:

1. 1,1,1 trichloroethane
2. Trichloroethylene
3. Pentachlorophenol
4. Hexachlorophene
5. Carbon tetrachloride
6. Polychlorinated biphenyls (PCB)
7. Vinyl chloride
8. Chlordane
9. Chlorobenzene
10. Heptachlor

Note that all ten are chlorine-based chemicals. Most are found in pesticides, cleaning agents, and preservatives. Remember the handy little bottles of "carbon tet" that were used for home spot removers? I used to think they were miracles *except for the headaches that went with them.* I was delighted to replace them with club soda and Quick 'n' Bright!

But many have *not* been replaced by anything and are still used ubiquitously and continue to be created. It is frightening to consider the ramifications of their presence in our atmosphere, water, and earth, as two recent authors have done.

The Toxicity of Dioxin: An Accidental Industrial By-product

In addition to the chemicals listed above, other organochlorines are formed whenever chlorine is used to bleach fabrics, paper, and even laundry. These chemicals can then form dioxins, a deadly class of compounds that can cause toxic health effects at levels thousands of times lower than most other chemicals. Seventy-five different forms of dioxin exist, all as accidental by-products of industrial processes that use chlorine or burn chlorine with organic matter.

Lois Marie Gibbs, in her book *Dying from Dioxin,*[8] says that dioxin now occurs ubiquitously in our polluted world. She highlights the U.S. sources of dioxin with informative maps, tables, and figures. As briefly summarized, she lists health effects as follows: cancers, male and female reproductive toxicity, effects on fetal development, skin disorders, metabolic and hormonal changes, nervous and immune system damage, and others. Dioxons don't break down in the environment, and they accumulate in our bodies' tissues. The EPA says that using bleached coffee filters alone can result in a lifetime exposure to dioxin that exceeds "acceptable risks." The agency admitted, as early as 1979, that dioxin (TCDD) was the most acutely toxic substance yet synthesized by man, confirmed to cause cancer in lab animals at only five parts per trillion. (For alternatives to products containing dioxin, see Appendix 14C.)

Hormone Havoc

As early as 1962, in her famous book, *Silent Spring,* Rachel Carson wrote that she suspected that some of the "miracle" pesticides such as DDT were somehow interfering with hormone levels, perhaps even leading to cancer. More recently, scientists have discovered that there are, indeed, chemicals that "mimic" hormones, and they suspect that our bodies *react* to those chemicals as if they had abnormally high estrogen levels. This raises serious concerns about whether this chemical bath we are giving our earth's fragile life-support systems is interfering with human reproduction and a causative factor in the "estrogen diseases" such as breast cancer. Chief among the suspects as hormone mimickers are dioxin, PCBs, and, of course, Carson's original nemesis, DDT, still present in the environment even after being banned for decades in this country (although not in Mexico, where *it was just banned in 1997!*).

In somewhat of a sequel to Carson's book, environmental scientist Dr. Theo Colburn, writing with John Peterson Myers and award-winning journalist Dianne Dumanoski, have gathered evidence of the damage wreaked by synthetic chemicals in their book, *Our Stolen Future,* which reads something like a sci-fi thriller. They document a 50 percent world-wide decline in sperm counts, rising numbers of birth defects, and other evidence gathered over 40 years of research.

Colburn began researching suspicious abnormalities that were beginning to occur in animal populations in widely diverse areas of the world, including our Great Lakes, California, Florida, and Europe. As she slowly accumulated the puzzle pieces in her research, continually asking herself where patterns seemed to exist, she stumbled on a plethora of earlier, very applicable, research. A Wayne State University study of women who had eaten Great Lakes fish regularly had found evidence that a mother's level of chemical contamination affected her baby's development.

The children of mothers who had eaten two to three meals of fish a month were born sooner, weighed less, and had smaller heads than those of mothers who did not. Moreover, the greater the amount of the family of industrial chemicals called PCBs in the umbilical-cord blood, the more poorly the child scored on tests assessing neurological development, lagging behind in various measures, such as short-term memory, that tend to predict later performance on intelligence tests.[9]

Colburn continued to dig, and she found that the same chemicals kept showing up in tissue analysis done in species demonstrating reproductive failure, as well as in human blood and body fat, and in particularly high concentrations in human breast milk. PCBs, a close relative of dioxin, can increase in concentration *25 million times* as they move up the food chain from water, to plankton, to small fish, to large fish, to birds and other predators, she said. This kind of "bio-accumulation," or magnification, makes persistent chemicals devastating to larger creatures, including humans. If this magnification makes concentrations of persistent chemicals (those which resist natural biological breakdown in the environment) accumulate in body fat at concentrations 25 *million times greater* in a top predator (such as the herring gull) than in surrounding water, what happens in humans who can be, depending on their diets, exposed to the *highest* concentrations in the food chain? This is definitely a question we should all be asking.

Meanwhile, the author suggests drinking clean or filtered water; raising or buying organically grown foods to avoid pesticides; heeding carefully warnings of fish and meat contamination; minimizing consumption of animal fats; setting standards to protect children and the unborn; knowing our own cumulative exposure; amending trade secret laws to reveal hazardous chemicals in products we buy; requiring companies selling any products we consume, especially food, to monitor for contamination; and shifting the burden of getting rid of these chemicals to the manufacturers.

Cleaning Up Chemicals: Conservatives vs. Liberals? Not Really...

Sometimes when I talk about these issues, I'm accused of being a "tree-hugging liberal." And I'm not the only one who gets attacked. Groups such as the Chlorine Chemistry Council, an arm of the Chemical Manufacturers Association, and the American Crop Protection Association, formerly the National Agricultural Chemicals Association., have launched an all-out campaign to discredit *Our Stolen Future,* just as they did 35 years ago when

Silent Spring was published. Many of their attacks are supposedly based on free-market idealism.

So I was relieved to see, in Gordon Durnil's book, *The Making of the Conservative Environmentalist,* an enlightened political statement, rare in these times, on the compatibility of conservative and environmental values. Remarkably, this book has been praised by entities at absolute opposite ends of the political spectrum: Dan Quayle, and Greenpeace. Durnil documents his transformation from a political lawyer—assigned by President George Bush to U.S. Chairmanship of the International Joint Commission (IJC), a U.S.-Canadian effort overseeing environmental quality in the Great Lakes— to a human being who was alarmed about the condition of our environment.

Arriving at his new job in 1989 with no "green" background at all, he studied, probed, questioned, and documented what he learned, using his legal training to evaluate the evidence on Great Lakes contamination. By 1992, after his simple and rational conclusion that toxic chemicals are polluting our environment, a major uproar erupted in the IJC, largely fomented by the major chemical companies. Largely because of industry opposition, his recommendations that toxic chemicals, including dioxin-generating chlorine, should be subject to a planned phase-out have not yet been enacted. Durnil writes:

> When a child molester molests again, we ask, "Why was he out on the street? Why didn't people keep him away from our kids?" But when an executive of some large conglomerate violates the laws by discharging some noxious substance into the water or air, or onto the ground, we pay little attention. We don't ask why he wasn't required to keep those unmanageable substances away from our kids. Science tells us of bad effects that certain kinds of discharges can have on our children, born and unborn, but we don't seem to see the analogy between a perverted individual sexually molesting a child and an industrial discharge affecting the basic sexuality of a child. I wonder why.[10]

Durnil would like us to know that the words *Conservative Environmentalist* do not constitute an oxymoron. As I've said for years, the root word for *conservative* is the same as for *conservation.* (This first just popped out of my mouth, almost without my being aware of it, when I was sitting next to Sen. Phil Gramm [R-TX] at a Washington, D.C., breakfast. He stared at me for a minute after I said it as if I were speaking Chinese. Then, without comment, he turned to the person on his right and changed the subject.)

It's high time we stopped seeing toxic contamination of the planet as a political issue and begin seeing it as a *serious problem for the future of all living creatures.* At the very least, we should insist that Congress require that the companies that produce these chemicals put biological markers on them so when they pollute our neighborhoods and we want to stop it, we know where to go. And maybe, just maybe, we should demand that Congress go beyond that, to demanding that industries "at the very least, do no harm." It seems like a reasonable request. After all, our nation's laws demand from *us* that we do no harm to each other!

Pesticides—The Ubiquitous Poison

As you read through the two lists of chemicals above, it probably dawned on you that not just one, but *many* of these toxins are in pesticides. Nine out of ten homes in America have brought in high concentrations of this toxic chemical soup in the form of some kind of bait, pest strip, aerosol spray, or pesticide solution. We tend to spread them around ubiquitously in our culture. Our children have been raised to be terrified of the slightest little black bug, as if they were invaders from another planet, not small creatures with whom we share this small planet in a huge universe. (Keep in mind that from that perspective, or even just from the view outside an airplane window, we are "bugs" ourselves!). It is doubly important that we become more aware of this problem, because, tragically, *one of the most frequent causes of childhood poisoning is pesticides.*

Chlordane, one of the most potent and harmful ingredients in pesticides, lasts almost forever because it accumulates in the body's fatty tissues. And it is just *one* of the poisons in the *hundreds of millions of pounds* of pesticides used annually in the U.S. I could go on here for pages talking about where chlordane is found and what it does to us but, trust me, you *don't* want to hear it. If anything about life on this planet will make you totally paranoid, this is it. Just don't ever use *ANYTHING,* pesticides included, *with chlordane in it, and especially, don't let your children get around pesticides or play in places where pesticides are sprayed EVER.*

The frightening conclusion that pesticides are skewing our immune systems to make an AIDS epidemic possible has not, as far as I know, been tested, but nonetheless, I believe its logic is inescapable. Many of the ingredients in this toxic chemical soup called pesticides are known to interfere with our immune systems. Because low-income people tend to live in older apartments that have colonies of cockroaches living in and around them, landlords tend to spray on a *monthly basis*, using the cheapest pesticide purveyor. The people wielding these sprayers are often temporary in those jobs, lasting until they can't stand the smell or the low wages. So most employers spend very little time training them. I've talked to several, and *not a single one I interviewed had had more than one hour of training in his job.* They are just told to go into apartments, spray all cupboards, and around the edge of every wall in every room—*no quantity specified.*

A short time after the sprayer finishes, the family returns, and the children begin to play. The little ones sit on the floor, rolling their toys over the carpets and against the walls, which have just been sprayed. Then they pick the toys up and put them in their mouths! They *ingest these chemicals—which ACCUMULATE in their tiny bodies in high concentrations for their weight.* This chain of pesticide spraying began ubiquitously about 25 to 30 years ago. *THAT GENERATION OF CHILDREN WITH WHICH PERVASIVE PESTICIDE SPRAYING FIRST BEGAN IS NOW THE GENERATION THAT HAS AN EPIDEMIC OF AIDS, AND THE EPIDEMIC IS MOST PROFOUND AMONG LOW-INCOME PEOPLE WHERE EXPOSURE TO PESTICIDES WAS GREATEST.* Although I have no proof, I believe that eventually a link will be made between concentrations of pesticide chemical poisons in our bodies and our vulnerability to the immune deficiency viruses.

Here are some ways to reduce your exposure to pesticides:

- Never assume that a pesticide is safe.

- Make your own lawn pesticide-free, and encourage your neighbors to do the same, or, at the very least, ask them to notify you when they are going to use lawn chemicals.

- Warn your children to stay *far away* from those lawn chemical service trucks or any lawn that has been recently treated by one.

- Find out how your local merchants treat their facilities for pests. Some supermarkets actually fog their produce with pesticides.

- Buy fruits and vegetables in season, preferably at your Farmer's Market. The closer produce was grown to your home, the less likely it is to have been treated with chemicals to keep it pest-free during shipping and storage.

- Thoroughly rinse all fruits and vegetables (no detergents— they leave residues, too).

- Peel any fruits with wax on them. There may be chemicals *under* the wax.

- Grow your own organic produce, or buy at an organic grocery such as Whole Foods.

- Always trim fat from meat and fish; pesticides build up in fatty tissues.

- Find out what pesticides are used in your office or your child's school. Do an education campaign to get them to use nonchemical pest-control methods. If that doesn't work, tell them you need to be notified when they are spraying, and you will not be able to be there at that time. Then wash any surfaces that the spray may have come into contact with.

- Hotel rooms are often sprayed with pesticides. Ask for a pesticide-free room.

- Find out if drinking water in your area has high pesticide residues. If so, encourage local officials to eliminate the sources of contamination, because water treatment systems that eliminate pesticides are very expensive.

- Golf courses present a great potential for exposure to unwanted chemicals. In particular, do not walk, sit, or lie down on one immediately after treatment.[11]

Aldrin—A No-No As a Termiticide

The last of a group of nasty chemicals we will talk about is aldrin, often used as a *termiticide* by builders around foundations during construction. Builders and lenders will often say that you *must use* termiticides. Fine. Tell them you will use *diatomaceous earth,* commonly used in swimming pool filters, or, a less expensive alternative, *00 sand-blasting sand* (pronounced double-ought sand-blasting sand). Filled around the foundation, it prevents termites from getting to the wood because the material is so fine they can't tunnel through it Their tunnels collapse around them, so they have to depart or suffocate.

One caveat when installing diatomaceous earth or 00 sand-blasting sand: Don't breathe the dust. Its labels warn that it is a carcinogen because it is silicon dust and can cause silicosis, or "coal-miner's disease." Silicon is another naturally occurring element—present in all sedimentary rock. Even though we live with plenty of silicon in our lives every day, getting tiny ground-up rocks stuck in your little lung sacs is not a healthy practice, as coal miners learned early in this century. Wear a mask. Obviously, the best foil for termites is a type of wall they can't eat, such as concrete, adobe, or masonry. But since that's not always possible or cost effective, the diatomaceous earth or 00 sand-blasting sand are the best alternatives. Specific installation instructions can be found at Greenbuilder.com/source on the Internet.

Boric Acid and Spiders

We haven't used pesticides for 14 years, and we have no bug problems—even in Texas where cockroaches are the size of mice—because we discovered boric acid and spiders, our basic Healing House "insecticide" system.

Residents of a Healing House use nontoxic solutions for pest control, including boric acid, spiders, and mousetraps.

Boric acid, in dilution with distilled water, is so beneficial it has also been used for generations to wash out the eyes of newborns in hospitals. That solution was my first—and second—contact with boric acid. Mother used it to wash out my eyes as a child. However, one of its most common uses now is as a pesticide. Actually, derivatives of the basic element, boron, are the planet's wonder drugs. Twenty Mule Team Borax is a nontoxic laundry "bleaching" additive and a fire retardant used in cellulose insulation and other products. Boric acid powder, used as a pesticide, works wonders by scratching the insect's shell and causing them to dehydrate to death. Completely harmless to the environment, boron is also used with its first cousin, silicon, to produce the electrical reaction in most solar electric (photovoltaic) cells.

Where do you find these miraculous products? Twenty-Mule-Team Borax is available at any grocery store, and you can purchase dry boric acid powder for pesticide use at any pharmacy for about $2 a large jar. You can also buy the handy plastic squeeze powder applicator (refillable forever) from the Real Goods catalog (see Appendix to this chapter). Granted, boron products require *our human assistance* to maximize their use. When you replace chlorine bleaches with it for a whitener in laundry, hanging the clothes in sunlight finishes the job so you will have, as the commercials would say, "the whitest whites." And believe it or not, there is really *not* any ongoing competition between you and all your neighbors to see who has the whitest underwear, despite what the commercials say! So if you can't hang clothes out to get them completely white in winter, just wait until spring. As my Grandmother used to say, "Who's gonna know?" And, simplest solution of all to ending the use of chlorine bleaches: *Stop buying white* towels, sheets, and other clothes that have to be bleached.

You also have to take one additional step when you wish to replace toxic pesticides with boric acid as a cockroach remedy. You have to keep nonrefrigerated foods in bug-proof containers and take garbage, especially food waste, *outside* your living space to the compost or trash *every night.* And even if you do everything perfectly, boric acid does take a little longer to get rid of roaches than spraying them with pesticides. With products such as Raid, you actually see the bugs curl up and die the second they are hit (which should tell you something about what pesticides do to living tissue!). With boric acid, you have to give it a full six weeks to get rid of all of them.

To administer it for the first time, clean cabinets and floors thoroughly. Sprinkle a fine coat of it around the back and side edges of all cabinets, around the baseboard of your kitchen, under cabinets, and in the pantry. Wherever you can, lay down a solid powder coat, not just around the edges. Typically, you could cover the entire area under the refrigerator, freezer, dishwasher, and washer/dryer with boric acid powder. Also put it on the floor behind toilets and inside the back and side edges and around water pipe openings inside bathroom cabinets. It will also work around windowsills or at baseboards where sugar ants and other ants come in. For flies, use a fly swatter. For other flying insects, use spiders, or open windows and let them out.

Using Boric Acid in Apartment Buildings

Our initiation gift to all new residents in our apartments is a jar of boric acid and a Pesticide Consent Form and Pesticide Information Sheet. We inform residents how to use the boric acid, and tell them they are responsible for keeping their apartments clean enough to keep out roaches (the main complaint in any request for pesticides). If they don't, and they insist on pesticides being used, they have to sign the consent form with a health warning on it that our managers read aloud to them when they move in. We recommend this process to anyone who owns rental housing to protect yourself from future pesticide health liability.

Spiders: The Best Natural Pest Inhibitor

It's true: People who haven't already learned to love spiders are stunned when I tell them that spiders make the best bug catchers around. In the 19 years we have used only spiders and boric acid as pesticides, the spiders have never once bitten, or even bothered, any human being in our house. Having said that, I first want to warn you to be able to identify *black widow spiders* and *brown recluse spiders*. I have never had either of them inside our house; but I have seen black widows in Scottsdale, Arizona, outside under our porch rail, and two brown recluses (about five years apart) in our garage here. Those are poisonous and should be removed or killed immediately.

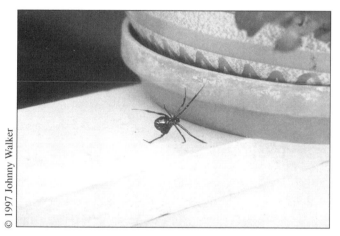

Black widow spiders, which venture out of their hiding spots under porch rails at night, carry a characteristic red hourglass on their underside.

© 1997 Johnny Walker

Brown recluse spiders have a characteristic dark brown violin shape on their heads. They are found in dirty, dark spots (but they can be gassed with hair spray and hauled outside for photos!).

© 1997 Barbara Harwood

Common house and garden spiders gained my respect from two incidents many years apart. In the early '80s, I was on a photography kick. Outside my son's window in Illinois, I found a most intriguing spider web with a large black and yellow spider tending it.(see photograph). I photographed the web over a period of an hour or two, fascinated by its creator. She danced around on her beautiful silk sculpture, up and down its zigzag path, waiting for her prey. Finally, she drew to her web a large wasp, and her work began. Within half an hour, the wasp, roughly the same size as she was, was bound up in a silken cocoon from which he would only emerge as food for her babies.

The elaborate web built by a spider who is a specialist in capturing wasps. She lived outside our window in the Harwood house in Northfield, IL.

© 1997 Barbara Harwood

The second incident happened in the corner of my kitchen. I would have been completely oblivious to it, down there under the cabinets and out of sight, if it hadn't been for the ruckus raised by the trapped dirt-dobber (a fairly harmless black wasp that builds its nests by sticking mud to walls, for those uninitiated in southern terminology). I was washing vegetables for dinner when I heard a frantic buzzing sound. When it went on for more than a few minutes, I followed the sound to a little spider web artfully spread over the corner recess. What I saw was captivating. A very tiny, but very determined little spider had captured a dirt dobber 20 times her size. When I first looked, she was sitting on the outside of the web, watching him struggle, loudly, to free himself. Finally, when he took a rest break for a few seconds, she moved in like lightning, tightly wrapping one leg at a time in her tough silk threads. Almost immediately he again began the battle to free himself, and she raced away to a safer spot. He would rest again for a few seconds, and she would move back in and wrap another leg. That cycle was repeated again and again until he, too, was a cocoon of food for her little ones.

Strangely enough, that little miniature theatrical performance by one of the tiniest visible creatures on the planet was very inspiring to me in a number of ways. First, and this almost goes without saying, I gained respect for the skill and speed of spiders against incredible odds. Secondly, I saw why they have little colonies of hollow bug shells, easily swept or vacuumed up, underneath cabinets or windowsills where they live. Third, I was, at that time, fighting a largely uphill battle to focus the attention of builders on the issues of energy efficiency, resource efficiency, and environmentally friendly buildings, as well as to focus the attention of the city of Dallas on the need for low-income housing. So I felt, in essence, like the tiny spider fighting the giant wasp. *And she won! Yes!* I thought of that in so many circumstances when I was the lone voice or the underdog: "Don't stop. Don't be afraid. Speak your truth. Do what you must for your children and grandchildren. The spider did, and she won!"

The moral of the story is: Leave spiders where you find them. If you don't bother them, they won't bother you. They will also kill all the other bugs in your space who come to their webs (most do) and leave them all together in a nice, neat little pile for your disposal. House spiders are the sign that you have an environmentally healthy house. And who knows, you might even see something in some incredibly unlikely place which will inspire you to do great things!

Radon Gas: Is It a Real Problem?

Radon gas is a radioactive gas that should be mitigated during the building process. It comes from the natural decay of uranium that is found in many soils. Use building techniques that keep radon gas from accumulating inside if your area has a potential radon problem. Since radon is a byproduct of rock whose origin is volcanic, it is probable that many areas truly *do not* have enough to be of concern. However, there are three factors involved in determining potential radon problems in addition to geology: aerial radioactivity, soil permeability, and foundation type. Sometimes radon gas can also enter a home through well water, but the main cause of radon gas in a home is soils.

The EPA's position is that one out of every 15 homes has radon problems, and therefore, every house in America should be tested for radon to see whether household levels are above four picocuries per liter (4 pCi/L). Nobody knows *exactly* what level of radon gas inside a building is tolerable yet, but common sense would tell us that the fewer contaminants in our houses, the better. Having said that, it is also common knowledge that we are in contact with very low levels of naturally occurring radiation every day. Our bodies have evolved *with those substances on this planet*, so, lest we obsess over this, there also may be less to be concerned about than some people think. So which way do we go? Start with your state radon office. Those numbers are available in a free EPA brochure: "A Citizen's Guide to Radon," available by calling (202) 233-9711. While you are at it, ask them to send you a companion pamphlet, "A Guide to Radon Reduction," in case you find out you have a problem in your area.

As a builder, I *must*, due to liability laws, defer to the experts, and you would probably be wise to do the same. On the EPA radon map, the darkest areas on the map are Zone 1, where there is a predicted indoor screening level of radon *greater than 4 pCi/L*. These are areas of greatest danger. The Zone 2, slightly lighter areas have a predicted level of between 2 and 4 pCi/L. The lightest areas, Zone 3, probably have a level less than 2 pCi/L, but the EPA cautions that "thousands of individual homes with elevated radon levels in Zones 2 and 3 remain undetected."

EPA MAP OF RADON ZONES

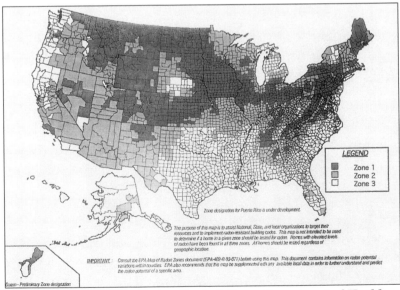

Courtesy Bureau of Radiation Control, Texas Department of Health

It may be worthwhile mentioning here that radon gas decays into radioactive particles that can be trapped in your lungs when you breathe. They continue to break down further, and as they do, they release small bursts of energy that damage lung tissue and can lead to lung cancer. *Please note that IF YOU SMOKE, the risk of lung damage or disease from radon is far greater than if you do not smoke and have never smoked.* There is special concern for children in the homes of smokers who may also have radon penetration, since children seem to have greater risk than adults for developing cancer from radiation.

Biological Contaminants

Eminent Canadian housing researcher, Oliver Drerup, author, with others, of the book, *Building Materials for the Environmentally Hypersensitive,"* and indoor air quality expert for the Canada Mortgage and Housing Corporation, has, in his slide show he uses in his lectures about indoor air contaminants, a video litany of horror in basements. They are not the monsters in the closet that scared Calvin and Hobbes to death, but they are truly monstrous, yucky pictures of black crud—creeping around on basement walls and poisoning the inhabitants who breathe the mold spores they emit. These particularly nasty molds are called stachybotrys atra (pronounced *stocky-botrus aatra*). As Drerup would say, "Not a pretty picture."

There are more of those around. Nearly all of them are caused by too much moisture *inside your house* where it doesn't belong. Moisture belongs pretty much inside plumbing pipes, on your skin so you don't age too early, and in the lettuce drawer of your refrigerator. That's about it. Other excess moisture gets in bad places: behind the tile on your bathtub, causing the drywall behind it to rot, and, eventually, disgorging your tile into the bathtub or shower bottom. It collects on your basement walls, causing yucky molds to grow, and inside the ducts of your heating system, spreading to your lungs every time you breathe. It also collects behind the wallpaper in your kitchen, causing it to peel off. And on and on.

As Drerup said:

> You can do solar and natural wind ventilation and rainwater collection and every other thing you've talked about here *exactly right,* but if you don't take care of moisture problems *in the design of the house,* you definitely will not have a Healing House. Chemical contaminants are *fairly easy* to control. You identify them and get rid of them—or don't build

them in to begin with—and they are gone. Biological contaminants, on the other hand, demand an in-depth understanding of how a building functions and intelligent control of moisture sources.

Therefore...

Moisture control is a primary concern in design for a Healing House, both in the building itself, and in the heating, ventilation, and cooling (HVAC) systems.

To check your existing house for the give-away signs of too much moisture in the wrong places, which grow into biological (mold, fungus) contaminants, check your basement for discoloration, dampness, musty smells, or moisture condensation, especially if your basement is not heated. Check old carpets, especially where you may have had plants sitting on them, even if the plants are in waterproof dishes. I was astonished a few years ago after we had a flood (a broken water-supply hose to the washer poured water into our house for seven hours before we came home and found it. Everything but our back teeth were floating by that time.) We pulled up all the rugs to replace them and found these nifty little, black, moldy circles where every plant in the house had been sitting. I realized then that the water wasn't from the plants, but from the house, being held in that little circle by the constant pressure of the plant.

This photo was taken by the author in Odessa, the Ukraine. When plants start growing out the windows, you can be absolutely certain that there is biological contamination of the building.

Old carpets, whether or not they have plants on them, get musty and full of molds and fungus spores because of the way carpets are made. Their little tufts are full of tiny openings. When dust, fungus spores, and molds in the air pass by, they are irresistibly attracted to the deep, dark home inside carpet fibers where they can grow, undisturbed by many types of vacuums that can't reach them. There they can settle in and multiply happily in the dark, passing out their nasty relatives to you as you walk by and stir them up. We have, in our own Healing House, gradually eliminated most rugs and replaced them with ceramic or wood floors for exactly that reason. My allergies were significantly improved by putting a wood floor in the bedroom and replacing curtains, also a good dust and mold collector, with Venetian blinds.

Piles of anything old—clothes, paper, furnishings (especially upholstered)—in your basement or any cold, damp place are also a prime breeding ground for nasty biologicals. (This is also a good place to breed brown recluse spiders, which you don't want any more than you want molds and fungi.) Get rid of any soggy piles of old stuff.

Floor drains collect hair and other waste materials that then nourish their own living, fungal cousins. Clean them regularly if they are used, replace them with an airsealing type, or pour a cup of baking soda and half of cup of vinegar down, seal the drain, and allow it to stand.

Make sure you have adequate ventilation in your bathroom(s) to remove moisture after baths and showers, either through a direct exhaust fan or a central ventilation system.

Cold walls in closets, where piles of boxes, clothes, or other fertile objects for moisture are collected, can also be a problem. Ventilate these with a central ventilation system, leave the door open in winter to warm them up, and, last but not least, make sure they don't look like Fibber McGee has lived there for years. (In case you're too young to remember the old radio show, *Fibber McGee and Molly,* this character, whose program opened with the clattering and banging of trash falling when he answered the doorbell at the wrong door, has inspired me *my whole life* to clean out my closets!)

Attics can also be a problem if they are not properly ventilated. Moisture from the house rises into the cold attic with the warm air from the heated house. There, the water molecules gather all their friends for a party in your insulation. At their parties, they drink a lot, getting really soggy drunk, and then invite over some of their less acceptable friends, the fungus of the earth—really moldy creatures. (Why does this sound a teenage party?) After a little while, you have a really smelly, soggy mess to clean up. Just seal the attic off from the living space, and ventilate it well so it doesn't have the odor of smelly socks or ancient gym shoes. The best non-motorized attic ventilation system is a screened ridge vent plus roof overhang vents to get continuous attic ventilation.

I'm sorry to recommend this to most people, because it was one of the scariest things I ever had to do, but check the tray under your refrigerator and freezer. You won't *believe* what's in it. If possible, do it in summer so you can make a dash for the outdoor hose with the power spray. Let it do the nasty work of getting the yuck off. Then resolve to do it monthly so it doesn't look like that anymore—or off-gas all that moldy refrigerator refuse (truly *biological* contaminants) into the air you breathe.

Change the filters on your furnace, air conditioner, and heat recovery ventilators as prescribed, or more often if necessary.

Remember that potted plants *can* support mold growth. If you are sensitive but still love potted plants, build a sunroom and isolate them there. And be sure you don't have them in your bedroom if you know that they bother you.

A few more tips from Oliver Drerup, the godfather of awareness about moisture problems and the ghastly biological crud with which they infect our houses:

- Don't dry laundry indoors unless you have a *really, old leaky house,* or you have vents in your laundry room. Better: hang it outside. Sorry, Canadians and Alaskans, the season is short. Alas, dryers may be a requirement in cold climates.

- Don't store firewood indoors.

- Keep wet surfaces very clean (showers, tubs, etc.).

- Take your shoes off before coming in the house (this from a man whose kids are, obviously, not yet teens!).

- Clean house regularly with a central vac or damp mop.

- Remove dust-collecting furnishings such as shag carpets and fuzzy furniture.

- Caulk and weatherstrip older homes to prevent entry of dust, pollen, and other spores that grow in moist areas.

- Don't smoke. If you must smoke, don't smoke inside the house.

And, if you have mold and fungus problems, you have to get rid of the moisture causing them. If you do all the things recommended here in your existing house and you still have problems, look at your outside down-spouts. Do they drain into depressions that flow around the foundation and basement walls? Is there a cracked wall that leaks only when it rains? If so, you may have to take more stringent measures, such as complete drainage and waterproofing the foundation. (If possible, check first to see if your home had this done during construction.) This could involve excavation around the exterior of the foundation and installation of a product such as bentonite clay. For this, call the experts. In new homes, foundation water-proofing is commonly required by code.

Other Indoor Air Quality Tips

In addition to ending pesticide use in your life, some other measures you can take to improve your indoor air quality are:

— Get a central vacuum system that exhausts to the exterior if you are building a house. One of the biggest problems with a regular vacuum is that microorganisms are small enough to flow through the pores in the disposable bag inside the vacuum. Therefore, when you vacuum, you're just moving the smallest particles from one place to another—and into your lungs if you are the one on the backside of the vacuum. A central vac system exhausts *everything*.

— If you're not building a new Healing House, get a vacuum that exhausts into water inside the unit, such as Rainbow or Filter Queen or a unit recommended by an authority such as *Consumer Reports*. Other regular vacuum makers will tell you that these don't help, but I'm here to personally testify that they help a lot. My respiratory allergies after the house is cleaned are significantly less with the Rainbow than they were with our previous air-vac model. And back in the '50s, my allergy doctor told my mother to get a Filter Queen, which at that time significantly lowered the number of my asthma attacks.

— Think twice or three times about using gas appliances in your living space, especially gas stoves. Anytime you have combustion of a fossil fuel inside a living space, you have combustion by-products in that space at some level, including carbon monoxide gas.

— There's been so much talk about dust mites lately that it gives you the creeps to go to bed at night. Sensitive people should take steps to rid your bed and your house of dust-mite doo-doo, the source of the problems. Put plastic covers on mattresses. Keep moisture levels in your home at less than 53 percent so dust mites cannot survive. Clean carpets, if you must have them, thoroughly. Better yet, get rid of carpets and use hard floors with rugs that you can remove to clean or wash. This will also help with dust mold, one of the major sources of allergic problems.

— If you are building a new home or replacing the HVAC system in your current home, make sure it is *sized* properly. I addressed this issue in terms of efficiency in the last chapter, but it has also been estimated that 50 percent of all IAQ problems could be prevented by keeping mechanical ventilation systems working at their properly designed capacity. If they are incorrectly designed or poorly maintained, they don't maintain the correct moisture levels in the living space, and moisture can be a key factor in the ability of fungi, mildews, molds, dust mites, and other microbes to flourish.

— If you need air cleaning beyond what you can do with these ordinary HVAC systems or Air to Air Enthalpy Heat Exchangers, buy an electronic air filter or an air purifier with a HEPA (High Efficiency Particulate Air) filter. They can be bought room size (14' x 20') for about $200, small house size (up to 1,500 sq. ft.) for about $400, or larger whole-house size for about $2,000. See the Real Goods catalog or a local HVAC supplier. The HEPA filters eliminate any impurities except odors, and a charcoal filter added to most units will get rid of those as well.

There are also HEPA filters available for vacuum cleaners, but the Canadian Mortgage Housing Corporation (CMHC) research has show that these do not function much better than a dirty vacuum cleaner bag. Oliver Drerup, of CMHC, said, "The vacuum cleaner bag pores, after use, become blocked by large particles.Therefore, for as long as any air will go through the bag at all, making it usable for vacuuming, you get pretty effective filtering of smaller particles."

As the author, I'm not sure I would recommend a *dirty* vacuum cleaner bag over a new vacuum that worked better, but it is genuine research by experts. As someone who has stood on the backside of a vacuum for more years than I care to think about, it seems to me the key question with that research is: "At what point does your vacuum, because the air through the bag is blocked, *do more damage than good* by not picking up dirt, molds, and spores because the biggest pores are blocked?" Therefore, my advice is still: Get a better vacuum.

MULTIPLE CHEMICAL SENSITIVITIES (MCS)

Multiple Chemical Sensitivities are, clinically, only applicable to those who have been so diagnosed; however, many of the chemicals that bother such people are also harmful to the rest of us. Many people are having health problems that may be, without their realizing it, connected to their living environment. This must be considered in creating any Healing House.

MCS is still a subject of debate among "experts" and people who aren't troubled by this problem. People who *have it and experience the symptoms* when they are in the presence of offensive chemicals, but *not* at other times, have no doubt that it is the chemicals causing the problem. So first, please understand that you could be at risk *even if you are not aware that you have chemical sensitivities.* There is a group of people in between those who are chemically sensitive and those who have no problem with any chemicals for whom the distinction is more subtle. Chemical sensitization has been recognized by occupational physicians for decades. The physical mechanism causing it is similar to the one that causes hay fever. Just as some people with allergies sneeze while others suffer life-threatening anaphylactic shock, so people's reactions to chemicals vary widely.

If a person has worked for a long period in a building that, over time, is becoming more and more contaminated with something, symptoms may arise so gradually that the connection between health and those contaminants is never made. The person may become sensitized through exposure that they're not even aware of. The health symptoms that concern them may have been written off as "just allergies," or "nothing to worry about," or "just one of those mysterious things that happen to us," by doctors. I have heard of all these explanations being given to patients by doctors who are faced with an illness they can't diagnose. Those people should probably consider thinking about the chemical environment in which they live, the chemicals they use in their lives, and the outdoor air and water quality where they live. This chapter may give them guidance.

My Personal Disclaimer

Please note that I am writing about MCS primarily from my own experience—not as a physician or other type of expert. I had many allergies as a child that resulted in severe asthma and atopic dermatitis. Additionally, as I recounted in an earlier chapter, I have become sensitized to certain other things—particularly cigarette smoke—and VOCs, especially formaldehyde, due to toxic exposure in college science labs. I would classify myself as either mildly or moderately chemically sensitive. In this section, I can tell you that what I have learned from practical experience works for me. I cannot, however, suggest that everyone's MCS or dermatitis is curable or even treatable with my ideas. I do know that they have helped several people I have told about them.

Some of the chemical sensitivities are becoming more common knowledge, as is the pesticide-exposure problem. Biological scientists are researching many connections between chemicals in our environment and disease, including, for example, the frequency of non-Hodgkins lymphoma among people who have been exposed to certain farm and yard chemicals, and the frequency of multiple sclerosis among people using certain water supplies contaminated by chemicals. However, the diagnosis of "unknown etiology" by doctors—meaning they don't know what is causing a problem—seems to me to be increasing. On a fairly regular basis, I hear of people who are floundering around in the medical and alternative treatment world trying to solve physical problems that doctors have labeled as unknown and unsolvable.

The Real Experts on MCS

The techniques for what have become known as "healthy houses" or "clean houses"—those as free of chemical contamination as is humanly possible—have been researched quite thoroughly and are known to be helpful. I have addressed some of the numerous sources of chemical and biological contaminants: the building materials, furnishings, and occupant activities, in the section on IAQ. The balance, I will briefly address in this section. However, for truly authoritative and very detailed information on MCS, see *Healthy House,* third edition, due out in late 1997[12] by John Bower; or *Building Materials for the Environmentally Hypersensitive,* by Oliver Drerup, et al., at the Canadian Mortgage Housing Corporation.[13]

MCS—The Evasive, Frustrating Puzzle

Often problems with MCS are diagnosed as "psychosomatic," the explanation mainstream doctors use whenever the find something they can't understand or cure. Symptoms can also masquerade as other illnesses, and when they become chronic, doctors suspect something else is going on. Better they should stop blaming it on hypochondria (psychosomatic illness), and start asking about air quality. Common symptoms of MCS include headaches, nose bleeds, anxiety, fatigue, concentration difficulties, irritability, disorientation, memory loss, depression, dizziness, or light-headedness. Cases have also been recorded of gastrointestinal ailments arising from MCS and poor indoor air quality, including nausea, abdominal bloating, diarrhea, constipation, and colitis. Architect Gary Olp describes some findings from his research:

> Continued long-term exposure to commonplace chemicals or biological effluents in the indoor environment seems to be correlated with the diminishment of the human immune system's ability to protect and cleanse the body. Some people can metabolize or purge contaminants from their bodies more effectively than others, while some simply can't tolerate any.[14]

> Millions of Americans have and continue to suffer from MCS—the number could be as high as one in five Americans. Allergic reactions to solvents, pesticides and chemicals . . have been researched . . . since the early 1950s. MCS cases have mirrored a rise in accepted allergic disease and asthma in the past decade. Drs. Nicholas Ashford and Claudia Miller, in *Chemical Exposures: Low Levels and High Stakes,* describe MCS as "an acquired disorder characterized by recurrent symptoms, referable to multiple organ systems, occurring in response to demonstrable exposure to many chemically unrelated compounds at doses far below those established in the general population to cause harmful effects."[15]

Helpful Hints for Mild MCS

Whatever your level of sensitivity, if you have any, I wish to share with you everything I have learned about how one can live fairly comfortably with mild to moderate multiple chemical sensitivities, as I have. Some of these tips have been given to me by two exceedingly bright dermatologists who have worked with my atopic dermatitis.[16] Others I have learned through experience, which, over time, has been my best teacher. Many are related to *both* skin and breathing (odor from either chemicals or biological contaminants.) There aren't very many authoritative sources around on the subject of everyday avoidance:

— Get rid of all the cleaning chemicals in your house, particularly those with any perfume or sprays or any of the chemicals or products listed above, and substitute natural, perfume-free materials from Seventh Generation, Real Goods, health food stores, or other local sources. Whatever you use for laundry detergent, double-rinse things that you breathe or that touch your skin, and don't use fabric softeners.

— Check your makeup, including everything on your dressing table. Smell it all. You probably already know if it causes skin problems, but if it smells, pitch it. Some regular market cosmetic substitutes can be used by persons only mildly afflicted, such as Clinique non-aerosol, nonperfumed hair spray and some other Clinique products, and some Prescriptives or Physicians Formula makeup products.

— Be on the watch for "hidden" contaminants, such as the powder inside rubber gloves and condoms. Or that antique perfume bottle of your mother's sitting on your dressing table because it's pretty. It may be leaking vapors. Dump the perfume, soak it in vinegar, and put in pretty colored water, or, if you want it to look like real perfume, use weak tea with a drop of yellow food coloring.

— Don't walk down the "soaps" aisle in supermarkets, and don't buy perfumed soaps or shampoos. If "beauty parlor" odors bother you, go when nobody else is there and sit in the most ventilated place. We all have to get our hair cut *sometime*, but this can be a real problem for very sensitive people.

— If you are stuck in a public place breathing somebody else's too-strong perfume, move or leave. (For me, the symphony is the killer. Why do women have to *smell* like a flower pot to go hear music?)

— Never go into a smoky environment. If somebody lights up, move or leave.

— Don't breathe the air behind 18-wheelers or old cars.

— Walk in outdoor, unpolluted air regularly, and breathe deeply to cleanse your lungs and your spirits.

— If your house is connected to your garage, make sure it is well ventilated, and get rid of all chemicals in your garage that could "blow" through leaks into your house, such as pesticides, lawn chemicals, paint cans, de-rust chemicals, and benzene or gasoline derivatives (gas and oil for vehicles and lawn mowers). We've already discussed the fact that you should get rid of all these things, anyway, but even I haven't quite accomplished that because there are just certain things my husband thinks he can't live without, principal among them being WD40 and leftover paints and varnishes that are *exactly* the right color. So if you, too, have MCS and still have some chemicals in your garage, just make sure you don't breathe any of them, and try to seal your house from exposure to your garage.

— Don't warm up your car *inside* your garage.

Two extremely healthful things you can do immediately are:

1. *Start drinking bottled, reverse-osmosis, carbon-filtered water. Drink eight glasses a day for a while, even when you're not thirsty.*

2. *Do breathing exercises four times daily, in clean air, as follows.*

After you have all the sprays and chemicals out of your space, try these exercises, which take about two minutes, four times a day. Dr. Andrew Weil, the Harvard Medical School graduate who is now teaching at the University of Arizona Medical School and has written a bestselling book called *Spontaneous Healing*, says this breathing technique is the single most beneficial healing practice he knows of:

Sit upright with your back straight. Close your eyes. Breathe in through you nose to the count of four. Hold it for the count of seven. Breathe out through your mouth, making a whooshing sound through your "o lips, to the count of eight. Repeat three more times, and do it four day. Increase it to eight each time when you want. *I predict you w doing it.* I love the energy it gives me, the natural, relaxed high I feel afterward, and the effect it has had on my sometimes cranky lungs.

Your Temporary Housing When You Need It: On the Road with MCS

For people with MCS, the nightmare of the week is trying to find someplace besides your own, desensitized room in which you can survive temporarily. Hotels and motels have been notoriously insensitive to individuals with any medical conditions in the past, although that is changing somewhat, particularly in the higher-priced chains.

There are two primary causes of air-quality problems in motels and hotels: the carpets and the heating/cooling system. Unfortunately, it's hard to know about these until you check in, particularly if you book a reservation from some other city and have no idea what the place is like. Another problem is *new* hotels and motels. Again, some of the larger chains of higher priced hotels have become more aware of air-quality problems, probably at the recommendation of their attorneys. However, in lower priced motels—even the chains, from my personal experience—this is not the case.

I recently had to be in a small Midwestern town for a family emergency. There was only one chain in town, one of America's oldest and best known motel chains, and they had a new building, open only a week. My assistant reserved a room for me. When I walked into the lobby, the formaldehyde smell nearly knocked me over. I told the desk clerk, and she said, "A lot of people complain about it, but I can't smell it." Of course not. She was in it all day, so she was experiencing a phenomenon known as "masking" or "adaptation response," a unique survival trait in humans that allows us to become accustomed to an initially offensive smell until we no longer smell it.

I left as rapidly as possible and found an older, yet clean motel with a nonsmoking room and a through-the-wall heating/cooling unit. It seemed fine, except that somebody had sprayed the room with an air freshener. I turned off the heat and opened the window, even though it was 26 degrees Fahrenheit outside. Then I went to find the housekeeper to give her my list of do's and don'ts.

- Don't use any sprays in my room for the duration of my stay.
- Don't use chlorine bleaches.
- Leave the heating system where I have it set.

- Don't change the sheets every day. It's a waste of water and electricity.
- Don't allow housekeepers to smoke in my room while they are working.
- Don't put perfumed soaps in my room. I have my own soap.

I returned and did the usual "cleansing" of the space with my little travel kit of personal touches, and it worked fine for my week-long stay.

Hospitals As Indoor Air-Quality Offenders?

Believe it or not, perhaps the worst offenders of all for air-quality offenses are hospitals. From time to time, when I have traveled, it is because I have had to spend time caring for elderly relatives and children who are in a hospital someplace. The last time, my beloved aunt was in a regional hospital in the Midwest. She had just had surgery to replace a broken hip, and at 79 pounds, she was weak and prone to pneumonia, from which she had almost died after the last surgery. As I sat with her, a housekeeper came into her room to clean, bringing a tray full of sprays—mostly chlorine products. I explained that she would not be allowed to use any of those in this room, and I told her why.

"These chemicals can be very damaging to *healthy* lungs, so they are a double hazard for someone who is already vulnerable to pneumonia. I don't want her breathing them, and I don't want to breathe them either," I said.

She asked, without a hint of malice, "How do you know this?" I told her I was writing a book on the subject and pulled some of my IAQ research out of my briefcase, offering to let her take it and read it during her lunch hour.

She came back and said, "I think you were sent to me as a miracle. I have had many of these symptoms ever since I started working here, and a couple of the other people have them too. I've been to the emergency room at this very hospital several times with dizziness, breathing problems, headaches, and rashes, and they keep telling me it's all in my head because when I stay off work for a week, they go away. Now I know why!" She vowed to work through her local union representatives to present this to management and ask that they be allowed to use nontoxic cleaning materials. I'm happy it helped her, but I'm really hoping that no other members of my family end up in that Nebraska hospital, because I'm sure I'm not too popular with management!

Building Materials for Those with MCS

I will not pretend to give you complete information here. Again, I would refer you to *Healthy House* by John Bower, and *Building Materials for the Hypersensitive* by Oliver Drerup et al.[17] In brief, in addition to all the chemical avoidance we have already talked about in this chapter, the 17 recommendations below are *generally helpful* for buildings housing people with MCS, and have been taken from the above-referenced publications:

1. Pure woods should be used except by those sensitive to the terpenes naturally occurring in some woods. Those people should use steel.

2. Concrete for interior use should be specified without admixtures and fly ash.

3. Trusses should be softwood, such as kiln-dried spruce or hemlock made without glues.

4. Any glulam lumber, waferboard, (OSB), or fiberboard products should be tested by the user and sealed if they are intended for interior spaces.

5. Some of the moisture-proofing in gypsum drywall, such as asphalt, may cause problems for some people, and users should test it.

6. Acrylic sheets (Corian) or natural marble or slate for countertops are generally better than most other products.

7. Laminates such as Formica can generally be used, but the glues with which they are attached are the problem. Users should test and then use low-toxicity sealant.

8. For caulking and sealants, see the above-referenced publications.

9. Metal insulated doors, and aluminum, steel, or wood windows are generally tolerated, and the gas in insulated windows is not a concern.

10. Hollow-core and wood doors should be sealed.

11. Kitchen cabinets should be sealed or made from easily tolerated soft woods such as birch.

12. Flooring: Hardwood flooring, ceramic tile, and natural stones such as slate or flagstone are generally well tolerated. Other woods must be sealed, and veneer products can cause problems. Vinyl sheet flooring is not recommended.

13. Wall surfaces: Large-size ceramic tiles with acrylic modified mortars are generally acceptable. Unpainted plaster is also usually tolerated well.

14. Oils should be washed from HVAC ductwork before installing.

15. Radiant electric heating or radiant hot water systems are probably the least offensive heating systems. Air conditioning with high-efficiency filters can help clean the air.

16. Copper plumbing pipe and porcelain-coated bath fixtures are generally preferable.

17. Metal and concrete or clay tile or slate roofs are recommended.

◆   ◆   ◆

Sustainability: What Does It Mean Anyway?

Sustainability is the re-establishment of natural systems for our living environment in which humans are totally integrated and nondisruptive. Therefore, it is beneficial to both the natural habitat and its life systems, and the humans and their habitat. Healing Houses must be built in the context of a sustainable environment, and healing cannot take place without a connection to that sustainable environment.

We understand that we need a sustainable environment in order to heal ourselves, but what are the rules we should follow to obtain it for ourselves, our towns and cities, and our nation? In the summer of 1994, a group of 20 individuals from across America convened at The Nature Place outside Florissant, Colorado, to answer the question. It was clear to them that buildings could not be analyzed and made sustainable alone—that is, segregated out of an entire living system in which the house functions and without which it cannot survive. They, as we now do, saw the need for a holistic sustainable environment, not only for our neighborhoods and our country, but for our planet. John Knott, a developer and member of this esteemed group, eventually called the "Sanborn team," tells the story of a woman in his Dewees Island development who survived pancreatic cancer. She was so grateful to be among the 5 percent who do survive that she has devoted her life since to studying the causes of illness in the human body and why some people heal and others don't. According to Knott, she has decided that sunlight, or the lack of it, is a primary factor in human health, and she pinpoints natural breezes, especially salt breezes, as natural healers.

© 1997 Emily Jenkins

The natural outdoor environment enhances living the natural life, close to earth, sky, and water. This small freshwater lake is a harbor for wild birds.

The Mt. Pleasant, NC, Sweetgrass Basketmakers' Association has an agreement with near-by Dewees Island. They are allowed to harvest sweetgrass on the island in return for teaching island residents how to make baskets with it. Sue Middleton prepares to teach a beginners' class by harvesting the sweetgrass at just the perfect level of development.

© 1997 Emily Jenkins

© 1997 Emily Jenkins

On Labor Day, 1996, Mary Rose Pritchard of Dewees Island, NC, learned the delicate art of sweetgrass basketweaving from Sue Middleton.

The chemicals that people introduce into their living environments, she believes, have a pervasive negative impact on humans; thus, to improve health, she targets totally eliminating toxicity from buildings, leaving the native habitat alone, eliminating the use of fungicides and pesticides in her immediate exterior and interior environments, and eating only naturally grown produce. According to her research estimates, 50 to 60 percent of the natural nutrients that bolster and support our immune systems are no longer present in most commercially grown produce, so we have tremendous increases in diseases such as breast and prostate cancer. "If you look at the five-year curve in breast and prostate cancer, it's not too bad," she told Knott. "But looking at the ten-year curve makes it graphically apparent that there is a significant increase in both diseases." In addition to food-nutrient deficiencies and chemicals in the environment, she cites other environmental factors, such as chlorine in water and microwaving in plastic, which causes toxic chemicals from the plastic to leach into foods.

Why is this so important to John Knott that he talks about it with the conviction of a traveling evangelist? This woman now lives at Dewees Island, Knott's sustainable development off the coast of South Carolina, where she doesn't have to worry about any of those things. And it seems that at that locale, she and the developer are making believers out of the residents and others around the country who hear their message. He doesn't go so far as to claim that the place *heals* them, but he does say:

> They are fascinated with how they *feel* at Dewees. There is such a positive feeling in your whole body. It's hard to describe, but my office is two miles away on the same waterway, and it doesn't feel the same at all. Dewees feels so natural, so together, and so well protected and well defended from all unsustainable intrusions that it is complete. When you are there, you feel complete, and after you have been here, other places somehow feel disrupted.

What are unsustainable intrusions? First we have to understand the word *sustainable*. Instead of defining *sustainable* by the usual phrase: "Using only the resources you must, and saving the rest for future generations," let's let Knott's Dewees Island development do it for us by showing you *what sustainability in development and lifestyle can be.*

© 1997 Norman LaRusso

Dewees Island, SC

Dewees Island is a private, oceanfront island retreat dedicated to environmental preservation. The island itself is 1,206 acres, with environmental covenants prohibiting the construction of more than 150 homes. The driving force behind the development's plans is simple: Humans and nature can co-exist in harmonious balance, without negative impact on either, and with positive benefits to both.

You might think that to remain environmentally "pure," that is, sustainable, at Dewees Island, you have to "look-but-not-touch." Actually, that's not the totally the case. Diverse ecosystems are marked, some as amenities, and some as areas that are not intruded on by humans. In such sustainable developments, management must actively work to educate homeowners on the uniqueness of their environment and how they can enjoy it and integrate themselves into it without doing any damage. For example, there is *no* golf course with its requisite chemical overload at Dewees Island, but there is plenty of fishing, shrimping, oystering, crabbing, boating, sailing, biking, birdwatching and exploring—the kinds of things which, if done in moderation, do not harm the environment.

In the natural, set-aside ecosystems and wildlife corridors, intrusion is forbidden. Over 65 percent of the island is protected from any development whatsoever, with over 350 acres on the northeastern end of the island designated as a wildlife refuge. The development employs a full-time Environmental Programs Coordinator and a full-time Landscape Ecologist, and strict measures have been taken to protect *all living systems*. Oceanside beach dunes have been managed to encourage the growth of beach grasses and to promote natural dune growth, including the planting of sweetgrass and sea oats, flora native to the area. The salt marsh on the landward side is protected. The maritime forest on the highland is the only area where building can occur. Natural sand roads are substituted for concrete and asphalt, and only electric vehicles are allowed on the island. The only island access is by ferry, and disturbance of areas abutting wetlands or the saltmarsh is prohibited. Landscaping is required to be native vegetation and only rainwater, collected in cisterns, can be used to water it.

In addition to addressing issues of sustaining the natural outdoor environment of the island over the long term, design guidelines for buildings are also strict, encouraging the use of passive and active solar heating, natural daylighting, shading devices, and natural pathways for prevailing summer breezes, which minimize the consumption of energy resources and prevent pollution associated with energy use. Waste-management programs are in place and required for both the construction phase and for home occupants, including source reduction, reuse, recycling, and composting. The use of environmentally responsible building materials is strongly encouraged. Before construction begins, homeowners and builders are all educated to understand that *all of the earth's resources* are limited, and, in order to reduce use of these resources in buildings, homes must be viewed entirely differently than they have before: *They must be built and lived in so they are resource providers, not resource users.* And they must be durable enough to last for a very long time so new resources do not have to be used in 20 or 30 years to produce new homes in their place because the original ones have deteriorated beyond repair—a common problem in coastal areas.

In other words, although *sustainability* as a term relates to resource use, it is a bit more. There is another whole dimension that is *holistic*—the blending of all *natural* systems into a whole in which humans and their dwellings have their small place and in which each system and the humans are interdependent and respectful of each other. I realize that I risk having this sound like a commercial for Dewees Island, but it is true that sustainable development is defined most easily by having an actual project described to you. And even then, just reading the facts about how it's set up doesn't tell the whole story.

"There is an incredible *spiritual* dimension to Dewees which can't be communicated in words," Knott said. "It seems, over time, to affect the lives of every single person who lives here. It's something we feel, but we can't quite *say* what it is. You just have to *be out there to know what it feels* like."

Knott says he can't locate an obvious, observable source for this extra dimension people experience there, even though he has traced its history all the way back to the Seewee Indians who lived on these coastal islands. Perhaps, he speculates, it's because the natural systems have been left so intact. But the beauty of it, he emphasizes, is that everyone who lives there seems to be affected positively by the environment. "One doctor, a researcher, moved in," he said. "He was such a sourpuss. He never smiled. Now he smiles all the time. He's outdoors a lot working with others, involved. He *looks and acts happier.* People have told me they move here and find things inside themselves they didn't know were there."

Maybe that's the great discovery about sustainability as a holistic environment: Our bodies have a remarkable ability to reconnect with the earth and sky in that kind of place, and when they do, they first heal our chronically flagging spirits, and others see it in our observable behavior. We just *look happier,* smile more, and seem more relaxed. Medical science has shown that the more relaxed and happier we are, the more physically healthy we are. Healing our spirits in that environment begins *our own holistic healing*—mentally, physically, and spiritually. After all, we as humans have evolved to the point where we are precisely because we, as a species, had the ability to heal ourselves from anything that interfered with our survival. Maybe we just haven't used that innate healing capacity for so long that we've forgotten, even genetically, what it feels like. We've lost the "cell memory" of what our bodies require for healing to happen. Maybe, frighteningly, that sixth sense that allowed our prehistoric predecessors to heal for eons is *evolving out* of our genetic makeup through disuse, like wisdom teeth and little toes. And maybe the *only way* to relocate it and heal ourselves of the pervasive neuroses over illness is to reconnect with the place where we originally evolved, where we developed the immune systems that allowed us to survive. Or maybe we still crave that connection deep in our subconscious, but most of us just haven't figured it out yet.

I believe we literally have to reconnect with *the natural environment* as it existed before the intervention of manmade systems in order to ensure the continued survival of our species. And that's what I believe to be the true meaning of sustainability: the re-establishment of *natural systems* in which humans are totally integrated and nondisruptive, and in which they and all other living creatures can thrive and evolve. When we reconnect with our source strength, we will not only heal, *we will also create healing for all other systems we touch because we will learn to feel their energies and to sense when they are disrupted.* We will again be able to sense, from them, the removal of a sustenance that provides constant healing and strength for ourselves. George Lucas aptly named it "The Force."

People who meditate describe the sensation as a "flow of energy" from the earth, plants, animals, water, sky—many natural systems—into their own bodies, and an outflow from themselves into those other systems. We have discussed the movement of wave action in Chapter 5, and we know from physics that for *any action there is an equal and opposite reaction* somewhere in the universe, even if we don't see it at that moment. I taught that principle to my small children by saying that when you punch your fist into the air in Texas, somebody in China falls over. They laughed and remembered it because it was a funny visual trick. But in a sort of extended physical sense, it is true. The easiest real example is that when we breathe out, we exhale carbon dioxide, which is received by plants. When we breathe in, we breathe 80 percent nitrogen and 20 percent oxygen, which is exhaled by plants. They give and we take. We give and they take. It is a simplistic example, but *the natural systems that were here at the origin of human life are what still sustain us today.*

Going beyond that, there is an actual energy transfer from one living thing to another that is far more than just dreamy metaphysics. When animals give out heat, a form of energy, they warm us. When they "smile" at us and lick us or cuddle with us, they give us positive energy, which is why it is a medically documented fact that elderly people with pets are healthier than those without. When mothers give off body heat and warm touches, their babies thrive. When babies are not touched and warmed, they not only do not thrive, sometimes they actually die. We exchange energy with each other in all kinds of ways. When we meet and mix with others and chat for hours, we *expend energy* that makes us tired even though we may have been just sitting while we do it. We are transferring energy through the act of simply conversing because we are sending others the energy of communication—sound waves with an energy level attached—whether in enthusiastic, sad, or just indifferent words.

It is those waves of energy that touch us every day. In the natural, *sustainable* environment, *all systems are giving us positive energies because they are able to grow and thrive, not just fight for life against evolutionarily destructive intrusions.* These are the positive energies of the original creation that formed all life as earthly entities capable of the ultimate form of self-healing: survival and development of new, more advanced forms.

When we think of the opposite of healing, we think of illness, then we think of viruses and bacteria, which most of us believe cause illness. Yet viruses and bacteria are some of the most primitive forms of life that have been here longer than any other life form. Human beings developed, survived, and evolved in an atmosphere filled with them. When you sit on the forest floor, you are literally surrounded by millions of types of viruses and bacteria, molds, and fungi. Our bodies *know*, in the deepest form of knowing, how to survive with viruses and bacteria and to evolve as a species, anyway. Yet, in the absence of our bodies' ability to heal themselves naturally, we have now created "antibiotics" (which means anti-life), and we think they are going to help us survive longer. (They were accidentally discovered when a piece of moldy bread fell on a petri dish containing a bacteria culture in Alexander Fleming's laboratory, and he noticed the bread killed the bacteria. Penicillin was the result of that mold.) In individual cases, that is true and sometimes almost miraculous. And in my own individual case, it makes me very happy when I think that I am alive now because, during at least two life-threatening illnesses, antibiotics saved me.

But what are we *ultimately* doing with these drugs? Doctors say that our bodies grow immune to them. What they mean is that *the bacteria* in our bodies grow accustomed to them. In other words, they *evolve* around them. They *learn to survive* in an environment where antibiotics are present by changing themselves and adapting, *exactly as everything on earth has since the beginning of time.* That will not change, no matter how many drugs we invent, no matter how much we reassure ourselves that science has an answer. And someday—in some cases it is happening already—we will pay the piper for the folly of dismissing nature. Two recent classic examples are the newly discovered existence of an antibiotically resistant form of tuberculosis, and a resistant strain of hospital staph. We keep trying to make our lives, our world, *artificially* sustainable, outside the natural systems, and that can't go on forever. No individual living system can survive without acknowledging and cultivating its interrelationship with all other living systems.

There is a better solution than stopgap medical intervention to postpone the inevitable, though. There are people who *rarely or never get sick* because they have *reconnected* with the source of all life: people who live in places such as Dewees Island, and others who do it individually, through meditation or in other ways—wherever they live. They have developed *Healing Houses, healing lifestyles, and healing life systems.* To sustain life on this planet over the long term, we must all learn how to do it. We must learn how to make that great, divine connection between ourselves and our planet. When we finally see how that connection works, and perhaps, more importantly, *feel it* with our bodies, we will begin to create a sustainable society because we will, universally, understand its importance and *insist* on it!

*"Will you ever begin to understand the meaning of the very soil beneath
your feet? From a grain of sand to a great mountain, all is sacred.
Yesterday and tomorrow exist eternally upon this continent.
We natives are guardians of this sacred place."*

—Peter Blue Cloud, Mohawk[1]

Getting to Sustainability–
The Sanborn Principles

"Our vision sees a world in which protected wildlands and biologically diverse ecosystems are amply represented across the landscape, and in which vigorous and healthy populations of all native species flourish, carrying on the ancient task of evolution . . . It would be a world in which diverse urban and rural human populations and the cultural and political institutions that guide them would adhere to the principles of sustainability and social justice, and in which people would work with one another to preserve, restore, and pass on to future generations an environment unimpaired by their presence in it."

— T. H. Watkins, The Wilderness Society

In 1994, the Sanborn team developed what has become known as *The Sanborn Principles,*[16A] guidelines for sustainable development that are printed, in total, in the Appendix to this chapter. Remember, a Healing House is, among other things, a sustainable building, as defined using the Sanborn Principles for buildings, which are incorporated into Chapters 13 and 14. Since a sustainable house must be placed in a sustainable environment, we will deal here with those principles that guide us to a sustainable environment *outside* our Healing House.

One small, but very important example of the necessary synergy between the Healing House and its outside environment is that when you use mechanical *controlled ventilation* to bring just the right amount of fresh air into your house, you can't bring in *polluted* outside air or you will no longer have a sustainable environment inside. Therefore, the air outside must be unpolluted, too. The Sanborn Principles *can* lead us to a *sustainable environment outside the home itself.* Let's examine them.

Note: Underlined text used in the balance of the chapter constitute the original written Sanborn Principles. The rest of the text was derived from verbal presentations made by the two Sanborn teams on July 7, 1994; and from elaboration by the author, a member of Sanborn Team II.

<u>Ecologically Healthy</u>

"<u>The design of human habitat shall recognize that all resources are limited and will respond to the patterns of natural ecology. Land plans and building designs will include only those with the least disruptive impact upon the natural ecology of the earth. Density must be most intense near neighborhood centers where facilities are most accessible.</u>"

"<u>Buildings will be organic, integrate art, natural materials, sunlight, green plants, energy efficiency, low noise levels, and water; and not cost more than current conventional buildings.</u>"

<u>Features of the buildings and their surroundings will include:</u>

<u>No waste that cannot be assimilated</u>. We consume too much, and we waste too much. Each of us consumes 36 pounds of resources a week. We discard 2,000 pounds of waste of all kinds per person, per week. This includes the by-products of production we don't see and aren't usually consciously aware of, such as CO_2 and dioxin; as well as things we see, handle, and use, such as packaging materials, old shoes, and worn-out toasters.

Paul Hawken, in his provocative and practical book, *The Ecology of Commerce,*[1] tells us that there is no such thing as waste in nature. One species' waste is another species' energy or food source. He says we must *fundamentally* alter the way we think about products if we are to solve our waste problems. We must think about the multitude of *things* in our lives in three categories:

1. **Consumables**: Products used and *completely consumed,* such as soap and tomatoes. (In order to qualify as consumable, a product's waste must be wholly biodegradable, and capable of transforming itself into food for another organism with no toxic residue that would cause harm or be accumulative when it is discarded.)

2. **Products of service:** Commonly called "durables," although some nondurables such as packaging are included. What we want from these products, he said, was to *use their service*—transportation from our car, cold beer from our refrigerator, news from our TV, packages for our gifts.

3. **Unsaleables**: These are products *nobody* wants to own, which we have no idea what to do with once we are finished with them—such as toxic chemicals, radiation, PCBs, and heavy metals. There is no "cycle" to these products within the environment, and no continuous or cyclical process into which they can be integrated that will not cause harm.

So, if we want no waste that cannot be assimilated, what should we do? First, as Hawken and the Sanborn team suggested, we have to require that things which, in their normal state, are biodegradable (for example, silk blouses and ties, which we now chemically alter by impregnating them with tin and zinc to give them their "hand"; and shoe leather; which is now tanned with chromium), be made *without chemicals*. Thus, Consumables would either be consumed or biodegrade into food for some other species.[2]

Lease, Don't Own, In Order to Clean Up Toxic Landfills

Second, we should change the basic underlying system of product distribution and ownership for Products of Service. Ownership should be retained by the manufacturer. The products should then be leased or licensed to a user. Attached to your television set, when you purchase it, would either be a transferrable license for its use, so the license can be sold or given away, or it would be leased. Under either system, the TV set could not be thrown away or destroyed. Return to its manufacturer, presumably at the same location where you bought it in the first place, would be required. Comparable systems for leasing are already in place for many products, such as furniture and cars.[3]

However, as Hawken said, fundamental changes in our thinking will be required. At the moment, we think of leasing a TV set as something people do when they can't afford to buy one. Thus, the current leasing consumer often gets a poor quality set that is vastly overpriced. If we changed our thinking so we recognized, as a society, how much better for our waste stream it is to lease—particularly when we are talking abut items with high toxic content like TVs—and we promoted the idea that when TV sets are returned, the materials in it are re-used, leasing would become socially acceptable overnight, and the quality of leased TVs would be the same as that of purchased TVs.[4]

The benefit to society at large by eliminating just *this one* product, TV sets, from our landfills is graphically described by Hawken when he tells crowds, with the passion of an ecological Billy Graham:

> A television set in 1992 had 4,000 chemicals, 500 to 600 grams of lead, and an explosive vacuum tube. There was no way to dispose of it safely. If you transport 20 TV sets in a truck, you are technically required to be licensed by the EPA as a toxic waste hauler. A new lease-license system would literally convert, overnight, a TV set from toxic waste to positive human service because *all its components would be returned to its maker to be assembled into another television set.*[5]

You Don't Want It, I Don't Want It . . .

Third, we have to mark Unsaleables with some chemical tag so that the company that manufactured them will have to come and get them when they end up where they shouldn't be. This can be done with molecular markers which, in fact, are already being considered by the EPA for certain chemicals. If my well water is contaminated by an organochlorine,[16B] a heavy metal, or a dioxin leachate from a landfill upland from me, I will know *what is in my water,* and I will know who to call to do something about it. At the same time, these chemicals should be required to be "parked" in a parking lot that is paid for in perpetuity by the manufacturer. Once that happens, it is possible that the companies manufacturing products *using those chemicals* will find a better way—such as *not using them at all!* [6]

The Swiss Miracle

The case of Ciba-Geiger of Switzerland is a classic example of the kinds of action that should be taken by governments and manufacturers to rid our atmosphere and water of toxic chemicals. The Swiss government required that the Ciba-Geiger corporation clean up the wastewater being expelled from their textile plants into a beautiful Swiss river so that it was *drinkable* when it exited their plant. Environmentalist and designer/architect Bill McDonough of the University of Virginia, and German chemist Michael Braungart were involved in the discussions to find a way to clean up the waste, but rather than attacking that single problem head-on, they changed the protocol. Instead of cleaning up wastewater, they suggested that Ciba-Geiger *eliminate the chemicals that caused the wastewater to be toxic.*

So, Ciba-Geiger researched 8,000 chemicals used to make upholstery fabrics. Of the 8,000, only 38 were found to be nontoxic. The company then looked at all the materials that could be used, eliminating any that required any chemicals *other than the safe 38.* The result was a wool and ramie[7] blend from which their entire fabric line is now made.

In addition to cleaning up the wastewater, there were other, surprisingly, cost-saving benefits to Ciba-Geiger, and to companies in Holland that have now adopted the same toxic-free system for textile manufacture, called the McDonough-Braungart Protocol.[8] These industries that make the fabric *are not regulated,* so they can make and ship these 38 chemicals and their fabrics without filing regulatory paperwork and arranging special shipping and handling, which reduces their cost of doing business.

The American company Design Tex is now producing the William McDonough line of wool-ramie-blend upholstery fabric, using totally biodegradable and nontoxic dyes and manufacturing processes. Design Tex, Inc., based in New York City, has also recently introduced a polyester workstation panel fabric made of 100 percent recycled soda bottles. (One linear yard of the 66"-wide fabric contains roughly ten, clear two-liter soda bottles.) They are continuing to work with McDonough to improve all the industrial processes used in production of their fabrics, whether recycled or not.

Junglified Surroundings, Both Exterior and Interior

The Sanborn team recognized the physical benefits derived from trees and plants, as well as the more metaphysical, nonquantifiable bonuses they might bring to any environment, as we have discussed in previous chapters. When a member of our team, Amory Lovins, first said "Junglified," I first thought of rain forests with monkeys swinging on branches overhead and elephants lumbering around beneath. But I have since learned that jungles and rain forests are different. Rain forests are areas that get over 100 inches of rain a year, whether they are in the Pacific Northwest, Alaska, New Guinea, or Costa Rica. Jungles, on the other hand, are thickets of natural vegetation, typically high grass, reeds, vines, brush, and/or trees, with tangled undergrowth—something like our "junglified" sunroom in winter, when we bring all the plants indoors where they twine together and threaten to capture passersby.

Thermal Passivity (Responsiveness)

In Chapter 13, we talked about the fact that passive solar heating is an integral and necessary part of the design of a Healing House. However, thermal passivity applies to the *outside* of buildings and to the construction of cities as well. A thermally responsive environment would work with natural conditions—the sun, wind, rain, or snow—in ways that assist in the overall goal of reducing energy use to heat and cool buildings, making the temperatures more comfortable for people living and working there.

First, and probably most important in this modern age of megalopolises, with hundreds of thousands of cars crawling side by side along ribbons of freeways so gigantic they can be seen from spaceships at night, we should think about what cars and highways do *thermally to their environment.* For one thing, freeways, combined with the absorbent, mass surfaces of smaller streets and buildings that they link together, create what is called the *urban heat effect,* a term used to explain the difference between summer temperatures in the country where trees and the natural landscape absorb the heat and cool the earth, and the cities just miles away, which are often ten degrees hotter at the same time. The more that asphalt and concrete are gathered together, the more heat they radiate back into the environment in the summer. The hotter it is *outside*, the more we have to spend on utility costs to keep ourselves cool *inside.*

If you think *natural*, you will have most of the concept of thermal passivity—land instead of hard surfaces; gravel or crushed rock instead of concrete or asphalt; radiant barriers, trees, ceiling fans, and architecture that draws cooling summer breezes, instead of air conditioning (or, in terribly hot, humid climates, *augmented* by air conditioning). Think natural materials, brick, rammed earth, adobe block for building materials—left dark in colder climates, and made light or painted light in hot climates. Think tree planting in all climates; evergreens on the north side of buildings to block north winds in winter in cold climates; and large, thick deciduous trees to block hot summer sun in the southern areas.

Know that dark buildings and roofs absorb more heat than light buildings and white roofs, so the dark roofs are good in Alaska where heat is needed, but terrible in hot climates where white, reflective roofs should be used to keep out sun. Dark streets (asphalt) absorb and reradiate more heat than light or white concrete streets, so ice melts faster on them when the sun is shining in winter, but they are baking ovens for cities in the summer. A gravel road or driveway is better for thermal passivity than either an asphalt or concrete, and it has the added benefit of being a free burglar alarm, as well as draining better during rainstorms, creating less run-off into creeks and rivers. Better than either of those is the untouched land that absorbs more heat than either of those, *but does not reradiate it,* so it is cooler than gravel, crushed stone, concrete, or asphalt.

Access by Foot to Primary Services

Don't we *all* wish we had an ice cream store in walking distance from our front porch in July? In Dallas or Houston or Phoenix, almost no matter where you live, you *must drive or ride in a vehicle* to get to any kind of service providers. In New York City or San Francisco, it's a different story— until you get to their new, "modern" suburbs where you're forced to drive. If we all could walk to the corner for a Dove bar or a pound of fish, it would provide a kind of psychological steadiness, an anchoring for the soul in independent human action.

Jane Jacobs, in her great book, *The Death and Life of Great American Cities,* tells us that a neighborhood is not just a collection of buildings, but a tissue of social relations. It is the comfort we feel; the transfusion of energy we get from seeing familiar, friendly faces; talking to the druggist about our problems with the baby; asking the man at the meat market how to cook duck; and seeing the priest, the doctor, the baker, and the man from the hardware store walking down the street. As she said so poignantly:

> Sanitary, steam-heated apartments are no substitute for warmhearted neighbors, even if they live in verminous cold-water flats. The chat across the air shaft, the little changes of scene as a woman walks her baby or tells her troubles with her husband to the druggist, the little flirtations that often attend the purchase of a few oranges or potatoes, all season the housewife's day and mean more than mere physical shelter.[9]

In addition to just convenience, access by foot (or wheelchair) also gives individuals a measure of control over their own lives that does not exist when vehicular transportation is required. There is a vital and well-recognized psychological connection between the state of people's health and the measure of control they *perceive they have* over their lives: their jobs and homes in particular. We could spend a lot of time talking about perception here—how one person will perceive less control in the exact same situation as another who perceives he/she has more control. But that aside, there is no question that when you can rely on walking or "wheelchairing" outside your own door under your own power to get the food you need or other basic supplies of life, you do feel you are exerting a measure of control over your fate, which can be felt in no other way.

I learned this, first hand, when I spent a summer in Germany in the '70s. There, whether people work or not, they walk to the neighborhood stores nearly every day to buy bread, meat, milk, or whatever they need. They all have pull-along shopping carts in which they take things on their way: cleaning, shoes to be repaired, and so on, and they bring back their purchases. It's a way of life, and more than that, it's getting *outside* under our own power to do things we have decided to do when we decide to do them. It *feels* reassuring—like going to a bush to pick berries for the evening meal must have felt to our ancient ancestors. It's as if we are comforted by taking a glance, each day, at the threads of the social fabric from which we are woven. It relates us back to the group—the tribe—and reminds us of the pleasures of societal interdependence.

In an article for *New Yorker* in 1955, Lewis Mumford, probably this century's foremost architectural critic, proposed "walkable" neighborhoods separated from traffic:

> The principle of separating walkers from drivers, which involves planning whole neighborhoods at a time, is known to planners as the Radburn idea, after Radburn, New Jersey, but as a matter of fact, it was first embodied in the plan of medieval Venice, whose canals carried the swift-moving traffic of another age. Until Radburn was designed in 1928, no professional planner seemed to be able to understand that the extraordinary charm of Venice, which persists despite its overcrowding and decay, is due partly to the fact that each neighborhood was planned as a unit, for the benefit of the footwalker, and is not menaced by the rumble and roar of wheeled traffic, and that to go from one part of the city to a distant part, one uses an entirely different transportation system which never suffers any interruption by the pedestrian and does not interrupt his progress, either. Leonardo da Vinci proposed to overcome the congestion of Milan by a similar separation of wheeled traffic from pedestrian walks. The first modern planners to effect such separation were Olmsted and Vaux, in their brilliant plan for Central Park.[10]

Speaking of Central Park, the Sanborn Principles emphasize our common need for the connection to the outdoors:

Natural Parks and Corridors for Wildlife

We discussed in Chapters 8 and 9 the connection between wildlife—all other life—and ourselves, so it should be obvious that we *need* this connection to wildlife. It is sometimes stunning to remember that there are people alive today in America who have no parks near them; who have never seen a duck; who couldn't tell a goose from a pelican or a fox from a possum; and who are repulsed by worms, snakes, and hawks because they don't understand the vital function they play in keeping the land healthy.

> *"For the Lakota there was no wilderness . . . nature was not dangerous, but hospitable, not forbidding but friendly."*
> — Luther Standing Bear, Lakota[11]

When, inevitably, buildings fall down (sadly, many built today, will fall down in 20 or 30 years) and our cities and towns have an "empty" space to be replanned, it is necessary that those doing the planning consider making wide corridors available for life other than human so *all* future residents can see some of the wonderful wild creatures on this planet for themselves. Heaven knows, when we want to relax, most of us don't race to the nearest inner city so we can stare up at the tall buildings or down at the concrete. We head for the parks, the corridors where rivers and streams run, where birds sing and ducks ride the slow currents, where flowers bloom along the banks. We sit in quite contemplation in those rare and precious pathways winding through the asphalt and concrete of our lives. And we hate to get up and leave when it's time. That should tell us something about what to *ask for* from our city planners. It should also lead us to recognize, again, in ourselves, our deep and recurring need to reconnect with the earth. Famed cultural historian and writer Jane Jacobs has an interesting anthropological observation about one reason why this connection is so necessary:

> From the days of Ur onward, city dwellers have always had the countryside close at hand. There, their homicidal impulses could be exorcised by digging and delving, or by shooting at destructive animals, and there, their need for spontaneous muscular exercise could be satisfied by swimming and boating and climbing, rather than by knives, brass knuckles and rumbles.[12]

Maybe if our inner-city kids had more time outside in safe parks and wildlife corridors where they could run and play freely, they would be able to exert more personal control over their lives when they are in the city—rejecting negative influences such as drugs, alcohol, and crime in favor of stimulation and physical activity outdoors.

We own an inner-city apartment complex in the Oak Cliff area of Dallas. I take the kids to the library every few weeks—whichever kids want to go. *Always, without fail,* when we are finished, they ask if I will take them "to the park." The beautiful, spacious Lake Cliff Park surrounding a small lake is nearby the apartments with its large expanse of grassy areas, its big playground, and little hills and bridges. It must feel very large to a child of 6 or 7, or even 10 or 11. I think it isn't so much the play equipment there that they love, although they do play on it periodically, it is the *big, open green space* of the place itself. They run up and down, inventing games for chasing each other, hiding behind trees, sometimes climbing into them, laughing, falling, scrambling up and running again until they are panting, sweaty, and exhausted. When they leave, they *never stop smiling* until I deliver them back home.

We should insist that every policy maker understand how much all of us, especially children, need outdoor green spaces in which our souls can reconnect with their source.

Individual Community Gardens

"Let us cultivate our garden."
— from *Candide,* by Voltaire

All over Europe, as you drive along autobahns and highways, as you enter and leave major urban areas, you see fenced areas of a few acres with bicycles parked around them and people tilling little sectioned-off areas containing their private gardens. These are city dwellers who are growing some of the food they eat in community gardens, many established by cities for use by their residents.

These gardens have all the benefits of reuniting their gardeners with the earth and sky that we discussed in Chapter 9, and, in addition, they provide a healthy source of vegetables and fruit for their family's consumption.

A friend of mine from England rhapsodizes about the benefits of gardening for her mother:

> I truly believe that what keeps mother alive is caring for her little vegetable garden out there. She has an old bicycle with a basket on the handlebars, and every day, she puts her little tools in the basket and rides out to take care of her tomatoes and squash. Often, she meets her friends there and they go for tea afterwards, so it's not just the plants, or the pride she has when she delivers tomatoes or cucumbers to her friends, but it's the *social* bit as well, the meeting of friends, the chatting, the making of new arrangements that she didn't know about when she awakened. It gives a little element of surprise and chance to the day that she wouldn't have if she just sat home and cared for the flowers on her windowsill—which are also beautiful, by the way.

The East Dallas Community Garden, set unpretentiously behind a fence of flowers, on two lots in a congested low-income neighborhood. Used by several Asian families who depend on it almost solely for their diets, the garden is operational year round.

© 1997 Barbara Harwood

Local Agriculture for Local Consumption

One of the great insanities of our time is that we buy, from our local supermarkets, "cardboard" peaches and tomatoes, picked while they are green and tasteless, sprayed with chemicals, and hauled to Texas from California in refrigerated trucks. The trucks use a double-dose of fossil fuel, part of it to get the truck here to Texas from California, and the rest to run the refrigeration (which requires that the truck be kept running *even while the driver stops to eat or sleep!*).

And that is just the beginning of a litany of sins this process of hauling food over long distances commits. Here are some of the others:

- That fossil fuel burned by the trucks pollutes the atmosphere and negatively impacts the trade deficit (2/3 of which is attributed to buying foreign oil. This does *not include* the cost of *wars* we fight to make sure we'll be *able* to buy it.)[13]

- The big trucks tear up the highways that we (and the truckers, through taxes) have to pay to repair.

- The peaches and tomatoes cost too much because all this fossil fuel, highway tax, truck maintenance, the drivers, and state agricultural inspectors in every state through which they pass, have to be paid for by us when we buy the produce.

- Many of the natural vitamins that would be present in tree-ripened fruit and vegetables are destroyed by this process.

- The fruit is often covered with pesticides and fungicides or have color or "ripeners" added so they look better to us, enticing us to buy them.

- And last, but not least, they are an insult to the tongue when you put them in your mouth.

How much better it is to go to a local farmer's market to buy fruits and vegetables *in their season* grown by local farmers and brought a few miles in their pick-up trucks or vans. Why doesn't this happen more often?

What Is Really Happening to Our Agricultural Land Near Cities?

First, agricultural land near cities is often taxed at rates that reflect its potential for development, rather than its value as agricultural land providing a variety of grains or vegetables. So the farmer can't grow produce there for our tables in the city because he can't afford to sell them at going prices and still pay those taxes. He *has to sell his land for development.* I often hear lobbying groups for developers say that urban sprawl and the death of agricultural land near cities is not their fault "because nobody forces the farmer to sell to the developer." I say, in response, that it's technically true that nobody is holding a gun to the owner's head, but city and county tax policy, which removes their ability to make a profit agriculturally, certainly holds the equivalent of a firearm to their financial futures.

© 1997 Barbara Harwood

Local agriculture, vegetables, and fruit grown 30 miles north of Dallas and sold locally at the Dallas Farmer's Market provide the entire income for Beth Buckingham and her family. A former racehorse trainer, Beth has had this stand for 15 years.

To remedy that, we must, in future city and county planning, tax farm land as farm land *no matter how close to the city it is* as long as somebody is farming it. And farming would include greenhouses in which somebody raised tomatoes or cucumbers or other vegetables year-round (as the Israelis do acre after acre in the Negev desert). There is no reason we couldn't do that near enough to our biggest cities so that people can have delicious produce with a small hauling cost much of the year. All it takes is a change in tax policy and the opening up of these kinds of markets.

There are a lot of young people who really want to continue farming traditions established by their parents and grandparents, but they can't see a way to do it and survive financially. This would be a whole new opportunity for them, and a growth industry for America.

Lewis Mumford understood local agriculture as a permanent part of regional land planning. I quote an address he gave in 1931 to the Round Table on Regionalism, Institute of Public Affairs, University of Virginia, called "The Regional Framework of Civilization":

> Regional Planning is the New Conservation—the conservation of human values hand in hand with natural resources . . . . Permanent agriculture instead of land skinning, permanent forestry instead of timber mining, permanent human communities dedicated to life, liberty and the pursuit of happiness, instead of camps and squatter settlements . . . .
>
> The people of Newcastle will no longer go to London for coals, as the people in the provinces have been doing this last century and more: There

will be a more direct utilization of local resources than would have seemed profitable or seemly to the metropolitan world which now has command of the market. In these varied utopias, it is safe to say, there would be a new realization of the fact that a cultivated life is essentially a settled life. [14]

To Each, in Its Own Season, in Its Own Time

Until we grow trees under domes of some sort, growing fruit is a different matter, and it will take something quite different from altered tax policy. It would take, first, our personal affirmation that eating fruit, grown naturally in our own area, is our desire. Then it will require personal, determined action. We, as consumers, would have to be willing to make that extra effort to buy from local producers and to eat fruits in season. By doing that, we would notify local peach tree growers (and pears, apples, and so on), that there is a willing and eager market out there so that more fruit could be grown profitably. Then we would have to tell grocery store managers that we will no longer buy tasteless, hard peaches and tomatoes so the grocery store chains would stop buying the ones that are picked green and shipped to us by the truckload.

Believe me, the resolve won't be difficult to find once you *taste* the difference. And it is possible that we, together, could really change the system by doing this. If farmer's markets around the country become big enough and successful enough to compete with the produce sold in supermarkets, maybe the supermarkets would start stocking *local agricultural products for local consumption.*[15] What a concept!

There certainly is no question about what *our* family prefers. We buy peaches every summer from Eloise Hunter at the Dallas Farmer's Market, a little hot spot of burgeoning popularity. Eloise's little East Texas farm surely produces the sweetest, juiciest, most delicious peaches God ever created on this earth. They come in first in late May or early June, and only last through July. There is great joy when we buy the first batch, and great sadness when she announces we have bought our last for the year. But you must buy them weekly because they *cannot be refrigerated—ever—*or it spoils their flavor and texture.

Our family has come to recognize another advantage to buying fresh peaches: a new awareness of their sweet, transient juiciness. They last such a short time, so they are a treat saved for certain times of the year. Because they taste so wonderful when we finally get them, we actually eat them differently from the "cardboard" supermarket variety. In what's become something of a summer ritual on warm summer evenings, we slice a peach into a bowl, put milk on it, and sit on the back porch watching the sunset while we eat it. We really *taste* the incredible sweet peachiness of each bite. It makes me remember my gratitude *for this time of year.* In this hectic, deadline-driven world, I actually remember to taste the difference between this time of year and any other time . . . all because of a sweet little peach grown by an African-American family in east Texas and brought to us through the farmer's market!

Local Produce for Local Consumption

There are those who will object to my advocacy of growing produce locally, saying that I don't understand that huge "agribusinesses" developed because of economies of scale, buying and selling in quantity from coast to coast. However, I point out to them that a major factor in the calculation of those economies of scale was the inherent assumption that fuels would be inexhaustible and cheap. That piece of the calculation will dissolve when we run out of fossil fuel to operate all the machinery and trucks required to keep huge distribution systems in place. And although we may not have actually *run out* of fossil fuels yet, they are certainly causing us severe environmental problems even today, not to mention the costly repair to highways and streets damaged by big trucks. Once those imbedded fuel costs, including their environmental side effects, are factored in, the "economies of scale" aren't so economically beneficial and will grow less and less so as years pass. *We need to consider some options for unhooking ourselves from a food supply that requires a fossil fuel-based transportation system!*

Growing New Businesses along with Food

Extending the concept of local agriculture for local consumption a bit further than a farmer's market would also mean, for example, that local wheat farmers could haul a portion of their grains to the local miller where flour would be ground, and then a local bakery could make bread for local consumption. Some of the grain could be used by local small businesses to make pasta or pie crusts. Once you eliminated all the shipping and intermediaries, the food would be priced reasonably in addition to being truly fresh.

As a bonus, some of the inedible by-products of local agriculture could also be used in small local businesses. For example, the straw separated from the wheat during harvest (and normally discarded) could be baled and used to build homes and barns (see Chapter 14), as well as for such local farming needs as bedding for animals. Whole crops could be used *in that local area*. In addition, it is a golden opportunity to train local laborers in need of jobs in these small farming communities to use local agricultural waste to build homes for those who need them.

Socially Just

Habitats shall be equally accessible across economic classes.

I have what I call Barbara Harwood's Fourth Law of Thermodynamics: The poorer you are, the less energy efficient the house you live in will be, until, at the very bottom of the income ladder, you live *outdoors*. There could be a corollary law: Even though we don't have, in America, what Lewis Mumford would have called "squatter settlements," the poorer you are, the worse the quality of the house you live in until, if they were all clustered together, the worst ones would *look like* squatter settlements.

I advocate, along with the national Low Income Housing Coalition, that "Housing Is a Human Right." I do so because I am convinced that *it is impossible to heal your body, mind, and spirit unless you are completely comfortable in the place you call home* . . . just like it's impossible for a child crowded with seven other children to a room or without a home at all to learn in school. Can't happen. Life's basic processes are interfered with in a very fundamental way when we are cut off from the ability to completely relax and feel safe *someplace* each day and night. Until we get that straight as a society, we will have people who function at a disturbed level—disturbed in behaviors that overwhelm teachers in crowded classrooms and eventually create stressed-out, abusive, often nonproductive parents.

Social justice for all demands that, together, we find a way to provide decent, affordable, and safe housing for all Americans.

Culturally Creative

Habitats will allow ethnic groups to maintain individual cultural identities and neighborhoods, while integrating into the larger community. All population groups shall have access to art, theater, and music.

Cultural creativity would allow individuals to express their own personality and identity within a cultural framework that is comfortable for them—a community of like individuals who choose to maintain their heritage and culture. At the same time, its benefits would be open to others from outside—such as Chinatowns, Italian or Irish neighborhoods, Jewish communities, Germantowns, and others that are firmly integrated into the larger social patterns so there is constant access and interchange between those inside and those outside the neighborhoods. When those old neighborhoods disappear, as has happened, for example, in the old Italian neighborhood in north Denver, the whole community loses—the Italians themselves who were able to maintain some of their language and heritage there, and the larger city that has lost a cultural resource—not to mention some great restaurants with the world's best Italian sausage sandwiches.

Cities without clearly defined ethnic neighborhoods, such as Dallas, are the poorer for it. Sometimes, in other cities, instead of individual ethnic areas, they are all blended into a colorful, heterogenous melting pot. Washington, D.C., for example, has melded together many ethnic groups, spreading them from Dupont Circle on up Columbus to the Adams Morgan area. In Adams Morgan, you can hear ten languages in the space of a block, and eat anything from Cuban to Thai to Arabic to a wonderful mixture called African-French.

I don't even need to mention the Chinatowns in San Francisco or New York as perfect examples of my point, but I do *think* about them when I eat in restaurants such as May Dragon in Dallas and *wish* I could walk outside afterwards and stroll through the red and green lanterns, go into shops with wonderful Asian art until 11 or 12 at night, and smell the strange cooking odors coming from the flats above the street. If variety is the spice of life, then ethnic neighborhoods are the spice of cities and need to be encouraged.

Culturally creative, to the Sanborn team, also had a second meaning:

Cities and towns should provide access for all their citizens to the great aesthetics: art, theater, and music.

I often wonder whether "Mozarts" and "Beethovens" have been born in this century but have never been discovered because that naturally talented young child was *never* exposed to great classical music. Many of you may think that nobody misses a lot in life by not hearing it, but I submit that when tests prove that students who listen to Mozart do better on test scoring than those who don't and plants grow faster and healthier in the presence of classical music than rock music, there is something more to this music than we might think. To me, as an amateur musician since I was preschool age, it would be a real tragedy if a Mozartian talent was wasted just because there was no time or place to tune the child's spirit to its ancient purpose.

Exposure to great paintings, drawings, and sculpture cultivates an artistic spirit in much the same way. Luckily, art is taught, at least to very young children, in their schools. A bit more than that is required, however. Often great artists say that they were inspired by some other artist during their developing years. A great work of art in a museum or gallery triggered some sort of emotional response that produced in them the same kind of creativity, though not necessarily the same product, that the original artist demonstrated. In a great and sustainable society, we must make sure we do not lose this talent because we have not exposed children to these aesthetic influences. As Lewis Mumford, great commentator on American cities and culture, said, "There is no end to the number of things which we do badly in the modern community, for want of the artist to do them."[16]

And last but not least, theater is, and has been since the early Greek theater, society's way of commenting safely on itself. It is a mirror in which we see reflected *something* going on outside our own experience. Vicarious living, yes. Thinking about things that we otherwise might not have thought about, yes. Being forced to deal with tough subjects, yes. But perhaps most important, having a couple of hours to have reflected back to us some of the complexities that make up the collective *us . . . that make us who we are as human beings.*

If we could look back to the beginning of human time, I'll bet we would see people "play-acting" . . . maybe playing charades as the first human game. Children mimic others with happy abandon. Little ones do it daily, as part of learning "how" to do the business of living. For the same reasons, art and music should be nurtured in adults as well as children so they can draw or compose what they feel but cannot say. After all, these are the things that differentiate humans from apes, and, according to Lewis Mumford, they are what differentiates between great cities and "anonymous jerry-built" ones:

At the height of the Middle Ages, as in fifth-century Athens, the arts formed together a living unity. A citizen did not go to a concert hall to hear music, to a church to say his prayers, to a theater to see a play, to a picture gallery to view pictures; it was a mean town, indeed, that could not boast a cathedral and a couple of churches; and in these buildings, drama and music and architecture and painting and sculpture were united for the purpose of ringing changes on the emotional nature of men and women and converting them to accept the theological vision of otherworldly utopia.

It is out of the vivid patterns of the artist's ecstasy that he draws us together and gives us the vision to shape our lives and the destiny of our communities anew. . . . [17]

Beautiful

The Sanborn Team wrote no description after that word. Nothing more was said, because nothing more needed to be said about incorporating beauty into sustainable development. When he asked that the word *beautiful* be included in the list, Sanborn team member Amory Lovins said, "It's a given in physics that the most simple and sensible solution to a problem is also the most beautiful."

© 1997 Holly Kuper

The stained glass window in the master bath of the author's affordable housing development, Esperanza del Sol (Hope of the Sun). Beauty in their living environment should be accessible to people in all income levels.

Lewis Mumford, in an article for *New Yorker* in 1968, said:

It is the beauty of great urban cathedrals and palaces, the order of great monastic structures or the university precincts of Oxford and Cambridge, the serenity and spaciousness of the great squares of Paris, London, Rome, Edinburgh, that have preserved intact the urban cores of truly great cities over many centuries.[18]

But perhaps those who said it best were our own Native Americans:

> *This covers it all, the Earth and the Most High Power*
> *whose ways are beautiful.*
> *All is beautiful before me.*
> *All is beautiful behind me.*
> *All is beautiful above me.*
> *All is beautiful around me.*
> — Navajo Song[19]

Physically And Economically Accessible

All sites within the habitat shall be accessible and rich in resources to those living within walkable (or wheelchair-able) distance.

Narrow, curving streets have been shown to significantly reduce speeds of cars through residential streets. Another popular traffic-calming technique in Europe, slowly catching on here, is using obstacles such as trees in the middle of streets.

Accessible characteristics shall include:

Radical Traffic Calming: "Traffic calming" is a new phrase that means putting obstacles of some sort in streets to slow down fast drivers. And though it may be a new phrase to us, it by no means a new concept. Early Europe created it for dual purposes, described by Lewis Mumford in his chapter on Medieval Cities:

> In general, the street was a line of communication for pedestrians, and its utility for wheeled transport was secondary. Not merely were the streets narrow and often irregular, but sharp turns and closures were frequent. When the street was narrow and twisting, or when it came to a dead end, the plan broke the force of the wind and reduced the area of mud. Not by accident did the medieval townsman, seeking protection against winter wind, avoid creating such cruel wind tunnels as the broad, straight street. The very narrowness of medieval streets made their outdoor activities more comfortable in winter. But likewise in the south, the narrow street with broad overhangs protected the pedestrian against both rain and the sun's direct glare.
>
> Though Alberti (Leone Battista Alberti in *De Re Edificatori*) favored straight and broad streets for noble and powerful cities to increase their air of greatness and majesty, he wrote, of the winding street: "Within the heart of their town, it will be handsomer not to have them straight, but winding about several ways, backwards and forwards, like the course of a river. For thus, besides by appearing so much longer, they will add to the idea of the greatness of the town, they will likewise be great security against all accidents and emergencies. Moreover, this winding of the streets will make the passenger at every step discover a new structure. . . ." [20]

European countries of our own time recognized the value of these walkable, safe, slowly traveled streets long before we did. They recognized after building only a few autobahns that if you have big, wide streets with four lanes, people are going to drive *fast* on them. And if you have streets on which people drive fast, pedestrians don't feel safe on them—either crossing them or walking near them. Old, winding streets are best for that.

Astonishingly, most city planners here in America don't seem to understand that if we want quieter neighborhoods, we have to change our city-planning policies so that residential neighborhoods have narrow, curving streets, sometimes built around trees or other natural obstacles. Not *everybody* wants to be able to rush to and from their house. Some people would actually prefer a neighborhood where it is safe for children to ride their bicycles and tricycles because traffic *can only go 15 mph or less*. The added benefit of traffic calming to all residents is that everything is much quieter in their neighborhoods without the roar of speeding engines!

Clean, Accessible, Economical Mass Transit

"Clean" obviously means using something other than fossil fuels as a power source, in addition to the obvious requirement for cleanliness on the train cars themselves. Economical means that it should be affordable to everyone to ride all the time. Accessible would provide access, as a right, for everyone—walking, bicycling, or wheelchairing—and beyond that, would provide access from anyplace in a city to anywhere else. Many people, currently, are cut off from transportation by poverty, age, or economic class. If you don't have a car, and there's not mass transit nearby or you can't afford what there is, you're isolated. As one low-income woman said, "I don't think people understand how it feels not to be able to go to the store, if you need medical aid and you don't have taxi fare or whatever— that feeling of isolation and anger."

When this issue comes up, I hear people say: "Mass transit has just gotten too costly. We can't afford to build it now."

Of course, I reply, it would have been better if we had built it back when Washington, D.C. or Atlanta or San Francisco built the *Metro* or *Marta* or *Bart*, but we didn't, and it *isn't* going to get cheaper to build in the future, so if we have to have it, which we do, we'd better get busy now.

Dallas has developed a fledgling intersuburban-city electric train system by adding one percent to the sales tax for the last 12 years. It will be completed in 2010 and will cost a total of $2.5 million, about 20 percent of which is Federal Transit Administration Funds. The sad thing is that there aren't enough of those funds to produce mass transit at the rate it is needed. Conservative Paul M. Weyrich, in his report "Conservatives and Mass Transit: Is it Time for a New Look?" said, about mass transit, "The vast majority of transit systems were privately owned, received no government assistance, and paid taxes." He said it wasn't until 1980 that government assistance to mass transit could even be accurately compiled: "In that year, it amounted to $4.8 billion. In contrast, government provided $39.7 billion to highways in 1980. By 1990, government transit assistance was up to $14.2 billion, but highways got almost $74 billion."[21]

Lest you think that all this highway money comes from users, as highway lobbies would like us to think, it doesn't. Only about 60 percent does.

The rest comes from us, the taxpayers.[22] In addition to what it costs us to maintain highways for gas- or diesel-powered vehicles, there is the question of what highways, and the vehicles on them, do to our air. Transportation accounts for 66 percent of carbon monoxide emissions, 21 percent of particulate matter, 35 percent of volatile organic compounds, and 40 percent of nitrogen oxides—all are carcinogens and/or precursors to ground-level ozone and smog. Harvard University School of Public Health estimates that air pollution may contribute to the death of 60,000 people per year.[23]

Every commuter who *stops* driving to work alone, the average person's most "polluting" daily activity, and *starts* taking mass transit saves 200 gallons of gasoline per year. Every gallon of gas burned puts 19 pounds of CO_2 into the atmosphere and assorted other pollutants, 50 percent of which, nationally, come from automobile tailpipe emissions. If the nation as a whole increased transit ridership by only 10 percent, the U.S. would save 135 million gallons of gasoline a year.[24] Today, the Dallas system alone removes 60,000 cars from the road. It is equivalent to one lane of highway, 125 miles long, bumper to bumper, removed from traffic, and it's only just begun!

This question of environmental pollution from automobiles is a very serious matter for those who are concerned about healing their bodies. Up to 110 million Americans breathe air that is unhealthy. About 30 percent of Americans *live* in areas where air does not meet national air quality standards, it is estimated that the national health-care bill for air pollution-related illness is between $500 million and $4 billion a year.[25] Cities and towns that are too big for all residents to get where they need to go on foot need to begin thinking not just in terms of the cost to build mass transit now, but *the cost to human health—physical and mental—of not building it.*

Bicycle Paths

The Sanborn Team II combined *bicycles* with *mass transit*. The proposal was that a clean mass transit system be tied to a series of bicycle rental racks so that a person could ride a bicycle he/she had "rented," probably at no charge or at a very minimal fee, check it in by punching in the person's registration number and the number of the returned bicycle into a computer, and hop on the train. At the train stop where the person emerged, he or she would pick up another bicycle, punch in a personal number and a bicycle number to "rent" it, and ride away on a bike path to their destination. Tracking systems built into the bicycles would allow constant computer monitoring in case there were questions about where a bicycle or its rider were at any point, good for both safety and tracking bicycle use.

Bicycling seems to work well in China and the European countries where paths or streets amenable to cyclists are provided. People ride to work or to mass transit during the hot summers or on the coldest winter days. In my experience and from discussions I have had, many people would prefer to ride bicycles to work, even in quite cold weather, but they are afraid of the traffic because there are so few official bike paths. A duo train-bicycle system would do wonders for the air quality, and it wouldn't hurt our individual exercise regimens either!

Small neighborhood service businesses, such as bakeries, tailors, groceries, bagel stores, fish markets, kosher delis, coffee bars, ice cream stores, clothing shops, restaurants, hardware stores, cleaners, and so on.

If you are going to have truly walkable neighborhoods, then you have to have small neighborhood service businesses that are accessible on foot or by wheelchair. They must cover the range of services people would need in their everyday lives—food, clothing, repair needs for homes and bicycles and whatever else, and social needs—places for social meetings.

Places to go where chances of accidental meeting are high; that is, neighborhood parks, playgrounds, cafes, sports centers, year-round school learning centers, and neighborhood shops.

"Accidental meeting" is a new phrase for a wonderful old concept I encountered on a daily basis as a child without thinking about it at all. When I was small, I pulled my little red wagon two-and-a-half blocks to Preble's Grocery on Main Street (which was then Highway 30—a main artery through America) with a long grocery list and $5. As I passed by the fresh egg store, I saw John and Winnie April through the doorway and waved to them. They waved back. When I passed the apartments filled with elderly residents on the corner, I saw Mrs. Knox or Mrs. Beninghouse or Mr. Worth coming out the door on their way to somewhere, and we spoke to each other.

At the next corner was Hand's Dairy, where one of the Hand girls was behind the counter and could see me walk by through the window as I saw her busy inside. We, too, waved. At the corner, I might see Jack Lowe, the editor of the *Sidney Telegraph*, coming from the post office; or Al Jorgenson, the bank president, walking back from the coffee shop. Across the street, I might bump into John Elwell and his handsome teenage son, Johnnie, or someone else from Elwell Motors.

So it went until I got to Preble's, where I ran into more people I knew—people who would help me reach things I couldn't from the high shelves or ask me about this or that in my family. Those were all "accidental" meetings I hadn't planned and they hadn't planned, but which enriched both our lives and, in addition, gave a child a great sense of something for which there is no word, so I will invent one: *protectedness.* When you encounter a lot of people you know on a daily basis, you somehow feel very safe.

Accidental meetings are one of the saddest losses of big-city desocialization, the "in your car, drive to work, drive home, get out of your car and go inside" lives. They are the color in the weaving that is the social fabric of our lives. They are so often taken for granted by small-town folk, and rarely experienced by city folk. We who have them no more are the poorer for it. We should try to bring them back into our lives and the lives of our children through the conscious creation of village-sized neighborhoods with neighborhood services and meeting places, outdoors and indoors.

Evolutionary

Habitat design shall include continuous re-evaluation of premises and values, and shall be demographically responsive and flexible to change over time to support future user needs. Initial designs should reflect our society's heterogeneity and have a feedback system. They shall be:

Multigenerational

The benefits elderly people receive from being in the presence of animals and children is being documented by medical researchers even as I write, including William H. Thomas, M.D., in his book *Life Worth Living,* which describes what he calls the Eden Alternative:

> The core of the Eden Alternative, a new paradigm for nursing home care, is the commitment to infuse nursing homes with huge numbers of companion animals, indoor plants, gardens, and children, while at the same time, reorganizing the management of the nursing home around the needs of the residents rather than around bureaucratic priorities.[26]

It wouldn't take a professional to tell most of us that the elderly thrive in the presence of *new life,* whether plants, animals, or children. I have seen the faces of my elderly parents and aunt light up when a great-grandchild enters the room; their obvious joy when a child climbs up on their laps to hear a story or pull at their ears or eyeglasses; their relaxed, happy laughter when they are in the presence of children.

I see, too, the enrichment of the child who is *so loved* by those grandparents and great-grandparents, who is cared for emotionally on a very fundamental level by that connection of generations. I see parents who are relieved of the constant pressures child-rearing brings for a few moments, or hours, by baby-sitting grandparents, so they can appreciate their own children more when they return. I see the enormous psychological benefits to both the elderly and the very young from this intergenerational nurturing.

I have seen the elderly snuggling with a puppy or caressing a kitten, as a contented smile crinkles the corners of their lonely eyes. I have seen an old companion dog, broken from its earthly bond with an elderly human when its master could no longer care for himself, left as alone and bereft as the master himself becomes in a nursing home.

And I have known that there is a better way.

Grandparents and great-grandparents don't belong in nursing homes or congregant housing. They belong in a societal structure that appreciates their gifts of wisdom, their ripeness of attitude, and their patience with life. They belong where we can all learn from them. They belong in the *multigenerational* village with the younger parents and their children where they can remain an integral part of the activity of all people of all ages—where they can *remember* that they, too, belong here in this place in the universe, and where we can appreciate the phenomenal wisdom they have gathered from their years of living in this place before us.

Nonexclusionary

In America, we have tended to isolate people into groups based on age and income. We have planned and built subdivisions with housing all the same price so all the people who live there are more or less the same—the same income levels, the same values, the same lifestyles. We have even gone so far as to *gate* some of those communities to keep out those who are different from ourselves. Boring, boring, boring—and destructive of the larger fabric of the community, because what it says is: "I'm in, you're out. I'm better, you're worse. I'm richer, you're poorer."

The town I grew up in had the largest house in town, a mortuary, next to a small, conventional, two-story, wood-frame house with seven children in it. The doctor with the biggest house in town lived between an old one that was falling down and a little tiny one that was thinking about it—a one-bedroom frame home occupied by an elderly man. You had your house *in the village* somewhere—nobody was shut out from seeing it (and commenting on it, one way or the other). We all walked by homes of the rich and the poor, and it never dawned on us that they should be separated from each other.

It is time to go back to patterns of housing that do not exclude anyone. These patterns should recognize, and celebrate in, their architecture and our differences so that when we finally have *walkable* streets within little "villages" in our cities, we will have something more interesting to look at than walls and gates.

Villagified

Let's think about some of the advantages of *villages* we've already considered in this book, even though we may not have used the word *village* in discussing them.

In a village, small by definition, everybody knows everybody else, so both the chance of accidental meeting and the "protectedness" quotient for children are high. Villages are walkable from one end to the other. Precisely because people get outside and walk more, they know each other better, so they tend to help and support each other more than in larger cities.

This is not to say that *everything* is rosy on that score. There is the village gossip hotline, and if you ever commit a "violation," people *never* forget! But the irony, or perhaps the cohesiveness, of it is that even those people who are roundly criticized at the local coffee shop or vigorously opposed in town meetings will be supported in their tragedies and rejoiced with in their victories by the very same people who have opposing viewpoints. This tribal behavior is, according to anthropologists, how human beings have interacted for eons in communities all over the world. *But to nourish and access those tribal behaviors, we must have "village"-sized habitations.*

Villages have access to land outside them for local agriculture, for walking and bicycling, wildlife, and community gardens. They have small neighborhood businesses that are physically and economically accessible to all residents in a completely synergistic arrangement. Without the businesses, the residents couldn't survive, and vice versa.

Perhaps the key words in defining the desirability of a "villagified" society are *comfort* and *coziness*. Most humans are more comfortable when they exist in the kind of interdependent tribal atmosphere a village provides. It is human shelter and provision for human needs built on a human scale. When a "village" grows over time, as small neighborhoods of village-size have in Europe for a thousand years, they develop a personality—what might be in Holland called a "gezellig" environment. Andrew Moskos, sociologist, former Amsterdam resident, and member of the American improvisational comedy group "Boom Chicago," describes it:

> A gezellig environment is one that allows good times to happen. It's almost like a vibe. A gezellig place is cozy and inviting and full of things that make it gezellig. McDonald's or the gas station minimart, on the other hand, would not be gezellig. The Dutch just love gezellig things and places, and their whole society is geared toward it.[27]

Our cities of today can't be cut apart and moved into the countryside, but they can allow individual neighborhoods that are "villagified," to develop naturally. These small "villages" could be divided by greenbelts, parks, and natural corridors for wildlife, created naturally when buildings fall into disrepair and have to be destroyed. The self-sustaining villages within the city could gradually be transformed so they use no outside energy resources. They would be walkable or bicycleable and connected by clean mass transit to all other villages that make up the great city. Within its green corridors and on lands surrounding it would be local agricultural production for local consumption.

Ideally, the sustainable society that would have been encouraged to develop gradually around the larger city would have as its primary criteria the recognition of all human habitat as an integral part of the larger living system that is our planet. Let's let that great, wise teacher, Lewis Mumford, have the last word on how the land itself expects us to create our habitat upon it:

> What drove (Henry) Thoreau to the solitude of the woods was no cynical contempt for the things beyond his reach. "Before we can adorn our houses with beautiful objects, the walls must be stripped, and our lives laid for a foundation. A taste for the beautiful is most cultivated out of doors, where there is no house, and no housekeeper." The primeval woods were a favorable beginning for the search, but Thoreau did not think they could be the end of it. The land itself, however, did stir his imagination

when he wrote: "All things invite this earth's inhabitants to rear their lives to an unheard-of height, and meet the expectation of the land.

The expectation of the land! One comes upon that phrase, or its equivalent, in almost every valid piece of early American thought. One thinks of moorland pastures by the sea, dark with bayberries and sweet fern, breaking out among the lichened rocks; and the tidal rivers bringing their weedy tang to the low meadows, wide and open in the sun; the purple pine groves, where the needles, bedded deep, hum to the wind, or the knotted New England hills, where the mountain laurel in June seems like upland snow, left over, or where the marble breaks through into clusters of perpetual laurel and everlasting; one sees mountain lakes, giant aquamarines, sapphires, topazes, and upland pastures where the blue, purple, lavender, and green of the huckleberry bushes give way in autumn to the fringe of sumach by the roadside; volcanoes of reds and crimsons, the yellow of September cornfields with intenser pumpkins lying between the shocks, or the naked breasts and flanks of the autumn landscape, quivering in uneasy sleep before the white blanket puts it to rest. To smell this, taste this, and feel and climb and walk over this landscape, once untouched, like an unopened letter or lover unkissed—who would not rise to meet the expectation of the land? Partly, it was the challenge of babyhood: how will it grow up and what will become of it? Partly it was the charm of innocence; or again, it was the sense of the mighty variety that the whole continent gives, as if between the two oceans every possible human habitat might be built, and every conceivable variety of experience fathomed.[28]

◆   ◆   ◆

CHAPTER 17

In Love with the Earth

Instead of an intellectual search, there was suddenly a very deep gut feeling that something was different. It occurred when looking at Earth and seeing this blue-and-white planet floating there, and knowing it was orbiting the sun, seeing that sun, seeing it set in the background of the very deep black and velvety cosmos, seeing—rather, knowing for sure—that there was a purposefulness in flow of energy, of time, of space cosmos—that it was beyond man's rational ability to understand, that suddenly there was a nonrational way of understanding that had been beyond my previous experience.

There seems to be more to the universe than random, chaotic, purposeless movement of a collection of molecular particles. On the return trip home, gazing through 24,000 miles of space toward the stars and the planet from which I had come, I suddenly experienced the universe as intelligent, loving, and harmonious.

— Edgar Mitchell, U.S. astronaut[1]

Without exception, everyone I know who has begun working in the sustainability movement has done so because sometime, someplace, something has happened to them to make them fall in love with the earth. Some magical mental metamorphosis has caused them to see anew what they have often seen before. The burst of tiny, perfect redbuds on a tree in springtime, the transforming miracle of birth or death, the grandeur of a mountain or a mammoth waterfall, the simple beauty of a random piece of crystal quartz, or the long and graceful lope of a wild antelope has taken their consciousness to a new level of awareness. They have had an epiphany experience in nature.

Often people came to this different level of awareness from a simple transformation of perspective. They, as Thoreau, looked at a pond and saw it teeming with life in a breathtaking aura of placid beauty. Or, they looked up one bright night at the planets and stars charting their course through space as they have for eons, signaling an order beyond understanding, a wonder beyond comprehension, and suddenly felt their own relationship to it all. With that realization, that we are a tiny speck in a huge universe, often comes an awkward, but sharply defined new understanding: that we truly have been given the awesome power to make a difference in what the future of this planet will be like for all living creatures through the next decades, centuries, and perhaps even eons. At that point of new awareness, many of us have felt called upon to be nurturing parent figures to this earth we have fallen in love with, to transform into something of a Mother Teresa to a planet crying out in pain.

From that realization comes commitment. So it was with California inventor and designer, Stephen Heckeroth. Immediately after graduating from college at the tender age of 21, Steve came to the hills high above the coast in Mendocino, California. Drawn by a mysterious force he didn't understand, one day he walked through a falling-down gate into a circle of ancient, blackened redwood stumps. As he stood among the ruins of the giants, staring down into a valley and beyond to the Pacific Ocean, he knew it was here that he belonged. Through some miracle—some would say it wasn't a miracle at all, but was simply the fulfillment of his earthly intention—he was able to negotiate the purchase of the land for exactly the small amount of money he had available.

Almost immediately, he started building. His first home was a tipi (teepee), made of canvas sewed on an old treadle sewing machine on top of poles he cut off the land. His first building was an outhouse, which he now calls a "fruit tree hole privy." When the "hole" fills up, he moves the privy and puts a fruit tree in the hole. I can personally attest to the success of his system. On our visit there last summer, I ate, off one of those fruit trees, several of the most delicious plums I've ever tasted.

Every building material Stephen used was indigenous—either taken from the site or recycled from nearby areas. He spent a year preparing for an Amish-style barn-raising, and in the summer of 1973, 100 of his friends and neighbors helped put up most of the barn in a single day. His family's first real home was a one-bedroom apartment upstairs in that barn loft. It now houses his daughter and her friend. That barn, downstairs, served as a home to goats and cows that Steve milked twice a day for eight years. It is now a barn only in the sense that it is home to a flock of chickens that the vegetarian family keeps for their eggs. The other side holds some of his miscellaneous inventions, and his two electric vehicles, a converted 20 horsepower (HP) electric tractor, and a 144 V. 400 amp Karmann Ghia. The roof of the barn supports 60 photovoltaic (solar electric) panels that provide all electric power for the house and barns all year long, and for the vehicles on sunny days.

When his young family outgrew the apartment, Stephen built a water tower house designed to include many of the same features as the homes of the young Frank Lloyd Wright, with whom Heckeroth shares a June 8 birth date. Most of Heckeroth's furniture, designed and built into the walls of the same unpainted natural redwood as the rest of the interior surfaces, was simply oiled to preserve and enhance its natural beauty. Wright, in 1954, explained his intention when he built in the same kinds of furniture:

> We now build well-upholstered benches and seats into our houses, trying to make them all part of the building . . . In organic architecture, there is little or no room for applique of any kind. I have never been fond of paints or wallpaper or anything which must be applied to other things as a surface . . . when you gloss over it, you lose its nature—enamel it, and so change the character of its natural expression, you have committed a violation according to the ideals of organic architecture. Wood is wood, concrete is concrete, stone is stone. We like to have whatever we choose to use demonstrate the beauty of its own character, as itself.[2]

The Heckeroth "water tower" house above the Northern California coast. The home, built by the owner from indigenous materials, needs no outside energy resources.

Passive solar and wood heat provide all space heating for the Heckeroth house. The roof of the sunspace on the southeast corner of the house holds two 4' x 8' panels, built of corrugated metal and copper tubing painted black and covered with glass, which, in connection with the coils in the wood-stove, have provided all the hot water for Steve's family for 20 years. Gravity flow brings water to the house from the water tank on top of the tower. The second-story shower in the house is directly over a downstairs toilet and sink, for plumbing efficiency. All graywater from the shower, sinks, and washer flow into a drip system that waters their 1/4-acre vegetable garden. All blackwater flows into a septic system that waters the fruit trees from underground.

The fruit trees, vegetable gardens, and eggs from the chickens provide all the food for the family except grains and dairy, which Steve's beautiful wife, Christiana, buys on her weekly trips to town in her electric car. The only other products she has to buy are family toiletries and toilet tissue, which are carefully chosen for their environmentally friendly qualities.

Late at night, Steve and Christiana are often at work—she on the computer powered by solar electricity, and he in a solar-lighted and powered "invention workshop" full of sophisticated tools. Recently awarded a contract by a European firm to develop the commercial electric tractor he invented, Stephen also has been hired, with Christiana, to design a health/rejuvenation spa in the old village of Patagonia, Arizona.

They labor, with tenacity and uncommon passion, at their first love—giving the rest of the world the same vision they have and live—a future dependent only on renewable energy. Clearly, the house they occupy, as well as their holistic five-acre site, comprise a Healing Place. From it, they are inspired to go forth into the world, making change one project at a time, laboring under the same caveat as all the rest of us: We can only do our little part, never knowing, at that moment, how it will really turn out.

> *"One thing is sure; we have to do something. We have to do the best we know how at the moment. If it doesn't turn out right, we can modify it as we go along."*
> — President Franklin D. Roosevelt.

What the Heckeroths do, we all can do. We can learn as much as we can about how the future will be shaped, then do our small part. To do that, we have to understand the technologies of the future. We have to clearly understand what makes a Healing House completely independent of outside energy sources and how we can move toward that goal for our planet.

The Heckeroth's house and all outbuildings are:

- built from indigenous materials;
- heated by passive solar windows and a sunspace;
- cooled by natural ventilation;
- provided with solar heated water;
- provided with electricity by photovoltaics (solar electric); and
- provided with food by a vegetable garden, fruit trees, and chickens.

Their car and tractor are electric powered and are charged from solar electricity, using no fossil fuels.

The family homestead, which needs no outside utility connections and no fuel supplies other than the sun, brings us to the Healing House principles not yet covered in other chapters:

A Healing House, should have incorporated into it every renewable resource that is physically and financially possible.

Soon, all Healing Houses will need no energy source other than the sun or wind or falling water.

Residents of Healing Houses will soon be able to recharge their own electric cars and all electric vehicles necessary for grounds maintenance and food production silently from the sun, wind, and/or falling water.

In order to help you understand how these systems work, and how future technologies will give energy independence to Healing Homes, I need to answer some questions about these technologies and where they will be accessed.

How does a solar hot water system work?

There are several different types of solar hot water systems. First there is the "passive" group, which has no auxiliary power needs. Second, there are combination types, in which the collection is totally passive, but power is used to get the water into the tank. And the third type has lots of "bells and whistles," which require power.

The simplest "passive" system is the homemade "batch" type that uses a large, single barrel-shaped metal tank painted black and placed in the sun to heat water in a "batch." These are the least efficient, but also the least expensive. In order to use this type system year-round in a cold climate, you have to heavily insulate all the pipes leading to your house, and place the tank in an insulated box with an insulated glass cover that faces south. This is called a "breadbox" solar water heater.

Another open-loop "passive" system utilizes the simplest flat-plate collector consisting of black-painted pipes in an insulated box covered with glass. Typically, insulated pipes connect a tilted flat-plate collector to a well-insulated water tank mounted above the collector. The water in the collector is heated by the sun and rises, by natural convection, into the top of the tank. The colder liquid in the bottom of the tank settles to the bottom of the collector. So it is the heat from the sun that causes the water to flow. When the sun is shining, the system is operating. This is called a "thermosiphon" system, and it requires freeze protection in most areas.

In a closed-loop system, the fluid in the collectors isn't water. It's some nonfreezing mixture that flows through a heat exchanger in the water tank. This protects the collectors from freezing. There are advantages and disadvantages to each. To find out about them, or to access more information on all active solar hot water systems, see *The New Solar Home Book.*[3]

What are the advantages of the ones that use more auxiliary power?

With a pumped system, you can have collectors on the roof and a tank anyplace in the building, and the water can be drained down into the tank to prevent the pipes in the collector from freezing.

The newest systems combine the simple effectiveness of closed-loop antifreeze systems with state-of-the-art photovoltaic technology. The small pump that circulates the mixture through the collectors and the heat exchanger coil in the hot water storage tank is powered by photovoltaics, or solar electric energy. This makes the system totally solar and gives it the advantage of successful operation during utility outages that might otherwise cause controller failure, the single largest cause of call-backs for gravity-fed active solar hot water systems.

Why should I want to put in an active solar hot water system in my Healing House?

First, it's clean energy. Second, it will save you money. Keep in mind that on your *annual* utility bills, you spend 37.5 percent on home cooling and heating, *30 percent on water heating*; and the balance for refrigerators (9 percent), cooking (10.3 percent), lighting (4.8 percent), television (2.7 percent), clothes drying (2.1 percent) and other things, including hair dryers, curlers, and so on (3.6 percent).[4]

If you use solar electricity to supply 80 gallons of water a day (average for a family of four), you save 3,300 kWh of (utility supplied) electricity per year. Every one of those kWh produces 2 lbs. of carbon dioxide, .2 lbs. of sulfur dioxide, .25 lbs. of carbon monoxide, and .01 lbs. of nitrogen oxide, or a total of 2.46 lbs. of pollutants per kWh. Your system, which saves 3,300 kWh/year, will save the air from 4.06 *tons* of pollutants.

And, best of all, if your system costs $2,500 (average cost), and you save $30 per month, or $360 per year on hot water-heating costs, your return on investment, before tax, is 20 percent.[5]

What exactly is photovoltaic (solar electric) power?

Quite simply, it is a system of producing electricity through the movement of loose electrons between two basic elements (usually silicon and boron) caused by light (photons) from the sun. Microthin slices of the two elements are placed together in tiny cells. Many of these cells are collected together to form PV panels and placed where they will be exposed to sunlight. For example, the entire top surface of the now famous little Sojourner, which just explored Mars, is made of photovoltaic electric cells—its sole electrical source, backed up by batteries. In addition to being made into modular panels, solar electric cells are now laminated onto roofing materials so you get a roof and clean energy at the same time. The most common photovoltaic panels have been tested to withstand one-inch diameter ice balls (hail) at 70 mph. The electrons created by a photovoltaic system produce direct current (dc), that can be stored in a battery for future use, or converted to alternating current (ac) for use in a standard electrical system.

At the moment, many local electric utility companies are required to buy your extra photovoltaic electricity. With a good power inverter, you can feed it into your local power lines to be credited to your account for future electric use when you need *their* electricity. This system, called "net-metering," eliminates the need to purchase costly batteries to store your own. Net-metering, however, may be lost in utility deregulation. (See the next section.)

© 1997 Barbara Harwood

These photovoltaic panels covering the Heckeroth barn roof provide all electricity for the family's home, computers, EVs (electric vehicles), and Steven Heckeroth's invention workshop.

Since solar is clean energy, why doesn't everybody use it?

Geographic location is one reason. The percentage of sunshine determines how much power you can generate with photovoltaic cells. A home in the southwestern U.S. gets a much higher percentage of daily sunshine than one in the Northeast or coastal Northwest. A residential PV system in Arizona, for example, will generate almost twice as much electricity as a similar system in New Hampshire.[6]

The second reason is a lack of availability of PV cells and the marketing of them to the general public. They have been "in development" for many years, that is, getting to the point where it is fiscally viable in the energy marketplace. PV power is steadily coming down in price and increasing in efficiency. PV panels are now available for about $4 per watt of power.

There are even larger issues when we evaluate the cost of solar electric as a total system power resource (a power "plant"). It must be measured against coal, natural gas (fossil fuels) and nuclear power, which have been subsidized to the tune of billions of dollars over the past few decades. When someone in the utility industry says "Photovoltaics are not cost effective," I say, "They would be if we stopped subsidizing other nonrenewable energy resources." And, in fact, there are striking new developments in the commercialization of PV worldwide.[17A]

How much does photovoltaic electricity cost?

Dennis Creech, founding director of Southface Energy Institute in Atlanta, says that it costs $5,000 per Kw to install—about $12,000 to $24,000 for a whole house, including storage batteries.

It costs between $.05 and .10/Kwh for a utility to buy as a large-scale power source, so it is not generally competitive with natural gas or coal. However, it would be cost effective for individual homeowners *if a power company would install the PV roof and lease it to its customers, letting them pay each month exactly as they did for power supplied from their large power plants.* The Sacramento Municipal Utility District (SMUD) leases PV systems to residential users for a premium of about 15 percent on their utility bill. For this 15 percent, from $4 to $6 per month, the homeowner becomes a "PV Pioneer," sharing in the privilege of being the first to have clean, solar electric energy produced on their own rooftop. SMUD says their cost is about $28,000 per system. Texas Utilities, which serves about 1/3 of the state of Texas, and a few others around the country, are evaluating similar PV leasing programs.

What about battery storage?

Batteries are still lead-acid, but deep-cycle industrial batteries will last from 8 to 12 years. These are the batteries used in forklifts and stationary applications by phone companies. They sell for about one dollar per amp hour, and they can be returned and remanufactured into new batteries. The prohibitive cost of large independent battery packs makes being hooked up to the power company (and using their backup as necessary) more economical for a homeowner if inexpensive hookups are available. It is also58 better for the power companies because solar electricity helps offset peak air-conditioning loads. Solar functions best when the sun is brightest, the same days that need the most air conditioning.

How does Steve Heckeroth recharge his electric vehicles (EVs) off the PV cells on his barn roof?

He does it in the same way you would power any electric appliance in your house. He just plugs the EVs into an electrical outlet. In his case, that outlet is powered by photovoltaics. Voilà! In eight hours, he can drive his

Karmann Ghia 70 miles on that one charge, or, after his tractor charges for four hours, he can rototill a half-acre garden or mow over two acres of lawn. And PV power provides the same performance "oomph" to an electric car as gasoline does to a gas-powered car. An electric "James Dean" Porsche, built by Steve's company, Mendomotive, goes from 0 mph to 60 mph in seven seconds—on a dirt road yet—fast enough to make a passenger hold her breath! Steven estimates that he saves 800 gallons of gasoline, or about 15 barrels of oil, every year with his electric cars.

Recharging vehicles is not limited to just an occasional residential automobile either. On May 23, 1994, Governor Howard Dean of Vermont turned on a solar recharge station to power a state electric mail truck for delivering state mail. Solar Works of Montpelier, Vermont, built the 1.75kW station, which will also be used to power an S-10 electric pickup jointly purchased by the state and the Vermont Electric Vehicle Demonstration Project (EVermont).[7] And this year, the famous Northeast Solar Energy Association (NESEA) solar electric car race in Maine had one entrant ticketed for speeding!

You mentioned barrels of oil. Is there really any danger of oil running out anytime soon?

Interesting question. An article in *Futurist* magazine written by L. F. Ivanhoe, a geologist, geophysicist, engineer, and oceanographer who heads the M. King Hubbert Center for Petroleum Supply Studies at the internationally known Colorado School of Mines, says that there is a very good chance that there will be serious shortages by 2010—*12 years from now!*

He explains that the numbers relied on throughout the world for establishing petroleum reserves come from *Oil and Gas Journal.* They, in turn, come from questionnaires sent out to each country's energy officials. There is no verification process. First of all, anybody who thinks countries who are hostile to the West, such as Libya, Iraq, and Iran, would tell the truth about their oil supplies is a real optimist. It benefits them in several ways to inflate their reserves: access to world bank loans collateralized by those reserves, economic power in negotiations with other nations, and status inside and outside their own countries. Not to mention that we, in the West, bend over backwards to save relationships with these oil-producing behemoths no matter how diplomatically obstreperous they become, sometimes to the detriment of our own citizens and world law and order.

Second, there is terrible confusion among the terms used, and many categories are bundled together and called "petroleum reserves" when they are, in fact, not proven to be there at all.[17B] This leads us, Ivanhoe says, to dangerous complacency when, in fact, we need to prepare for serious oil shortages at least by the year 2010, and possibly by 2000.

And lest we are too skeptical of nay-sayers such as Ivanhoe, who remind us that oil supplies are finite (and both politicians and economists are often unwilling to recognize that fact), an article in the prestigious, quite conservative *Wall Street Journal* in June of 1997 seemed to confirm some of what Ivanhoe said—at least his hypothesis about easily accessed oil becoming more and more scarce:

> Oil companies, including several from the U.S., have paid $2 billion for the right to exploit 20 oil fields in Venezuela, about twice the total expected . . . Drillers' eagerness to pay up for Venezuela points out an essential truth about international oil exploration today: Most of the low-hanging fruit has already been picked. Many major oil nations, such as Saudi Arabia, Mexico, and Kuwait, remain essentially closed to foreign participation at the wellhead. Those that are open offer either poor long-term prospects, unattractive fiscal and legal regimes, or too much political uncertainty, as in Russia and Algeria.[8]

What about fuel cell- or hydrogen-powered cars?

There are reportedly two functioning types of systems for providing hydrogen (very clean energy) to fuel cells that would power vehicles. Phoenix Gas Systems, a subsidiary of Hydrogen Burner Technology, has a patent on a reforming unit that can easily strip pure hydrogen from any hydrocarbon fuel; that is, gasoline. Apparently, according to Tom Dickerman writing in *Hydrogen Technology*, this is the system being used by Chrysler's new prototype fuel-cell car.

The air-pollution benefits of a system that burns hydrogen instead of straight gasoline would be significant (Chrysler claims a 90 percent reduction in emissions and a 50 percent increase in fuel efficiency), but the hydrogen is "reformed" from a nonrenewable source. Splitting water, a renewable resource, into hydrogen and oxygen may someday be a solution, but currently, this requires too much energy.

Are there other renewable energy sources that my Healing House could use?

Windmills. Although today's windmills look a little different from the one that I used as a very young child drawing water at our farm, wind power is now the world's fastest-growing energy source, according to the Worldwatch Institute. Global wind power generating capacity rose to 4,900 megawatts last year, an increase of 32 percent in one year. Since 1990, its use has increased 150 percent. Unlike coal, the leading source of electricity today, wind power (and solar power) produces no air pollution, acid rain, or CO_2 (carbon dioxide), which causes global warming.

Poor countries are also beginning to see the benefits of wind energy. Construction is set for one of the largest wind farms in the world on a windy hill near Tangiers. Eighty-four wind turbines, each capable of producing 600 kilowatts of electricity, will generate 2 percent of Morocco's total electricity within three years.

A windmill used to pump water at the author's farmhouse in Nebraska...still operational. The building is the old milkhouse where the author used to skim the "spoon cream" off the top of her grandfather's milk cans.

© 1997 Barbara Harwood

The newest version of the old windmill, called a wind turbine. This TU electric array, manufactured by Carter Wind Turbines of Burkburnett, TX, generates 800,000 KWh of electricity annually, which powers 80 homes.

© 1997 TU Electric

The world's largest wind turbine went into service last year in Emden, Germany, generating 1,500 kilowatts, two to three times as much as any previous wind turbine. The French-built machine consists of three 105-foot blades, each weighing three metric tons.[9]

Wind is an excellent alternative where wind blows hard enough. Not all areas, therefore, are appropriate. Additionally, wind power is cost effective on a large scale, but sometimes the cost of an individual wind generator is prohibitive, and it does have to have back-up power because there are times—even in the windy city, Chicago—when the wind doesn't blow. In addition, most urban and suburban neighborhoods have restrictive covenants against something as large as a wind generator sticking up out of your backyard. Not so on farms or ranches in the country. Sometimes, it can be very cost effective for a group of homeowners to cooperate in the cost of purchasing and maintaining a large windmill.

What will utility companies of the future look like?

Many experts who have studied the industry think utility companies will primarily be *service providers,* rather than *power suppliers* in the future. One company (probably still a monopoly) might retain and maintain distribution lines for an area (what one of my power-company friends calls a "poles and wires" company), regardless of who produced the power that was used on those lines. So if company A owns the power lines, company B can sell you power and get it to you.

Yet another company might provide service for the power you receive. That is, if your power goes out at a location in the "territory" of company A, even though company B provides you power, company A will come to your house to see what the problem is, take care of customer inquiries, meter reading, marketing, energy efficiency programs, and other miscellaneous services. Another company might just buy and sell power resources—called "purchased power"—like a real estate broker sells property—and resell it to the end user. That company could buy small natural gas generator plants, wind or solar power, or portions of power from larger old coal and nuclear power plants.

As we head into this new era of split-up power companies, there are a couple of things for us, as consumers, to beware of. First, if deregulation occurs and a new power provider comes into an area selling power at a lower cost than we currently pay, that seller is going to try to get the *biggest power USER* in the county onto his service. Obviously if you sell 100 MW to one buyer, it's easier than selling 100 MW to 1,000 buyers in terms of service, meter reading, billing, and every other thing power companies do. If this happens, and new, low-cost power providers take away the biggest industrial and commercial users from the system, it will leave us, as residential users, holding the financial bag for the costs of the big power plants built in the past.

Some state governments, in deregulation talks, are asking all of us as taxpayers to share the cost of "bailing out" the existing utility companies from those big power plant costs. Some plan to leave it in our rates. Either way, it could be very uncomfortable. Even though "deregulation" sounds good as a buzzword, this bail-out issue could haunt us financially for years and years. Perhaps it would be better to deregulate a little at a time, letting a standard or speeded-up (called accelerated) depreciation get rid of these costs as it now does.

Second, as we move into this free-wheeling atmosphere of five companies for five parts of what used to be all together at our local utility, who will be our power provider of last resort? What if our little residential community isn't "cost-effective" for the local utility to service anymore, and no other company has come to our area soliciting our business? Will the old company be required to stay and serve us even though they are now deregulated and free to go wherever they want? To counter this, there needs to be provision for a "provider of last resort" included in deregulation language.

Third, if the only incentive is the bottom line, à la Wall Street at the moment, where will be the incentives to conserve energy or to create cleaner energy? Who will do the research and development on clean, new technologies? Will power companies care more about satisfying their stockholders or cleaning up the air? You choose. Literally. You *will choose* by your input into this utility deregulation debate. Make your voice heard if you want clean, renewable energies. Don't be intimidated by all the high-fallutin' language. It *boils down to these five simple issues:*

- Who will have to provide me with electric power if no one wants to?
- What will happen to clean energy resources?
- What will happen to energy-conservation efforts?
- Will research and development to provide new, clean, power technologies be mandated to continue?
- Who will pick up the bill for the costly existing power plants?

Many believe that the relative success of renewable energy resources will depend on the degree to which they are embraced by utilities. According to the *Environmental Business Journal (EBJ)*, the public is increasingly concerned about global warming and dirty air. This is creating a surge of interest in clean, renewable energy resources among the public. But their success will not necessarily depend on more government subsidies, but lower cost capital and more joint ventures to give utilities of the future experience with them. As *EBJ* said, "What's missing is a comprehensive national energy strategy that either incorporates incentives for renewables or accounts for the environmental costs of traditional power sources."[10] That is, if we factored in the cost of damage from acid rain and global warming into the cost of burning coal to produce power, the price would be much higher, and renewables would automatically be more cost effective.

What things are even further into the future for a Healing House?

Obviously, the ideal goal for a Healing House is to help its occupants pay *no* utility bills, and not have to buy *any* fossil fuels for transportation, yet still have the same lifestyle they currently enjoy—to live as the Heckeroths live. That is probably 30 or more years away for most Americans. We are all hooked up to electric power. Most of us own cars, in which we have a considerable amount of money invested, that use gasoline. Many of us are also hooked to natural gas for space heating and, some of us, for cooking and water heating as well.

To unhook from those systems tomorrow, first of all, would cost a fortune in existing houses. Second, it would mean that we had to build a whole new house, and there is a problem with that *in addition* to the cost problem. Almost no builders would have the vaguest idea how to build a house for all renewable systems. We have to begin to demand these clean energy systems for ourselves in order to force builders to learn the technology. When we do, as more and more systems are used, the cost will come down, benefiting all of us.

Much of the larger establishment—that is, big building companies, big utilities, and big automobile manufacturers—are afraid of these renewable technologies. They fear something they don't understand, and they fear it will take market share from them. Which it will. If they don't get educated on clean technologies and begin to adapt themselves and their companies to this change, another Microsoft entrepreneur will appear in a year or two, figure out how to inexpensively implement the clean technologies that survey after survey shows Americans want, and make fortunes with them.

Some large companies, such as Exxon and Enron, who are both getting into the photovoltaics business, and Arizona Public Power and SMUD who are marketing PV cells, see that handwriting on the wall. Most do not. Some states, such as Arizona, are pushing companies toward clean energy. More will begin to as air pollution becomes more and more of a problem, and as insurance companies make demands on customers to reduce greenhouse gas emissions through insurance rate pressure.

Meanwhile, it is now up to you, who have become educated through reading this book, to pass on your knowledge to others and encourage them to participate in the activism that it will take to make our planet healthier through energy efficiency and renewable energy technologies.

As Roy McAlister, president of the American Hydrogen Association, wrote:

> The course of civilization will be determined by what we decide to do with the remaining fossil fuel reserves, what people are taught, what they experience, what they see, hear, think and believe. A worthy Grand Purpose for Civilization is the achievement of prosperity without pollution.[11]

◆   ◆   ◆

C H A P T E R 1 8

Healing Ourselves Where We Live

You shall love the Lord your God with all your heart, with all your mind, with all your strength. *You shall love the creatures the Lord your God has created; all the creatures of the earth and sky, and all the creatures beneath the sea; You shall love all the people created by the Lord your God, who are your neighbors on this earth, for though they not be perfect, they are created in the image the Lord your God has ordained.* Teach this *law of love* diligently unto your children; Speak of it in your homes and on all your ways; Remember it when you lie down and when you rise up. Bind it as a sign upon your hand; Write it on the doorpost of your house and on your gates. This you must do in order to fulfill all my commandments and be holy unto your God. For I, the Lord your God, who has created this bounteous land, am holy. *I command you to live together on this land in holiness.*[1]

(Author's changes from Biblical text are in italics.)

The Power of Meditation

"We are particles of this mystery which pours forth into the world."
— Joseph Campbell[2]

I told you at the beginning of this book that I meditate, and that I believe, in a very fundamental sense, that I was led, through meditation, to the work I do. In this chapter, I'm going to tell you about meditation, intention, wholeness, and love as your personal pathway to a Healing House of your own.

I believe that the *single most important thing I do*, in the quiet space I have created here in my own Healing House, is to spend time every day reconnecting in meditation with "The Force," whatever that is. When I meditate, it feels as though I have plugged myself into a big light socket in the sky from which energy flows into me. It seems to be, from our limited view of reality, some sort of magic. This is why people who see themselves as realists or scientists often reject reaching for it or touching it. They fear that it will somehow contaminate their reality.

And they are right. They will never again see the world the same way. They will never fear the same things. They will never again be as frustrated or as alone. They will find that there are a great many things they understand *less well* than they did before. And they will be enriched beyond their wildest imaginings by the experience.

Meditation As Teacher

From meditation, I have learned that there is some sort of indefinable cellular connection in which a physical presence in me speaks in some nonverbal way to a physical presence in other life, in plants, trees, animals, children—all people. It's as if there is a part of me, invisible to the naked eye, that has a welcoming hand reaching out to other living things exactly as I would stretch forth

© 1997 Holly Kuper

The author in her meditation space.

my hand to greet another person for the first time. These two entities connect in some very fundamental, life-sustaining way, replenishing both of us for as long as I consciously hold onto that connection, which is easiest when I am in direct contact with it in some way—leaning on a tree, sitting on the earth, and hearing the wind and birds. I have come to believe that a lot that's wrong in the world would be fixed, automatically, if that conscious connection were reintegrated into our bodies and minds.

Most of what is wrong with people who build the houses in which we live is the same thing that is wrong with society at large, and financial institutions in particular. Those who determine policy for them have lost touch with that part of themselves that, in meditation, can open up to establish that ultimate life-enhancing, life-sustaining connection. Because they have lost it, they believe that other things, such as material wealth, are the key to the kind of peaceful feelings of completion and fulfillment one receives in meditation. But that is not the case.

Money Is Not Real

Money is merely a means of barter we use to maintain ourselves in our social system, that is, the world as it exists. Study after study has shown no relationship between the amount of money someone has and their level of happiness. We have to have enough to sustain ourselves for our lifetime on this planet, but we don't need *more* than enough. We can only wear one set of clothes at a time, and we should only eat so many calories a day. We need shelter over our heads, but not *grand* shelter—only that which incorporates the Healing House principles, however small or large is required to accommodate the number of people we live with.

It is when all of us get caught up in the *popular*—that is to say, the advertising agency-created—vision of what we *ought to have* that we mess up our psyches and feel this pervasive discomfort about our lives.

Almost every day, I talk to people who have developed, through time, a vision of a basic, simple, healthy life. They want a house the right size, which is independently sustainable over time. They want bankers to give them a mortgage and not penalize them because their house isn't as large as others in their neighborhood, or because it has a gravel driveway instead of concrete, and no fireplace or garage. They want to deal with people who understand their simple, profound goals and the metaphysical learning process that led to those goals. They don't care if they're ever in a decorator magazine. *They just want a house that heals their spirits.*

Most corporate business people have forgotten their own way back to the earth, so they have forgotten how to see that *connection* in others. Although their conscious intentions may seem to them to be pure, they are not. If they are not personally in touch with the truth of this need for connection with nature, the unintended consequences of their decisions affect *all of us* every day of our lives. Somehow, we have to re-establish that connection with the earth and all its living systems in the next generation so that when they are business leaders, political leaders, and corporate giants, they take those values with them. We have to help people who are blind to the natural systems, that *in the end must rule all of us*, and understand their own evolutionary bond with those systems. It must become *their intention*, as well as our own, to honor people's spiritual connection to nature, and to recognize their need to reconnect with it physically in their homes.

I find it stunning to realize how many young people in fairly influential positions are reconnecting to these natural forces through meditation. At the last joint conference of the seven major groups involved in buildings and energy, the American Solar Energy Society, the Association of Mechanical Engineers, the American Institute of Architects, and others, four of us held a session called "The Spirit of Sustainability." The presenters talked about meditation and its life-supporting and inspiring connection to our work. The room was packed to overflowing. People were sitting not only on every chair, but every available square inch of floor space, and spilling out the door. And, the most astonishing thing was that everyone in the room was spellbound. Nobody moved during the whole two hours.

I learned later that the CEO of a powerful regional utility company, the CEOs of several architectural firms, and others with sterling credentials of national leadership were in that room. What this said to me was that there is a hunger for reconnection, for wholeness. The intention of these people to find wholeness, many said later, had led them to meditation.

The Power of Intention

The one metaphysical aspect of existence that continues to amaze me, perhaps more than any other, is the incredible power of intention. What I intend with my action seems to be almost as important as what I do, maybe because when I "intend," I create a visual image of what I want to happen. That visual image leads me to take the action that will, in turn, lead me to my intended goal, and will also help me share that goal, verbally, with others—"selling them," as it were, on participating in that goal.

If what we *intend* is to lead a *healing lifestyle* in our own, new Healing House, we have to define it and image it for ourselves before we can pursue it through all our actions. Hopefully, this book has helped you make pictures in your mind of your own Healing House. Now you can place those pictures in your meditation or even draw them if you have that talent, and begin to allow yourself to be led toward that house. If this sounds a little far-fetched, I challenge you to think how you have achieved other goals in your life. I'll bet, if you analyze the process you used, it was the same, although you may not have identified each step as I have here.

Perhaps you are saying, "She just doesn't understand. What I have to do is *survive* in my job and my life. I have to function each day as the system demands. I have no control." I think you will find that if you change your intention—in other words, your thinking about what you are doing— you *will see the kind of impact you intend to create.* Try a new way of thinking, and take that new thinking with you into a daily meditation. Before you begin visualizing your own Healing House, remember the healing that energy-efficient, resource-efficient, environmentally friendly houses give not only to ourselves, but also to the planet. Then recognize and remember the fragility of the life-support systems of our planet, as Russian astronaut, Victor Shatalov, described:

> When we look at the sky, it seems to us to be endless. We breathe without thinking about it, as is natural. We think without consideration for the ocean of air. Then you board a spacecraft, you tear away from Earth, and within ten minutes, you have been carried straight through the layer of air, and beyond there is nothing! Beyond the air, there is only emptiness, coldness, darkness. The "boundless" blue sky, the ocean which gives us breath and protects us from the endless black and death, is but an infinitesimally thin film. How dangerous it is to threaten even the smallest part of this gossamer covering, this conserver of life.[3]

The Sleepwalkers Here

How unaware we are, without meditation to ground us, as we walk through life. How oblivious we are to the wholeness all around us on this planet, the very wholeness we seek but always seem to miss as we search everywhere else for answers to our unfulfilled existence. We read and study, search the Internet, and question the TV gurus in the great intellectual struggle to find meaning in our lives. Yet what we find is not the missing pieces, but a greater enigma. From one place we find a tidbit, from another place a little more, and from somewhere else another hint. But somehow all the pieces don't quite add up to a whole *because we've missed the source of wholeness.* Why? Ken Blanchard and Terry Waghorn call it "spiritual amnesia":

> Every human being might be said to be suffering from a kind of spiritual amnesia. For most of us, the sense of mystery concerning where we came from and where we are going, which we knew and felt as little children, has been replaced in the process of "growing up" by a veneer of reasonableness and false certainty. Focused as we are on our day-to-day routine, we are sleepwalkers here . . . .[4]

Healing Our Spiritual Sleepwalking Through Meditation

If you wish to learn to meditate, find a quiet place from which you have removed nonspiritual distractions such as books, radios, TVs, and in which quiet and peace are the norm. That is, the middle of a room in which conflict resolution is done, or a place where tension-producing activities such as paying bills or doing income taxes are done, are not good places to start meditation. After you have established the meditation connection easily, you can do it anywhere, anytime, even standing up in a crowded room. But at the beginning, it will be easiest in the right atmosphere.

Get yourself some cushions or a comfortable chair, and sit down in total silence. Preferably, have plants around you, perhaps animals who will lie quietly at your feet, and a view of the outdoors in front of you. Or you can prepare, as one of my friends in Denver has, a small meditation area in a guest bedroom where she has put a little bench with her collection of rocks, shells, and feathers, an incense pot, a picture of an Indian, and assorted other meaningful items. It should be a space that is uniquely *yours*. Once you have meditated there for a while, it will be an almost magical space where you can feel the meditation connection by just sitting down and being silent for a few seconds.

After you have prepared your meditation space carefully, sit down when you can have a quiet half hour alone. (By the way, babies and very young children will not interfere with your meditation. I sit in yoga position and just place my tiny grandchildren in my lap. Small children can be provided with a "meditation cushion" of their own next to yours and given small, quiet toys to play with near you. If you explain to them that "Mommy" or "Daddy" or "Grandma is going to meditate, and you can do it with her, or you can play quietly here while she does it, you just can't talk to her," they will usually comply. Surprisingly often, they will sit down and imitate you in contacting "The Force," especially if they are old enough to have seen *Star Wars*.)

As you begin, close your eyes and ask, out loud, for the universe to help you start meditating. Then begin concentrating on your own breathing. Take what I call the Andrew Weil Breaths: Breathe in to the count of four. Hold it for seven counts. Then breathe out, through your mouth with a "whew" sound like you are trying to whistle, to the count of eight. Do this ten times. After that, just monitor your own deep breathing.

At the same time, picture the space behind your closed eyes as if it is a TV screen. Watch it. Colors may appear, or other shapes. If thoughts you don't want to think about appear, just let them float in and then lead them out again, and refocus on the screen behind your eyes and your breathing. You will automatically get deeper and deeper into this as you do it, and you will also—99 times out of 100—come out of meditation in a half hour if that is your intention.

Enjoy, and be enriched and quieted. Meditation is truly wonderful.

Thinking Holistically

If there was one thing I could communicate to you that you should focus on gaining during meditation, and only one, I would choose to have you remember *wholeness*, and to *intend* a wholeness that extends from the center of yourself all the way outward to the farthest reaches of your imagination—a wholeness that blends your spirit with a universe that is intelligent, loving, and harmonious.

To understand wholeness, you may have to change the way you think about *everything*. Since the days of Isaac Newton, discoverer of gravity almost 500 years ago, we have broken everything down to smaller and smaller particles. We've learned to separate, to segregate, and to classify by individual characteristics. We have broken the atom into its tiniest fragments. Every system we study, we take apart to analyze the smallest individual pieces we can isolate with our most powerful microscopes. We have *reduced* reality to the point that we have forgotten that once all things were whole. We have forgotten that *everything on this planet* is *part of a single system*, and we are just tiny chromosomes on it.

For a moment, take that soap bubble image and picture yourself, as creator, staring at this soap-bubble planet attached to a string hanging from a branch like a Christmas ornament in a tree that is our universe. Would you have put systems of life on that little planet-ornament that were incompatible with each other? Would you have organized life-support systems on it that had to evolve—*together symbiotically*—for three billion years if they were not compatible—*if they did not belong together?* Would you, when you created them, imagine that one of the life forms on it would later kill the others systematically?

Hardly.

Religion has complicated this matter of realigning our thinking about this planet in many ways. Western religions, which came to fruition in vast desert areas where humans were almost all that could survive, taught that "man," meaning the human race, had dominion over the earth. Even if it is true, surely that does not just imply control. It *also implies stewardship*, care for the other living things with whom we share our space.

Eastern religions, perhaps because they originated in more fertile areas, have taught that humans share this planet with other plants and animals. They believe that it is the duty of humans to promote balance and harmony, both in the immediate environment and in the universe. And they believe that *achieving that balance and harmony of mind and body that is called enlightenment requires great self-discipline and personal effort.* This is the same kind of discipline and effort that starts us with the practice of meditation. (After practicing it for six weeks or so, less discipline is required because we are hooked by the wonderful feelings that result from doing it, from its *enlightenment.*)

Obviously, one very vital step toward enlightenment and a vision of wholeness for ourselves, our planet, and our universe, is to live in a Healing House, because if the place where your body and spirit "headquarter" is not a place of respite, regeneration, and re-creation for you, it is harder than ever to conceive of a healing wholeness in the universe and beyond.

The second step is to recognize, as we seek to understand ourselves and our needs, desires, and responsibilities on this planet, that there is something beyond our rational ability to understand, and *to learn to trust our own instincts when we confront the nonrational ways of understanding truth that we encounter in meditation.* When we encounter that mystical reuniting with the earth, sky, and water of this planet, we are at the beginning of wholeness. When we feel that for ourselves, we will find new responsibilities toward the place we live.

> *"All things are transparent to transcendence."*
> — Joseph Campbell[5]

The Last Healing House Principle

HEALING HOMES IN A SUSTAINABLE SOCIETY BEGIN WITH THE THOUGHTS AND ACTIONS OF ALL OF US.

We see many who are following in the giant footsteps of Rachel Carson, a '50s-'60s era ecologist and author of the epochal and profoundly disquieting book, *Silent Spring,* warning of the same things: the contamination of the natural systems that sustain our planet. We are still overusing chemicals poisonous to all living things. When we can *see* the air we breathe, it is obvious we are overusing polluting fossil fuels for both electricity used in buildings and for most transportation. Our politicians and industrialists, for the sake of sales, encourage the use of old, polluting industrial machinery in Third-World developing nations that was discarded by modern industrial countries. We see the proliferation of fossil-fuel burning automobiles, trucks, and highways instead of electric vehicles or clean mass transit, and the loss of oxygen-giving forest lands.

We know that overpopulation is crowding out forestland in many areas and causing the destruction of trees, the only source of cooking firewood in subsistence-level societies. We see deserts gradually spreading throughout Africa because of statistically documented declines in rainfall in the latitudes of Africa, where repeated droughts and famine have killed tens of millions of people in recent years. We see chunks of ice the size of Rhode Island breaking off from the Antarctic ice sheet because of ocean warming. We hear about holes in the ozone layer that protects all living things from ultraviolet radiation. We see the destruction of South American rain forests due to human farming, tree harvesting, and cattle raising. But what does all this have to do with us and our Healing House?

Why Should I Care?

Bill Moyers asked Chief Oren Boyd of the Onadago Nation in New York that question one night in a PBS interview. The chief's response was:

> If you poison the water, you will die. If you poison the air, you will suffer. If you degrade the place you live, you will suffer. We live in the time of the human being. We should be living in the time of the mountain. A chainsaw cuts down a 400-year-old tree. No getting back that tree for 400 years. When life-giving forces that we give thanksgiving for turn on us, what do we do? When rain poisons lakes, when sun gives people cancer, what then? In my tribe, respect is learned through ceremony. Thanks are given to the King of Trees, the maple. We know we must respect the maple and preserve it where we live. Each person is born with a number of days in their hand. We shouldn't take ourselves so seriously. We have just two commands. First command: Give thanks. Second command: Enjoy.[6]

Doesn't it all, really, come down to that? Give thanks, and enjoy: life, the peaceful places, the loving people, the amazing diversity of life in our world, the stunning beauty of a sunset, the glory of a verdant, green springtime, the astonishment of birth. As we give thanks for this earth and its bounteous life systems, we will become truly aware. As we become more aware, we will learn to enjoy more fully, and then we will begin to care deeply about preserving this splendid place for ourselves and generations of those who follow us. If we do not learn to care, to be conscious of the work that comes to us *because we understand the value of all life,* future generations may never have a chance to see what we see.

George Schaller, one of America's most distinguished naturalists, believes that fighting long and hard is the only way to preserve the environment he loves so much. "As an ecologist, you walk around the world and see the wounds and scars, and your spirit just cries," he said. "But then you see the future, and you fight on, with hope. Nothing is ever safe. We have to protect what we still have."[7]

My favorite quote, perhaps of all time, comes from Rabbi Lawrence Kushner in his magnificently simple and wise book, *Honey from the Rock.* It is the summation of all the wonder, the incredulity, and the profound power of the desire I have to help heal this planet.

There are two directions of astonishment. Above there arches the immensity of the heavens. If the distance to the sun were represented by the thickness of this page you are reading, then the distance to the farthest point in the *known* universe would be a stack of papers 31 million miles high. Within each of us there breathes the intricacy of the human body. In each of the 100 trillion cells, there are roughly 100,000 genes coiled on a molecule of deoxyribonucleic acid (DNA) which, if uncoiled and unwound, would string back and forth between the earth and the sun over 400 times. Humans stand at the center of those two infinite directions. Within us, space and time are infinitesimal. Above us, space and time are astronomic. We will never see the farthest thing above, nor the smallest thing within.[8]

◆   ◆   ◆

The Responsibility for Sustaining All Life

If we believe it is our opportunity, our obligation, to determine how future generations can be sustained on this planet . . .

If we feel we can no longer run from the pain we see around us . . .

If we feel that we, as individuals, can no longer live for ourselves alone, but that we are part of a whole interwoven pattern of life, a system within larger and larger systems. . .

And if we believe that the healing of the <u>whole</u> must be preceded by the healing of the parts, then this is the time for us each to do our small part, whatever it is.

And my message of hope to you is that however small and insignificant your part may feel to you, it is very, very important, because every small act contributes to the sum of all goodness that impacts on this gigantic systemic organism that is <u>us.</u>

Every Healing House that is built impacts enormously on the people who live in it—people who are part of our system, who are part of us.

<u>If you teach one person what you have learned here . . .</u>

If you teach him or her how to improve their house in one small way, you have impacted that person, that family, and they, in turn, will impact their community and their world.

If you love others enough to speak out when you see things that are not sustainable on this, their planetary home, you become part of a larger voice saying those things. Ultimately, it is like throwing a pebble into a pond. It will spawn ripples that build on the ripples of others, flowing on and on, all the way to the edge of the universe.

If you lead one person to greater understanding, you will see new light in their eyes, which will illuminate their world, which is also our world.

<u>This world we share needs all the light and the love it can get!</u>

◆   ◆   ◆

"For one human being to love another: that is the most difficult of all our tasks, the ultimate, the last test and proof, the work for which all other work is but preparation."

— R. M. Rilke[9]

Technical Appendix

Appendix to:

THE PREFACE

**Three days after the murder, the University Park police, in an incredibly lucky break, found the killer. In the daily newspaper, a cab driver read about the murder, the first in University Park in many years. He remembered picking up a man covered with blood near the murder site that night. He tipped the police, and in a squad car, they took him to the location where he had dropped the man off. As they turned the corner onto the Oak Cliff street the cabbie had described to them, a young man with long brown hair crossed the street. "That's him! That's the guy," the cabbie exclaimed. The police arrested the man, the 28-year-old unemployed son of a middle-class local couple. He had a long history of mental problems. He said he thought he was stabbing Helena.

CHAPTER 5

5A - Complete text of poem at the beginning of Chapter 5:

Seated upon the spinning atom . . .

We spin
at once and always
circles lead us onward
from the atom
to the molecule
to the planet
to the solar system
to the galaxy
to the universe.

So with the life
from the tiniest invisible seeds
to the newborn
to the family
to the friends
to the neighborhood
to the town or city
the state, the country
and the planet.

Like a child's stacking toy
or the Russian dolls
which fit one into the other
until the game ends

with the smallest or largest
a child can find.

But in real time
real life within our planetary circle
is there structure we can predict?
Is there a different kind of gravity
holding it all together
down to the smallest units?
What is the point at which one small circle
one living creature
reaches critical mass in aberrant pathway
and flings itself outside this unnamed force field
like a renegade meteor?
And when it is gone,
rolling over and over into some strange void
what unbalance is left behind
in our field of consciousness?
What hole is made?
Is one circle distorted by an absence
which in turn
distorts a larger circle
and yet a larger one?
Is it for me, then, that the universe was created?

Is this intricate balance on some sort of massive time clock
so that when I become dust and ashes
a new seed is sprouted
and if my timing is off
this delicate pattern disintegrates?

What is it I do
I should do
to hold together
my unique spot in the circles?
Will I recognize the choice when it comes?

— Barbara Bannon Harwood

5B - Radio waves with short wavelengths can penetrate the ionosphere, an area of ionized gas above the earth's surface; therefore, they are used to communicate over long distances via satellites. Long-wavelength radio waves are *reflected* back to earth within the ionosphere, so they are used to transmit information from place to place down here on the earth's surface. Electromagnetic waves, which carry "radio" sounds, are actually *produced* when free electrons in radio aerials are made to oscillate (speeded up) by an electric field.

5C - Ultrasonic waves are waves with frequencies above the range of human hearing, or above 20,000 hertz. These reflected waves form echoes that are converted into electrical pulses, which form an image visible to the human eye on a screen. Unborn babies, for example, are almost always checked with ultrasound at about four months' gestation to make sure they are developing normally.

5D - X-rays are electromagnetic waves that ionize gases they pass through, causing phosphorescence, which brings about chemical changes on photographic plates. These photographic negatives are then "read" by doctors called radiologists to determine whether density changes in those tissues indicate disease states.

CHAPTER 12
How to Implement a Healing House Rainwater Harvesting System

You can do a rainwater collection system fairly simply. First, Charles Gibson said, you will need .62 sq. ft. of clear roof space per inch of rain per year, so you need to determine the annual rainfall in your area. The National Weather Service or a local meteorological service can answer that. The Green Buildings Conference panel rule of thumb was that 24 inches of rainfall a year is necessary to provide adequate water for *total* water use. Obviously, that number is dependent on how much water you use, something you can usually determine from your water bills. However, if you don't want total water use from rainwater, collection for plant care or a small garden can be done anywhere, regardless of annual amounts.

Elena Westbrook, for whom we built a custom home, and an environmental writer who has studied water and waste water issues extensively, said the formulae for determining the number of gallons of water you need, and then desired collection areas are as follows:

(Annual rainfall in inches)(horizontal roof area in square feet)(.6)=annual gallons of water.

Horizontal roof area (sq. ft.)=annual need (gallons) (0.6)(rainfall, in./yr.).

Collection area, she explains, is the *horizontal* area of the house footprint, not the amount of roofing material. A house with a steeply pitched roof will have significantly less collection area than actual roof area.

Calculating the recommended minimum of 24 inches of rain per year, a house with 2,000 sq. ft. of collection area will harvest 29,400 gallons per year. With 30 inches of rain/yr., they will collect 36,000. However, if rainfall in their area *averages* 30 inches/yr., they are sure to get a 24-inch year sooner or later, she said. Therefore, she recommends that anyone who is thinking of doing a whole-house rainwater system make backup arrangements—a well, a city that will refill the tank, or a potable-water truck that delivers.

Several different kinds of roofs can be used for rainwater collection, but the best is galvanized steel, or Galvalume, with a baked-enamel finish, certified as lead-free, which we have used on many custom homes. Care should be taken to use products with no lead when installing a Galvalume roof if it is to be used for potable rainwater collection. Older Galvalume roofs were often installed with nails and lead washers, from which lead can leach. Older metal roofs were often made of composites that included lead, so if you're not sure what the material is on your metal roof, or how it was installed, get the water runoff from it checked for lead before drinking.

Asphalt shingles can also be used, but they shed sand and petroleum-based chemicals, particularly when they are new, so the water should not be used for drinking, and screen filters should be installed at various points before water reaches the tank. Wood shingles are also acceptable, but if they are made of treated wood, they may leach toxic chemicals.

The type of roof also affects collection efficiency, so it has to be included in your calculations for roof space needed. A metal roof supplies 95% of the rainwater that strikes it. An asphalt roof, only 85%.

Try Some Old Grandad Rainwater Collection

You must have a solid -concrete or rock pad for the tank if it is to be above ground, or a very big hole if it isn't, and a tank. The 1,600-gal. HDPE tank that we used at our last custom home cost about $700, and we bought a 500-gallon one for our own home for $383, plus $60 delivery charge. In some locations, even less expensive tanks can be obtained by having your local septic systems dealer alter a tank for rainwater. David Omick of Proveto y fe Esperanza in South Texas gets a 500-gallon tank from his septic dealer *delivered to site* for $150. We were not able to find anyone to do that here, but we do know of areas where people even use, for rainwater collection, old barrels once used for aging whiskey and beer!

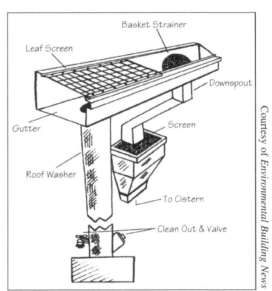

Courtesy of Environmental Building News

Schematic showing primary means for keeping leaves and pollutants out of cistern: Roof-washer fills with first 10 to 20 gallons of rainfall. After it fills, water flows to downspout leading to cistern. After the rain ends, the roof washer is drained—or the valve can be left open slightly so that water trickles out, even during a rainstorm.

Next, think about where the roof is located. If you are surrounded by oak trees, the oak "blossoms" will give you fits in your filtering system. (For those who haven't seen an oak bloom, they shed thin, worm-shaped pods covered with tiny seeds.) So will other seeds, flowers, leaves, and other detritus from trees, as well as the little gifts birds leave everywhere they perch (which may contain nasty fungi and spores, according to Elena Westbrook). You can either set up a "roof washer" system if you use rainwater for drinking and cooking (details are in the books recommended further on), or just put screen filters on your downspouts and gutters, which you will have to clean regularly.

Then run gutter and downspout from your roof into the tank and attach the drain valve 12 inches above the bottom of the tank to provide space for any sediment settlement. And, just for fun, find an old whiskey barrel at an antique store, put it under another gutter you can call your very own, and some summer day when you're *really hot*, get in.

For more detailed information on rainwater collection systems, see *Rainwater Collection,* book and video written, published, and hosted by John Dromgoole, 1995, $30; *Planning for Individual Water Systems,* written and published by The American Ass'n. for Vocational and Instructional Materials.

For more information on graywater systems, see *Create an Oasis with Graywater,* by Art Ludwig, Published by Oasis Design, 1994, 47 pages. All are available through the Real Goods catalog (800) 762-7325.

CHAPTER 13
13A - Understanding Passive Solar
To understand why passive solar works, you have to stop for a minute, close your eyes, and think about how the sun moves across the sky. It rises in the east, giving you morning sun on the east side of your house. At noon, the sun is at the highest point in the sky. Late in the afternoon, when temperatures typically are at their peak, the sun begins to set in the west. Thus, in summer, late-day heat on the west wall or windows can be fierce.

Now think about winter versus summer. Because the earth rides its annual circular pattern around the sun at a slight angle, the northern hemisphere is tilted away from the sun in winter so the sun is low in the southern sky, beginning its daily journey in the southeast, and ending it in the southwest. Winter sun is at a low angle. In summer, because our hemisphere is tilted toward the sun, the sun is at a much higher angle, about 90 degrees.

Natural Daylighting With Passive Solar in New Construction
A side benefit of passive solar design is natural daylighting, but *it is not necessarily automatically added to rooms that do not have a southern exposure,* so you do need to think about it during the design process. We have covered the reasons why natural daylighting is so desirable in Chapter 10, but it should be brought up with your architect or builder if you are planning to build a Healing House, or with your remodeler if you are redoing an existing home.

13B - Additional Natural Ventilation Techniques
Two other useful passive ventilation techniques are a whole-house attic fan, and continuous ridge and soffit vents for ventilating the attic only. In efficient houses in most climates, there should be an airtight membrane between the house and the attic Ask your builder about the vents, but whole-house fans are often installed after a house is built. It can draw cooler nighttime air through doors and windows of a house by pulling hot house air into the attic to be exhausted outdoors. Be sure the fan opening is one in which a pop-in insulation panel can be inserted for winter insulation, and *do not use one in a house with combustion appliances unless*

they are atmospherically decoupled.

13C- **Thermal Mass Buildings**

Where cliffs were not available, often other ancient cultures constructed their shelters with thick earthen walls. These thermal mass walls, made with highly dense material such as adobe, rammed earth, mud; or mixtures such as sand and mud, grass and mud, or straw and mud (called Cob), are slow to heat when the sun shines on them, and they release that warmth slowly during the night as they cool down.

13D - **More Thermal Mass Methods**

You can even create thermal mass in an existing space fairly cheaply and easily if you want to. A friend of mine wanted some reliable nighttime heating for a little sunspace (greenhouse type) building in which he was going to house some new employees. He bought some old oil barrels, painted them black, filled them with water, and put them immediately under the sunspace windows at the edge of the main room where, years later, they still provide all the heat the building needs. They heat slowly during the day, then release their heat at night. Almost any kind of watertight container painted black or a very dark color will do. When these black barrels filled with water are also used to provide hot water for a house, they are called "batch" hot water heaters. The water is heated all at once in a "batch" instead of being heated by panels through which water flows and is stored in a hot water tank. (See a full explanation of active solar hot water in Chapter 17.)

To illustrate for yourself how well that "batch" heating works, you can use an old camper's trick called a "solar shower," which is nothing more than a black bag filled with water, hanging from a tree limb in the sun. It heats up during the day and makes a wonderful evening shower. You can buy a "solar shower" from the national Real Goods catalog, (800) 762-7325, or at many local camping supply stores.

Or, in your backyard, you can make a "solar bath," a fun science experiment for you and your kids. Fill two simple, heavy-duty black garbage bags with water. Tie them tightly and leave them in the sun all day. For a warm bath, disrobe and climb in. Use one for washing, the other for rinsing. (As you can imagine, the trick is getting into the bag *without* spilling out all the water—not something you will see a picture of me doing in this book!) But if you try it, you will be astounded how warm the water gets in one day.

If you are redecorating, the easiest solution to additional thermal mass is probably to put ceramic tile under your sunny windows. It works best where the slab edges or basement walls have been well insulated, but if the sun strikes it, it gives you benefits in *some measure*, no matter what.

Giving Your Own House a Passive Solar "Fix"

To do your own passive solar analysis, start with a "window check." Do a rough sketch of your home and its windows. If you're not sure where direct south is, and you don't have a copy of your building plans, look at the sun early in the morning. In winter it will be slightly south of east; in summer, slightly north of east. On September 22 and March 22, it will be *exactly* east. When you have found east, stand with your outstretched left arm pointing east, and your right arm pointing west. Your nose will be pointing due south.

Once you determine how your windows are placed, note what you're doing with your south windows. Are they covered with closed draperies or blinds during the day in winter? If they are, uncover them. Let the sun shine in. If you're worried that the sun will fade your furniture—a problem with colors in the blue-green range—cover the furniture fabric with sheets when you don't have company, or buy pretty throws or bedspreads to use as throws. If those same windows don't have summer shading, consider getting awnings to shield them, which will allow you to leave drapes or blinds open for daylight.

If you have *too many windows* in the wrong places and you are overheating any time of the year, try mini-blinds. Obviously, they are going to help keep out heat when they are closed. But the National Renewable Energy Laboratory found in testing that they reduce solar gain by 50 percent *even when they are open,* especially when they're pointed downward (so when you look outside, you see the ground, not the sky).

Add-on sunspaces or sunrooms are a popular way to add passive solar heat, particularly in existing houses without south-facing windows. Caution is advised, however, because sunspaces can be a problem in moderate or warmer (mixed heating and cooling) climates *if they have curved glass at the top.* This will cause overheating in spring, summer, and fall. A better choice is a sunspace with vertical windows and overhangs of the proper width.

13E - **More Information on Radiant Barriers**

Radiant barriers on attic rafters protect houses against summer heat because the sun's rays (radiant waves) heat *things,* not air. These rays warm whatever surface they hit. When the sun's rays hit your roof, they heat it. It radiates heat down that heats your attic insulation, which, in turn, heats your ceiling. A radiant barrier interrupts that cycle by re-radiating those rays away from your house.

Radiant barriers are made of two layers of aluminum foil with something to add strength between, usually a nylon mesh. It should be installed so it doesn't gather dust which, over time, can reduce its effectiveness by 50%. Therefore, it should *not* be installed laying down on top of the attic insulation. In new construction, a product called Kool Ply can be installed as roof decking. Kool Ply is foil laminated to the underside of plywood or OSB (oriented strandboard) roof decking and adds very little additional cost over regular roof decking. It is installed over the rafters just like ordinary roof sheathing, with the foil facing downward. Energy savings depend on climate and the amount of conventional insulation in the attic. Kool Ply decked attics were an average of 21 degrees cooler than attics without it when tested. There is an additional benefit. If you install a radiant barrier, you can reduce the amount of attic insulation in some climates. If we use radiant barriers, we reduce the attic insulation to R26 from R38, without losing efficiency.

To install a radiant barrier in your own home, buy the least expensive one available at the local lumber yard. Using a staple gun, staple it upside down against the rafters. It's cheap and very easy to do. Florida Solar Energy Center tests indicate it will save 30% of the heat coming through your roof in summer; about 8%

on your overall cooling bills. The only better material for reducing sun penetration is tree cover.

13F - Insulated Sheathing Materials

There are many kinds of sheathing. In a "stick-built" house—one where the individual pieces of lumber are put up one at a time to create a "frame"—building codes require corner bracing to prevent wall sway. Most builders just use plywood. One commonly used product is called "Thermoply," but don't let that fool you. There is no "thermo" value here—only cardboard covered with tar paper.

A better choice is an insulated sheathing with thermal *resistance* value (called an "R value") combined with an L-shaped or T-shaped metal corner brace. Among the exterior sheathing materials are expanded or extruded polystyrene or polyiso-cyanurates. (poly-iso-cy-an'-urate). We no longer use extruded polystyrene, a pink, blue, or green foam -looking product, or polyisocyanurates because they are made with CFCs (chlorofluorocarbons) and HCFCs (hydrochlorofluorocarbons). These CFCs are bad for the environment because the chlorine atoms in them break down far above the earth and destroy the earth's protective ozone layer.

Expanded polystyrene, or white beadboard, which my company uses, is made without CFCs or HCFCs, often using recycled materials such as packaging waste from Motorola. Its shortened moniker is "EPS," and it is the same material from which the little portable beer and soda coolers we take to ball games are made. At R4 per inch, it is the most cost-effective sheathing, as well as being the most resource efficient because it uses recycled materials in its manufacture, and the most environmentally friendly because of the absence of CFCs and HCFCs. This sheathing can be taped at the joints to create an air barrier.

13G - More about Insulation

The most common insulation material is fiberglass—pink material usually installed in pre-cut panels or "batts," either with or without paper attached, or blown in to create a blanket in the attic. It has an R of 3.6 per inch, so a common 2" x 4" wall, which most builders use, can hold a total of 3-1/2 inches, or an **R 12.6.** *This is not enough insulation anyplace except in far southern climates.* A 2" x 6" frame wall, which we use, holds 5-1/2", or an R19.8. However, fiberglass is not our company's insulation material choice, primarily because it is not an effective air barrier, and because it is a potential carcinogen. Air moving around the batt, as well as through it, can dramatically reduce the insulating effect in walls, although it works well when blown into attics.

Neither is our choice mineral wool, sometimes called rockwool, also made from very fine inorganic fibers chopped up in a hammer mill to produce a fluffy, loose material suitable for blowing, and very stable after installation. It is, however, the choice of some builders of Healthy Housing for the chemically sensitive, because it is inert, has large particulate size, and can be obtained without any oil on it.

Our current wall insulation choice (when we do frame houses) is *cellulose*—either wet-spray or dry blown, both of which are manufactured from finely shred-ded **recycled** newsprint and cardboard with borax added to resist fire, fungal growth, and rot. Ask your architect to specify cellulose, a fluffy, low-density material that has a higher resistance to air infiltration than most other loose fill insulation. Once it is installed, air infiltration can be reduced slightly with dry-blown, and quite significantly with wet-spray; however, wet spray cellulose should *not* be used in a house for a chemically sensitive person. Dry blown cellulose can. Installed correctly, it has an R value of 3.6 per inch and does not have the air convection problems of fiberglass.

Ned Nisson, esteemed editor of *Energy Design Update*, a builder's bible of energy efficiency and renewable energy techniques, described why the Natural Resources Defense Council (NRDC), a leading US environmental organization, issued a report at the end of 1996 emphasizing the health threats associated with fiberglass insulation. It called cellulose not only safer, but better in almost every other way.

> Environmentalists typically favor cellulose insulation over fiberglass for several reasons. It is made from 75% recycled newsprint, is not a suspected carcinogen, requires less energy and generates less pollution during manufacturing, and performs extremely well. Fiberglass, on the other hand, is classified as a possible carcinogen, has lower recycled material content, has documented poor performance in some situations, and is made in factories with huge smokestacks that consume lots of energy. [*Energy Design Update*, August, 1995, pgs. 9-10.]

There are some new systems, including cotton insulation made from recycled Levi Strauss manufacturing waste, that will probably be good choices once they are cost-effective and easily accessible.

Another new insulation product we love is *icynene* (pronounced "Ice-A-Neen"), one of the spray-on type foam insulations. Unfortunately, it is about four times the cost of other insulation materials, but it is definitely the most effective as an insulator combined with an air and moisture barrier that also windproofs and seals walls, floors, and ceiling cavities. And it is great fun to watch being installed. For just a second or two after the installer begins spraying it on, it looks like white paint. Then it begins to grow, like a cumulus cloud on fast forward, as the millions of tiny cells fill with air. It stops growing when it is 100 times its original volume. The first time I saw it installed, my reaction was just one word: "Wow."

In addition to being a wonderful insulator and sealant, it is also cited as a product which has no off-gasses, emits no CFCs or HCFCs, and is incapable of supporting bacteria or fungus. It is recommended by the American Lung Association for use in their new "healthy house" program, and is probably one of two insulations of choice for victims of Multiple Chemical Sensitivities (MCS), the other being rockwool, as discussed previously.

I have also used another polyurethane foam product called "Great Stuff," which comes in a can at any hardware store or can be sprayed on whole walls. When I was doing an energy-efficient retrofit on a shopping center in Indiana, I somehow left one of the doors, which had to be sealed off, out of my calculations on which the subcontractor had made his bid. So I was stuck with a very leaky, old, uninsulated door that I had to get rid of somehow. Instead of removing it and filling the opening with masonry before it was insulated on the interior (which we did with the other doors), I just cut and stuffed scrap blue extruded polystyrene foam onto the door, glueing it on with Liquid Nails, then sprayed the gaps with Great Stuff for a permanent seal. After spraying, I used the straight edge of a folded paper plate to even the edges (it's like working with banana cream pie —really a kick!), and voilà! A fully insulated and sealed opening for a few dollars and two hours work instead of $800. It still looked like a door from outside, and my only regret was I couldn't be there to see the first burglar who tried to break into it.

13H - **More About HVAC Equipment**
Geothermal Heat Pumps, a Mechanical Connection to the Earth:

A standard heat pump, called an air-to-air heat pump, is really nothing more than an air conditioner with a feature that lets it work "backwards" in winter. It takes the hot air out of the house in summer and dumps it back outside—which is why it's so hot when you stand by the outside part of an air conditioner in summer. In winter, a regular heat pump takes warm air from outside and puts it inside the house. As you can see, there are two problems with air-to-air heat pumps that led our company to recommend geothermal. When it's very cold outside, say 20 degrees, there's not very much heat to be taken from the air, so an air-to-air heat pump has to struggle mightily to keep you warm—*all at your own expense, of course.* In the summer, when it's 104 degrees outside, the hot air is dumped outside when it could be used to heat your hot water, the geothermal's "desuperheater" function.

We try to use Geothermal Heat Pumps in all our buildings, sometimes called Ground Source Heat Pumps, for several reasons. First, they are the most efficient system, with an Energy Efficiency Rating (EER) of 16+ on high speed, and 20.4 on low speed. Because our homes are so energy efficient, the units can operate at low speed most of the time. That means, at a 20.4 EER, you get $2.04 worth of heating or cooling every time you spend a dollar on your utility bill. Or, as a financial analyst would say: You get a 104% return on your investment in your local utility.

Second, they reduce the peak load for the utility, helping reduce air pollution on hot summer days when it's the worst. Third, the "desuperheater" feature takes the heat from inside your house in summer and deposits it into the hot water heater *before* it is transferred into the ground, giving you free hot water about half the year. Fourth, it's very quiet. And fifth, there is no equipment sitting outside to be vandalized, accumulate dirt, or just experience the wear and tear of normal weather.

A geothermal heat pump, instead of dumping the waste hot air outside, conducts the heat into a closed polyethylene plumbing pipe loop filled with water, which is underground. As the hot water travels deeper and deeper into the earth, where the temperature is a constant 55 to 60 degrees, depending on your area, the heat is transferred to the earth surrounding the loop, like a "heat sink." The loop is cooled, and that temperature is used to cool your house. As the summer progresses and more and more heat is dumped underground, the ground down there becomes warmer and warmer. Then, in the late fall, when you change the thermostat back to "heating," the loop flows the opposite direction, taking the heat out of the ground and bringing it back into the house. *The reason it is so inexpensive to operate is that the temperature of the earth is very close to the desired temperature in your house, so very little electricity is used to get the house temperature up or down the few degrees to your chosen thermostat setting.*

We most commonly use a two-speed, triple-integrated Waterfurnace Geothermal Heat Pump with the desuperheater for heating domestic hot water. The heating Coefficient of Performance (COP) is above 4.0, and the cooling Energy Efficiency Ratio (EER) is above 20. In fact, according to *Energy Design Update*, May, 1992, page 14, "with 50-degree Fahrenheit ground water temperature, the cooling EER can be above 30." A properly *designed* system should be able to operate at low speed 80 percent of the time. This provides about half the capacity of high speed. The optional "desuperheater" extracts heat from the refrigerant circuit and transfers it to domestic water in a coiled heat exchanger.

I should warn you that a geothermal heat pump may not function well in a house unless it is very energy efficient, with a tightly sealed envelope. Thermal conduction is too slow in the earth around the loop to take tremendous volumes of heat or cold. Where the water table is higher, they work better in a closed loop system.

I have had "experts" tell me that geothermal doesn't work well, and after we have debated for a few minutes, I inevitably find out that they are *not* talking about highly efficient homes, only in homes built to standard specification or less. There have also been failures with units that

The water furnace geothermal heat pump dumps the heat from the house in summer into your water heater, giving you free water heating during hot months.

© 1997 Barbara Harwood

depend on well water for an "open loop" system, which we do *not* use. The well water sometimes cannot keep up with the demand.

Does Gas Pass?

There are combination gas systems that work well and which some builders prefer. Both the Austin Green Builder program and a builder who does highly efficient homes in Chicago recommend a gas combination unit in which the hot water heater is also used as a space-heating system. However, I personally resist using any gas in my homes even though it is now designed so the flame is "sealed off" from the living space, simply because gas heat, as it ages, becomes less and less efficient and more and more dangerous. I understand that "closed combustion" systems are supposed to be totally safe, but I'm still not convinced. In homes built by our company that should last a hundred years or more, will the family who moves in long after I'm dead know what to do with an aging gas furnace, whether it is still sealed properly, or whether it is leaking dangerous fumes and needs to be replaced?

I'm particularly opposed to using gas appliances or heating equipment in a home built in an area laced with earthquake-prone faults. There are automatic shut-offs in gas lines from the street, but at whatever point the gas is shut off, there will still be some in the pipes beyond that point and into your house. That gas can burn and start a fire in your house during an earthquake.

Another problem with combustion appliances inside a home is that if you unintentionally create a negative pressure in your house high enough to backdraft any of these appliances and they are not sealed off from the living space, you can create serious air quality problems, including carbon monoxide poisoning. One documented problem situation was suction created by a power attic exhaust fan that was installed to replace a passive ridge vent. Even though the whole house attic exhaust fan was installed according to industry standards, it created enough suction, all the way to the basement, to pull outside air back down the chimney and cause the gas furnace and water heater to backdraft combustion gases into the basement.

In addition, when people ask for gas, it's usually because they want gas burners and a gas oven for cooking. These I'm really opposed to. You don't even *want to know* the quantity of poisonous fumes you introduce into your living space every time you cook in a tight house. Even worse is cooking something in the oven that takes five or six hours, like a Thanksgiving turkey. If you think about it for a minute, you'll know that anytime you *burn a fossil fuel*, poisonous gases—especially carbon monoxide—are emitted. Those, if they are going to be burned at all, belong *outside.*

Radiant Heating—Does It Give You Cleaner Walls?

Another option some people love is radiant heat, either under the floors so their feet are always warm in winter, or in the ceiling. A typical radiant heat system is comprised of some sort of water heating boiler, usually combustion, a heat exchanger, and tubing running through the floor or ceiling, either integral to the slab or in panels.

There are also systems available now as an alternative to combustion that use heated air in the tubing, sometimes from passive solar collectors (black glass plates over a "box" piped directly to the tubes). Air flow is either by fan or convection, depending on the volume needed at the time. We have not used them, because in our mixed climate, an integrated heating and cooling system is more desirable than separate radiant heat with an electric air conditioner; however, I have stayed in homes with radiant heat, and it is extremely comfortable and almost completely silent, so I would recommend it highly in climates where cooling is not needed.

Here, courtesy of Ned Nisson, founder of *Energy Design Update,* is an obscure bit of science about radiant heat that will impress your friends. Cool walls collect dust. Warm walls repel dust. Well, sort of. In a room with ceiling radiant heat, the walls tend to be slightly warmer than the air in the room because the heated ceiling radiates directly to the wall surfaces. Because they are warmer, a layer of convective air against the wall rises, so dust doesn't stick on the wall because it's blown away. A 1971 report published by US Steel explained that in such a room, the warm wall surfaces would create a dust-free barrier that would prevent airborne dirt from depositing on the wall surface. Wall and ceiling surfaces should also be slightly warmer with *floor* radiant heat. *Energy Design Update,* April, 1995, page 5.

13I - **More About Mechanical Ventilation**

There are two types: A heat recovery ventilator, and a heat and humidity recovery ventilator. The first is a simple heat recovery ventilator that removes heat from inside air before it is exhausted to the outdoors in winter, and removes heat from outside air before it is brought in during the summer. However, the type we use is a heat and humidity recovery ventilator [HHRV] also sometimes called an "enthalpy recovery" ventilator) that recovers not only heat from air either going out or coming in (depending on the season), but it also balances the humidity. During winter, it recycles humidity from exhaust air back indoors to keep the home from drying out. In summer, it extracts humidity from the incoming air stream to reduce the cooling load. They are *not*, however, *solely* de-humidifiers, so they won't reduce humidity in a home that isn't air conditioned.

The two advantages of a HHRV are that you *know* the air quality in your home is being controlled because a specific amount of fresh air, at an appropriate humidity, circulates at all times; and second, it saves you money.

There are two good HHRV products on the market I could recommend: AirXchange, which we have used in custom homes; and VanEE Duo, just as good but slightly higher priced in our region. They are very little more in cost than a regular HRV in most cases, and in the case of AirXchange, they charge nothing extra for the humidity feature.

For additional, detailed information, see "Mechanical Ventilation in the Home" by Don Stevens; *Home Energy* magazine; March/April, 1996; pgs. 13-19.

CHAPTER 14

14A - **Types of Framing Materials and Building Systems**

Framed houses are not resource efficient if they are built with trees cut from our old-growth forests in the Northwest United States and shipped in logs to Japan, where it's cut into lumber and shipped back here. It's not even resource efficient when it's shipped from Canada—unless you live on the U.S./Canadian border, and the trees and lumber mill are in your backyard. Wood framing is, however, resource efficient if, for example, east Texas yellow pine forests are used for building in east Texas, or if you use some of the alternative types of lumber made from smaller, lower-quality trees. These alternatives, *which have all the benefits of natural wood products,* are called "engineered wood," and they should be used whenever possible in a wood-frame style Healing House. They include:

• Finger-jointed studs, which utilize mill cut-offs and damaged wood to produce strong, usable- length lumber and trim boards. They are typically higher quality than conventional studs because knots are removed and they have less of a tendency to twist or bow.

- Oriented Strand Board—or OSB—made from wood flakes or chips, orienting them in crisscrossed layers to greatly increase strength. Small diameter, low-grade trees, such as aspen are often used. OSB is quickly replacing plywood that uses bigger trees. It is also made with *phenyl-formaldehyde*, which is better for indoor air quality than urea formaldehyde. Our company prefers using this product, particularly in Structural Insulated Panel walls, except that *chemically sensitive people cannot tolerate it.*

- Glulam Timber: Solid sawn lumber is glued together to create large structural beams.

Structural Insulated Panels (SIPS)

These panels, also known as stress-skin or foam-core panels, are our material of choice in 90 percent of our company's custom homes *because they are made primarily of waste materials, and they create the tightest building envelope with the least hassle.* The panels we use have 7/16" OSB board as the outside of a sandwich, encasing an expanded polystyrene insulation core made partially from recycled packaging waste. The panels (6" for walls, and 8" for roofs) are joined with tongue-in-groove joints for maximum air-tightness.

In a side-by-side monitoring test in Kentucky, a home built with foam-core panels was shown to use between 12% and 17% less energy for heating than a stud-frame home with identical dimensions and R-values. The test, conducted by the Florida Solar Energy Center (FSEC), confirmed claims by the SIPS industry that their homes are more energy efficient, but researchers are not *exactly* sure why. It is probably a combination of the same factors that caused us to choose this building system over others: less air leakage through the building envelope, no air circulation within or through insulation, and less thermal bridging by studs and other framing members.

There is a caveat to this, however, in low-cost housing. A house of 1,200 sq. ft. on two floors using SIPS will, based on the tested savings, use roughly 2.9 million fewer Btus of heating energy per year than the stud-frame house. At typical gas costs and 80% efficiency, that amounts to just under $22/year in savings. If the cost of the SIPS is 10% greater than a stud-framed home, which it is in our area, then it is not a cost-effective choice for low-cost housing. However, this cost gap is narrowing as the cost of framing lumber continues to soar, largely due to both demand and U.S. tariff policies with Canada.

Foam-Form Building Systems

There is a growing multitude of stay-in-place foam-form building systems available, including AAB, Argisol, Conform, Fold-Form, ICE Block, LiteForm, Polysteel 3-D, Blue Max, and R-Form, plus, no doubt, others I haven't mentioned. They are basically a foam form—parallel sheets (usually 2"+) of foam made into stackable units—like Lego blocks—which are tied together by either metal or plastic ties. Once they are set on the footings with metal rebar through the concrete holding them in place, additional metal rebar is inserted between the layers of foam. Concrete is then poured into the space. The plastic or metal ties, at their origin on the outside of the foam, create a nailing surface for drywall or sheathing.

We have found both positives and negatives with the one foam-form system we have used. On the plus side, it creates a well-insulated, tight wall (with 2-5/8" of foam on each side, the wall is R25—the same as our SIPS or stud-frame walls; with 2", it is R17) which is, no pun intended, as solid as concrete. It should hold up well to storms that might destroy less stable structures (tornadoes, hurricanes), and it is very good in situations where one or two walls of a house are "retaining" walls, holding back earth that is backfilled against them.

However, foam-form systems are very unforgiving about errors during construction. A slight, almost undetectable tilt to the foam forms can create a wall that will tilt in or out, and once it's poured, you can't exactly just walk over to it and give it a little push to make it stand up straight. It's more or less there for eternity. Luckily for us, a sharp foreman used a carpenter's level to check before the concrete was poured and found a slight deviation that was still correctable. The installing subcontractor *absolutely should have checked that,* but didn't. A second negative for some users is that the concrete mass wall is unusable as "thermal" mass because it is enclosed in foam insulation. A concrete wall that is insulated on the *outside only* would gather heat from inside the building into its mass—through the sun's heat on it or the heating system—and hold it constant for several hours even without a heat source, as we explained in Chapter 13. The last negative is that it costs about 15% more than SIPS.

Adobe and Adobe-Type Wall Systems

Adobe is the name given to certain clay formations or soils that cover thousands of square miles in Colorado, Utah, Nevada, Texas, New Mexico, Arizona, and California. They are composed of very fine particles of clay, quartz, and other minerals. When moist, adobe soils are plastic and readily worked. Their compactness and coherence make excellent building block when they are dried. Sun-dried adobe bricks have been used for thousands of years in hot, dry countries from Egypt to Mexico, but their first recorded use occurred when they were brought to Spain from Africa.

Adobe soil is sometimes mixed with a stabilizer like flyash (waste from the burning of coal, now sold by utility providers as a viable replacement for lime as a stabilizer in concrete and adobe block) to provide an even more solid material for flooring and building blocks. Adobe bricks, dried in the sun rather than being fired, and the most commonly used building material *in the world,* are stacked on each other and secured with mortar. They are enormously resource efficient and easy to make in areas with native adobe soil. In Saragosa, Texas, after the tornado, one frustrated victim who had lost his adobe grocery store wasn't about to accept the 2 x 4 wood frame building the Red Cross proposed as a replacement, so we went out into a field beside his house, dug up some clay soil, and, with the help of his family, made his own blocks and built his store the way it was before.

Adobe can be left uncovered on the interior and exterior, but it must be "remudded" every few decades. The greatest threat to unprotected adobe is erosion by water, typically in summertime convection storms with their violent, wind-driven torrents. So the best exterior "mudding" mixture is wet adobe with short pieces of straw (2" or less), which is put on using the heel of the hand to make an arc shape like half a rainbow. This keeps rain rivulets from running down the wall, cutting pathways as they fall.

One would not ordinarily think of ordinary, everyday, clay-fired bricks as part of an "adobe" wall system, but in Mexico, and throughout Latin America and South America, they are commonly used for total wall systems. Walls about 36 inches thick comprise both the exterior structure and interior walls. Very labor intensive and time consuming to build (good in an area with high unemployment), these walls have excellent mass and longevity. Both interior and exterior surfaces are typically white plaster.

Rammed earth as a building system is almost as old as adobe brick. Used in North Africa after all the trees became ships, rammed earth techniques were carried northward to France centuries ago where soil was perfectly adapted to it. Renewed interest in the material after a university student discovered hundreds of centuries old rammed earth homes sparked its revival there. Another recent hot spot of rammed earth activity is Western Australia, where over 20% of all homes and buildings are now rammed earth.

David Easton, in Napa, California, analyzes the soil in an area to see whether it would be appropriate for rammed earth by mixing some in a pan of water and watching settlement. Then he does a shrinkage test, then a "worm" test. "If you can make a worm six inches long of your soil, then it's good for rammed earth," he said. However, if the clay content is over 30%, the walls may have cracks. In California, the rammed earth must have steel reinforcement added to insure earthquake safety."

14B - Volatile Organic Compounds (VOCs) and Their Alternatives

Since some of these chemicals are *both* in building materials and multiple consumer products, the building materials containing these harmful chemicals are printed here in bold type, to help you avoid them when you are building or rehabbing your house into a Healing House.

Methylene Chloride is a solvent, principally recognized by the smell. It is commonly used in **paints and varnishes**, and it is in about 80% of **paint strippers**. It is also used in **refrigeration and air-conditioning equipment**, and **pesticide** aerosols. Its damaging effects are especially potent to people with angina and heart problems because our bodies convert it to carbon monoxide in our blood. It has also been known to cause kidney, liver, and nervous system damage, as well as heart attacks and cancer.

Better solutions:
• Use one of the low-odor, water-based acrylic sealers available at many paint stores and hardware stores in place of varnishes.
• Use low-VOC or no-VOC paints.
• Use a limestone-based whitewash.
• Use a cassein-based paint.
• Send furniture out to be stripped or use a heat gun or sandpaper.

Pesticide replacements:

- Use boric acid and spiders (see the next section)
- Baking soda and powdered sugar mix
- For ants: chili powder where they enter, or Terra Sugar Ant Remover (a boric acid derivative)
- For flea collars and sprays: Herbal collar or ointment, citronella, or add Brewer's Yeast to your pets' diet.

Rat and Mouse Poison Replacements:

- Mousetraps. Sorry, I've tried *everything* else—all these so-called merciful traps people sell—to catch these guys and take them outside. Nothing else works. (Except twice, I have been lucky enough to catch a mouse inside a paper bag. I quickly closed it and took it far away from the house to the woods to release it. Before I let it out of the bag, I gave it a little speech about not being welcome inside the house and told it that it should be darn glad to be alive (while my husband howled with laughter!).

House Plant Insecticide Replacements:

- Mixture of bar soap and water or old dishwater—spray on leaves, then rinse. If that doesn't get it all, especially for white flies, mix four cloves of garlic, minced, and half an onion chopped fine, into a gallon of water. Let sit overnight. Then spray on both sides of leaves, and, if possible, all the little guys will fly off as you spray. Two applications within three days got rid of a horrible infestation on my gardenias.

  For plant scale: If weather permits, simply put the plant with scale outside near an anthill. Ants will occupy the plant until the leaves are completely clean, then leave. If it happens in winter, as it did to one of my indoor ficus trees, isolate the plant so it doesn't infect the others, and wait until spring when you can take it outdoors. Ants cleared our tree completely in one month.

Dichlorvos (DDVP) has been under study at the EPA, which has been considering banning it from food packaging for almost ten years after an investigation at the National Toxicology Program of the Department of Health and Human Services identified a link with leukemia. It is also used in **pesticide** aerosols, as well as in **pet and yard** aerosol products.

4-Dichlorophenoxy acetic acid (2,4-D): The National Cancer Institute reports that dogs whose owners used this yard- and farm-related chemical on their lawns had an increased rate of a non-Hodgkins lymphoma-related dog cancer, and they have now linked the same disease to its use by farmers.

Hydroxides and lye products: Sorry, but these include many automatic dishwasher detergents, toilet-bowl cleaners, **paint removers**, and drain cleaners. Of course, eating or drinking it is disastrous, but even inhalation causes lung damage, and when it comes in contact with skin, it can lead to serious irritations or eruptions. It is also not great stuff to be putting into our water supply.

Better Solutions:
- **Automatic Dishwasher Detergent**: Seventh Generation Auto Dish Detergent** (author's note: I have tried other "natural" products, and none work very well except this one.)
- **Oven Cleaners:**
  —Baking soda, water, elbow grease.
- **Toilet Bowl Cleaners:**
  — Toilet brush and baking soda, then mild detergent.
  — ASTONISH from Real Goods (800) 762-7325.
  — Seventh Generation Toilet Bowl Cleaner**
- **Drain Cleaners:**
  — Bio-Free at Seventh Generation or Real Goods**
  — Baking soda and vinegar (one cup soda poured down the drain followed by 1/2 cup vinegar. Leave overnight. Flush with water.)
- **Disinfectants:**
  — 1/2 cup borax in 1 gallon water.

Trichlorethylene (TCE) is a solvent used in **waxes, paint thinners, rug shampoo, fumigants, and polishes**. Suspected of causing cancer of the liver.

Better solutions:
- **Rug Shampoos:**
  — Dry cornstarch sprinkled on rug, vacuumed up. White Wizard (for bad spots) from Real Goods or Seventh Generation**.
  — Citri-Glow (shampoo) from Real Goods**.
  — Quick 'n' Bright**—sold by individual dealers. (I have used this amazing product and recommend it very highly for almost every conceivable-cleaning purpose.) (800) 537-3450.
- **Fumigants:**
  — Refresh-A-Closet Bags—Real Goods**.
  — Smells Begone—Real Goods and Seventh Generation**.
- **Polishes for Furniture:**
  — One part lemon juice to two parts olive or mineral oil.
  — Amazon's Lemon Oil from Real Goods or Seventh Generation**.
  — Earth-Friendly Furniture Cleaner—Seventh Generation**.
- **Gold, Silver, Brass, Pewter, or Copper Polishes:**
  — All-in-one Metal Polish from Seventh Generation**.
  — Soak silver in boiling water with baking soda, salt, and a piece of aluminum.
- **Rust Remover/polisher:**
  — NOW Rust and Corrosion Remover—Seventh Generation**.

- **Wood Preservatives or wood floor polishes**
  — Mineral oil or olive oil and water (thoroughly dampen floor, rub oil in, let rest six hours, wipe off excess oil. (Good for your hands and knees when you do it, too!)

Paradichlorobenzene (PDB) a combination of benzene and chlorine—moth repellents, insecticides, germicides, spray deodorants, and room deodorants, and ohmygawd *nail polish!* (This is the ghastly smell in nail painting parlors—a potentially deadly combination of two of the most toxic chemicals in the world.) PDBs have the same list of health problems as formaldehydes (and are also often found in room and car deodorants, frequently used in hotels and, believe it or not, hospitals): headaches; and eye, nose, and throat irritation. At higher concentrations or for longer periods, they can cause weakness, dizziness, loss of weight, and liver damage. Known to cause cancer in animals, it is very resilient in the environment, lasting for years or generations.

Better Solutions:
- **Moth Repellants:**
  — Cedar chunks, or boards bought at a lumberyard and refreshed with Amazon's Cedarwood Oil from Seventh Generation**.
  — Cedar Rolls: Cedar shaved very thin and given a paper backing to use in drawers, closets, shelves, or on walls. Seventh Generation**.
  — Lavender flowers.
  — Have clothes dry-cleaned and sealed in moth-proof plastic bags, available at any cleaners, for summer storage.
  Caution: Never use moth repellants on anything for babies.
- **Germicides:**
  — NOW, Mildew-Away, or Super Pine - Seventh Generation**.
  —Rubbing alcohol.
- **Room Deodorants:**
  — Orange Mate, or Lime Mate - Seventh Generation**.
  — Small tray of grains: rye, wheat, barley.
  — Natural flower petals from your garden.
- **Spray Deodorants:**
  — Roll-on deodorant.
  — Natural crystal deodorant.
- **Nail Polish:**
  —Naked nails, now being made popular by Meryl Streep and others. (Stop painting 'em.).

Cyanide: Agatha Christie's favorite murder weapon, it is one of the most rapid poisons known and is used to kill insects and rats. It is also in silver polish, photographic chemicals, and some art materials.

Naphthalene: A derivative of coal, one of a class called "Aromatic Hydrocarbons," which includes xylene, toluene, and styrene. These are used in solvents and toilet bowl deodorizers, and are best known as a moth repellent, and are a by-product of burning tobacco. The chemical causes allergic rashes in people of all ages, and may also damage eyes, kidneys, liver, red blood cells, and become highly neurotoxic at high concentrations. They also cause anemia in children exposed to clothes and blankets stored in mothballs. Take a lesson from nature: Avoid these chemicals, just like moths do.

Benzene: The smell of gasoline going into your gas tank. One of the top five organic chemicals produced in the U.S., it is used as an anti-knock additive in gasoline. It is highly flammable, very poisonous, and a major irritant to mucous membranes, and *easily absorbed through the skin in harmful amounts*. It is the single best reason in the chemical pollutant world to **keep vapors from your garage totally isolated from your house**, and to buy an electric car as soon as possible.

Perchlorethylene: You can't read this on the label where it is most common, but you absolutely can smell it on your clothes when you bring them home from the cleaners. The most common effects of overexposure or normal exposure in a sensitive person are eye irritation, burning in the nose and throat, or rashes and burning on the skin when wearing dry-cleaned clothes. If you live in a Healing House and do not have any alternative but dry-cleaning of clothes or fabrics (drapes, upholstery) in your house with this chemical, hang your dry-cleaning outside to air before bringing it into the house. Or better yet, tell your dry cleaners you want your clothes dried longer in their dryers, which remove the chemicals. They don't want to do this because it costs them more, but if you convince them you need it for your health, they probably will because at that point it becomes a liability issue.

Better Solutions:
- "Dry-clean" sponges called Wonder Sponges—Seventh Generation**.
- White Wizard—Real Goods and Seventh Generation**.
- Quick 'n' Bright—sold by dealers in your area or 1-800-537-3450.

Ammonia: A powerful chemical irritant whose most common household use is in window cleaners.

Better solutions:
- For glass: plain water with a little vinegar added.
- Seventh Generation Glass Cleaner**.
- For other flat surfaces: vinegar, salt, and water.
- For bathroom: baking soda and water.
- Dilution of Quick 'n Bright or White Wizard.
- Seventh Generation All-Purpose Cleaner**.

**Most of these products can also be bought at local health food or natural organic food stores such as the Whole Foods chain. If you can't find them in your area, call Seventh Generation for their catalog at (800) 456-1177. Real Goods catalog: (800) 762-7325.

14C - **Ridding Your House of Organochlorines**
Better solutions:
- Don't use chlorine bleaches for anything, ever.
  Germicide:
  — 1/2 cup borax in one gallon water.
  — Rubbing alcohol.
  — Anti-bacterial cloth (used on space ships) from Real Goods**.
  Paper Goods:
  — Buy chlorine-free, dioxin-free papers, including paper towels, napkins, toilet paper, facial tissues, and paper plates from 7th Generation, Real Goods, or your local suppliers. (If the paper is also recycled, so much the better, because every ton of paper we recycle saves 17 trees and keeps 3.3 cubic yards of garbage out of landfills. Recycled paper also uses up to 95 percent fewer chemicals to produce.)
  Use cloth diapers, "bleached" with 20 Mule Team Borax and sunlight.

  Clothes Bleach:
  — 20 Mule Team Borax, available at any grocery store, added to laundry detergent (Author's tip: For the "whitest whites," this must be combined with hanging whites in sunlight.)
  — 20 Mule Team Borax can also be used as a "brightener" for colors in laundry. Alternate product: Any hydrogen peroxide nonchlorine bleach.

Other Cleaning Agents:
- Seventh Generation All-Purpose Cleaner.
- Citra-Solv—for tougher cleaning jobs—Real Goods.
- Oasis Biocompatible Laundry Detergent.
- Seventh Generation Concentrated Laundry Detergent.

Abrasive Cleaners:
- Rub area with 1/2 lemon dipped in borax. Rinse and dry.

Drain Cleaners:
- Plunger; flush with boiling water, 1/4 cup baking soda and 2 oz. vinegar.

** Most of these products are available at local natural food or health food stores. If they are not available where you live, see telephone numbers for catalog orders above in Appendix 14B.

CHAPTER 16
16A - **The Sanborn Principles**
1. Healthy Indoor Environment for Occupants
Create a living environment that will be healthy for all its occupants. Buildings shall be of appropriate human scale in a nonsterile, aesthetically pleasing environment. Building design will respond to:
- Toxicity of materials
- EMF
- Lighting efficiency and quality

- Comfort requirements
- Attention to the principles of Feng Shui

2. Ecologically Healthy

The design of the human habitat shall recognize that all resources are limited and will respond to the patterns of the natural ecology. Land plans and building designs will include only those technologies with the least disruptive impact upon the natural ecology of the earth. Density must be most intense near neighborhood centers where facilities are most accessible.

Buildings will be organic, integrate art, natural materials, sunlight, green plants, energy efficiency, low noise levels, and water and not cost more than current conventional buildings. Features of the buildings and their surroundings will include:

- No waste that cannot be assimilated
- Thermal passivity (responsiveness)
- Reflective surfaces
- Junglified surroundings, both exterior and interior
- Access by foot to primary services
- Natural corridors for wildlife
- Individual community gardens
- Local agriculture for local consumption

3. Socially Just

Habitats shall be equally accessible across economic classes.

4. Culturally Creative

Habitats will allow ethnic groups to maintain individual cultural identities and neighborhoods, while integrating into the larger community. All population groups shall have access to art, theater, and music.

5. Beautiful

6. Physically and Economically Accessible

All sites within the habitat shall be accessible and rich in resources to those living within walkable (or wheelchair-able) distance. Accessible characteristics shall include:

- Radical traffic calming
- Clean, accessible, economical mass transit; i.e. "cybertrans"
- Bicycle paths
- Small neighborhood service businesses; i.e. bakeries, tailors, groceries, bagel stores, fish markets, kosher delis, coffee bars, etc.
- Places to go where chances of accidental meetings are high; i.e., neighborhood parks, playgrounds, cafes, sports centers, etc.

7. Evolutionary

Habitats' design shall include continuous re-evaluation of premises and values, shall be demographically responsive and flexible to change over time to support future user needs. Initial designs should reflect our society's heterogeneity and have a feedback system. They shall be:

- Villagified
- Multigenerational
- Nonexclusionary

16B - **Organochlorines,** which are stubbornly persistent and last hundreds of years, include famous chemicals such as DDT, Heptaclor, CFCs, PCBs, chlordane, and dioxin, which is so potent that one barrel full of it could kill every person in our nation. They were discussed thoroughly in Chapter 14.

CHAPTER 17
17A - **Photovoltaics: the World View**
The saddest thing about photovoltaics is that Japan and Europe are way ahead of us in their development, as they were in fuel-efficient cars a decade ago. Of the 68.5 megawatts developed in 1995, only 12.5 MW were in North America, and only 7 MW in the US. Over 20,000 homeowners in Japan are waiting for their own PV rooftop systems. The Japanese PV research and development program next year is projected to be three times the size of the U.S. program.

As we approach the 21st century, 70% of the population in the developing world, about two billion people in four hundred million households, still use kerosene, wood, or batteries for light and power. When their poor governments have tried aggressive rural electrification programs, they have found the cost of massive power plants prohibitive. And even if they were built, the families who need the power couldn't afford it. Those areas desperately need safe, clean sources of electricity, such as solar and wind. [12]

17B - **More on the World's Oil Supplies or Lack Thereof**
There are several categories of oil supplies:
- *Reserves:* engineers' opinions of how much oil is known to be producible, within a known time, with known technology, at known costs, and in known fields. Banks lend money on these.
- *Active reserves:* same as above.
- *Inactive reserves:* those known to exist, but not considered producible within 20 years; i.e., inaccessible or producible only with not-as-yet-commercial methods. Banks will *not* loan money on these.
- *Political reserves:* the sudden, unsubstantiated reserve increases announced by any country, probably political "puffery" used to increase national political prestige or in negotiations for OPEC quotas or bank loans. An example of this is that units of natural gas are commonly converted to barrels of oil equivalent (BOE) and included in a company's or nation's reserves, even though it is not as convenient, safe, or flexible as oil. It is these political reserves, Ivanhoe suggests, that "tend to lull the public, politicians, and stockbrokers into complacency."
- *Resources:* geologists' optimistic opinions of all undiscovered oil theoretically present in an area. Banks will *not* lend money on these.

Ivanhoe says we have to go to *Oil and Gas Journal* to get "real numbers" on oil reserves. However, in addition to the fact that the numbers come from the country itself, they are, in most cases, comprised of *all* the categories above, verified and nonverified.

Some nations' numbers are obviously gross approximations. Iraq doubled its reported reserves from 47 Billion Barrels of Oil (Bbo) to 100 Bbo in 1987—the number that Iraq still lists for its reserves eight years later. Who could prove Iraq wrong? And what difference would it make to Iraq if the world's economists and planners were misled by Saddam Hussein's petroleum ministry?

Even more egregious than the exaggerations of political reserves is the economists' treatment of the U.S. Geological Survey's *resource* numbers. These are commonly added to the O&GJ *reserves* to produce a grand total of each nation's "oil endowment." The sum of the two (unknown) values give huge "fruit salad" numbers that are routinely and incorrectly called *reserves*.[13]

Ivanhoe says the critical date for concern is the time when global public demand will substantially exceed the available supply from the few Persian Gulf oil exporters. That is, he says, will be about 2010 if normal oil-field decline occurs, or as early as 2000 if the world's key oil producer, Saudi Arabia, has serious political problems that curtail its exports.

Thus, the question is not *whether* but *when* the foreseeable permanent oil crunch will occur [which] will not be solved by any redistribution patterns or by economic cleverness because it will be a consequence of pending and inexorable depletion of the world's conventional crude oil supply. Few economists can bring themselves to accept that the global oil supply is geologically finite.[14]

◆   ◆   ◆

Notes

PREFACE
1. Frank Lloyd Wright, *The Natural House,* New American Library, 1954.

CHAPTER 2
1. *Symbolic Landscapes,* by Paul Devereux, Gothic Image Publications, 7 High St., Glastonbury, Somerset BA69DP England, 1992.
2. *Honey from the Rock,* by Lawrence Kushner, Jewish Lights Publishing, 1977.
3. Ibid., Devereux.
4. Ibid., Devereux.
5. Brought to the Sanborn Conference by a member of the Sanborn team as a small poster. No credit except the name of the author, Chief Seattle.
6. Ibid., Devereux.
7. Ibid.
8. Ibid.
9. Ibid, pg. 56.
10. Quote Kathy Pulley, associate professor of religious studies at Southwest Missouri State University, in World Traveler, Nov., 1996, pg. 84).
11. Ibid., Kushner.
12. Nancy Curtis's research from 1875, collected in *The Indians' Book*, recorded and edited by Natalie Curtis; © 1987. OBC, Bonanza Books.

CHAPTER 3
1. Lewis Mumford, from *The Lewis Mumford Reader,* edited by Donald L. Miller, University of Georgia Press, 1995.
2. Frank Lloyd Wright, *The Natural House,* New American Library, 1954.
3. Author's notes, World Renewable Energy Congress, Denver, Colorado, June, 1996. Tombazis further discussed this connection in *Renewable Energy*, proceedings of the World Renewable Energy Congress, Pergamon Press, 1996, pg. 52.
4. Blessingway, from *Through Indian Eyes,* edited and published by Reader's Digest Publishing, 1996.
5. Frank Lloyd Wright, *The Natural House,* New American Library, 1954.
6. William James, English author.
7. Stewart Brand, *How Buildings Learn,* Penguin Books, USA, 1994, pg. 21.
8. *Portrait of Progress,* by Reba D. Grubb, Raim and Assoc. for Tucson Medical Center, 1995.
9. Ibid.
10. Author's notes, World Renewable Energy Congress, June, 1996.

CHAPTER 4
1. Frank Lloyd Wright, *The Natural House,* New American Library, 1954.
2. Ibid.

CHAPTER 5
1. Frank Lloyd Wright, *The Natural House,* New American Library, 1954.
2. Ibid.
3. Ibid.

CHAPTER 6
1. Spirit of the Smokies, June 1996.
2. Frank Lloyd Wright, *The Natural House,* New American Library, 1954.
3. Ibid.

CHAPTER 7
1. Faith Popcorn and Lys Marigold, *Clicking: 16 Trends to Future Fit Your Life, Your Work and Your Business,* Harper Collins, 1996.
2. *Through Indian Eyes,* published by Reader's Digest Assn., Inc., 1995.

CHAPTER 9
1. Saint Bernard of Clairvaux, French Theologian, *Epistle 106,* 1091-1153.

CHAPTER 10
1. "The Difference is Daylight" *Washington Home* cover story; Mike McClintock, Sept., 1996.
2. "Seasonality of mood in Italy: Role of Latitude and sociocultural factors. "*Journal of Affective Disorders*. Vol. 33(2) 135-139, Feb., 1995.
3. "Rhythm and Blues: The theory and treatment of seasonal affective disorder," by Dalgleish et al; British Journal of Clinical Psychology. Vol. 35(2) 163-182, May, 1996.
4. To ensure that this winter depression was related to length of natural light exposure and not to other factors, a study in Rigshospitalet, Copenhagen, Denmark, obtained local weather data from the Meteorological Institute in Copenhagen. They found no significant correlation between level of winter depression and cloud cover, rainfall, or atmospheric pressure. But they did find a significant correlation between depression and minutes of sunshine, global radiation, length of daylight, and temperature. "The influence of climate on development of winter depression," Molin, Jeanne, et al. *Journal of Affective Disorders*, 37(2) 151-155. April, 1996.
5. Labbate, Lawrence et al. "Influence of phototherapy treatment duration for seasonal affective disorder," *Biological Psychiatry*. Vol. 38(11) 747-750. Dec., 1995. Walter Reed US Army Med. Ctr., Dept. of Psychiatry, Wash., D.C., Labbate, Lawrence et al.
6. "A seasonal pattern of hospital medication errors in Alaska." *Psychiatry Research*. Vol. 57(3) 251-257, Aug., 1995.
7. Copyright by Sister M. Madeleva, 1927, renewed in 1955; reprinted by Helen Hayes and Lewis Funke, *A Gift of Joy,* M. Evans and Company, Inc., New York; and J. B. Lippincott Company, Philadelphia and New York, 1965.
8. Burke Miller, "Daylighting the Way in Oregon," *Solar Today*, Nov-Dec., 1996, pgs. 26-29.
9. Ibid.
10. *Wall Street Journal,* Nov. 20, 1995, pg. B7.
11. Ibid.
12. Burke Miller, "Way Station," *Solar Today*, July-Aug., 1994, pgs. 17-20
13. As seen in *Energy Design Update*, April, 1992. For more information, contact Broan Mfg. Co., P.O. Box 140, Hartford, WI 53027. (414) 673-4340.
14. Ned Nisson, *Energy Design Update,* June, 1992.
15. The SunPipe includes a clear upper plastic dome fitted with a non-airtight gasket that allows the tube to "breathe" a little to remove trapped moisture. The bottom diffusing dome is sealed tightly to the tube and ceiling to prevent air leakage. Standard flashing and a storm collar are designed to keep out rain.
16. Danny Parker and Lyn Schrum, *Results from a Comprehensive Lighting Retrofit*, Florida Solar Energy Center brochure number FSEC-CR-914-96, available from FSEC, 1679

Clearlake Road, Cocoa Beach, FL 32922-5703, or by calling (407) 638-1000.

17. Facts from the Rejuvenation Lamp and Fixture Company catalog. 1100 S.E. Grand Ave., Portland, OR 97214. (505) 231-1900.

CHAPTER 11

1. *"How Grateful We Are, O Lord,* by Rabbi Sheldon Zimmerman. Temple Emanu-El, Dallas, TX , May 3, 1996.

2. Noah Adams, *Piano Lessons,* Delta Publishing, April, 1997.

3. From *Through Indian Eyes*, published by the Reader's Digest Assn., 1996.

CHAPTER 12

1. Anders Nyquist, Sweden, presenter at the Third Annual Eco-city Conference in Senegal, January, 1996, had some interesting statistics on blackwater: "Human beings each produce in their urine, 6 kilograms of nitrogen, 1 kilogram of phosphorous, and 1 kilogram of potassium annually. Five hundred square meters of cultivated land can support 75% of a person's nutritional needs with an annual input of, guess what? Right. 6 kg of nitrogen, 1 kg. of phosphorous, and 1 kg. of potassium. Why not use it in developing countries to be self-sufficient? We are sitting on a valuable resource." From EcoCity Newsletter, Spring, 1996.

2. Ben and Jerry's plant is in Waterbury, Vermont, just off the freeway. (This is not a big town!) Their mailing address is 30 Community Drive, South Burlington, VT 05403-6828. (802) 651-9600.

3. Omick has since made changes that improved the graywater system and add only a few dollars to the cost. At the end of the PVC pipes in the mulch, he built little brick piles by stacking eight bricks, laid with the holes horizontal, in pairs. He passed the pipe through the center of a brick, but not all the way out the other side, and put a 12" square patio block on top of the brick formation. This makes a little brick chamber at the end of the water flow so that dirt doesn't clog the end of the tube. Prior to this change, refuse from the washer water (hair, buttons, etc., was caught at the end of the tube by the protective screen and blocked drainage.

4. From *Through Indian Eyes*, published by the Reader's Digest Assn., 1996.

5. Ibid.

6. Alex Wilson, Editor, Environmental Building News, Vol. 6, No. 5, May, 1997.

7. Author's notes from Green Buildings Conference (GBC) Austin, Texas, Nov., 1996.

8. Author's notes from the Green Building Conference indicate the UV purification system Gibson has requires a 40-watt fluorescent bulb, which runs on 1/2 amp, and a 5-micron filter has to be changed about every eight months. Larger UV purification systems or ozonation systems are also available at higher cost, but may be necessary for certain uses.

9. That system cost $250,000 according to author's notes from GBC.

10. Ibid., *Environmental Building News*

11. UV Waterworks, recipient of *Discover* magazine's 1996 Award for Technological Innovation (environment category) and *Popular Science* magazine's 1996 Best of What's New Award, is available from WaterHealth International, Inc. (WHI), 1001 Second St., Suite 325, Napa, CA 94559. (707) 252-9092. For more information, call Dr. Arthur Rosenfeld, Senior Advisor to the Department of Energy, (202) 586-6593, or contact him on the Internet at Arthur Rosenfeld@hq.doe.gov.

12. Winona LaDuke, "Like Tributaries to a River," *Sierra* magazine, Nov/Dec., 1996.

13. Baker Morrow, *Designer/Builder* magazine, December, 1995.

14. Janet N. Abramovitz, Senior Researcher at Worldwatch Institute, in *Futurist*, July-August, 1997.

15. *The Western Guide to Feng Shui* by Terah Kathryn Collins, Hay House, Inc., Carlsbad, CA, 1996.

CHAPTER 13

1. Zeno, from *Diogenes Laertius, Lives of Eminent Philosophers*, quote on a World Wildlife Federation postcard by Gerry Ellis, Ellis Nature Photography.
2. Burke Miller, Wamganoag Tribal Headquarters, *Solar Today,* Jan/Feb., 1995.
3. Ned Nisson, *Energy Design Update,* July, 1992, pg. 9.
4. Nadav Malin, "New Life for Old Carpets: Carpet Tiles Lead the Way," *Environmental Building News,* June, 1997, Vol. 6, No. 6.
5. Steve Loken, Guide to Resource-Efficient Building Elements, and *ReCraft 90 Handbook.* To order, call the Center for Resourceful Building Technology, (406) 549- 7678, or fax (406) 549-4100.
6. Product News & Reviews, *Environmental Building News,* April, 1997, Vol. 6, No. 4.

CHAPTER 14

1. Chief Flying Hawk, 1852-1931, as quoted by Gary Gene Olp, AIA, NCARB, Environmental Architect; "A Natural Approach to IAQ."
2. "Straw Daubs: How Fiber Cuts Erosion" by Ed Crocker, *Designer/Builder*, Nov., 1996, pg. 14.
3. "A steel-framed wall with R-13 fiberglass batts has an overall R-value of about R-7. The reason for the low R-value is that the highly conductive steel studs act as thermal bridges, carrying heat around or through the cavity insulation." (*Energy Design Update* July, 1995, pg. 6). "As for stopping convection in steel framing, icynene won't help there, either. Researchers at Oak Ridge National Lab concluded that the thermal bridge effect in steel framing is so strong it drowns out convection effects." Answer to Letters to the Editor by Ned Nisson, *Energy Design Update,* Oct., 1995, pg. 5.
4. "Ancient Cob Method Makes Comeback," *Designer/Builder*, Aug., 1996, pgs. 27-28.
5. For more information, see *The Straw Bale House* by Bill and Athena Steen, David Bainbridge, and David Eisenberg; Chelsea Green Publishing Company, White River Junction, VT; 1994.
6. For more information, see "Pliny Fisk III, The Rebar Revolution," *Designer/Builder* magazine, Sept., 1996, pg. 38. Or contact The Center for Maximum Potential Building Systems, 8604 FM 969, Austin, TX 78724. (512) 928-4786.
7. Paul Hawken, *The Ecology of Commerce,* Harper Business Publishers, 1993.
8. Lois Marie Gibbs, *Dying from Dioxin,* South End Press, 1995.
9. Theo Colburn, Dianne Dumanoski, and John Peterson Myers, *Our Stolen Future,* Dutton, 1996.
10. Gordon K. Durnil, *The Making of a Conservative Environmentalist,* Indiana University Press, 1995.
11. Colburn et al., *Our Stolen Future,* and Sharlene K. Johnson, "Pesticides: what you don't know can hurt you," *Ladies Home Journal,* June, 1997.
12. For "Healthy House," third edition, published by the Healthy House Institute, 1995, call (812) 332-5073. Healthy House has also recently published another book called *The Healthy Household,* by Lynn Marie Bower.
13. Published by CMHC/SCHL, the Canadian Mortgage and Housing Corporation, 1995. It can be ordered at (613) 748-2367.
14. "A Natural Approach to IAQ" by Gary Gene Olp, AIA, NCARP, Envir. Arch.
15. Ibid.
16. Nancy Furey, M.D., of Chicago, and Paul Bergstresser, M.D., of Dallas. Words could never express how grateful I am for the relief I have experienced as a result of what they have taught me. Many persons with Multiple Chemical Sensitivities also have Atopic Dermatitis (AD). A partial definition of AD is rashes or skin irritations for which there is no

known cause. In my own case, I have absolutely identified certain chemicals as part of the cause, including chlorine in bedsheets and towels.
17. Ibid., Bower and Drerup.

CHAPTER 15
1. *Through Indian Eyes,* edited and published by Reader's Digest Association, 1996.

CHAPTER 16
1. Paul Hawken, *The Ecology of Commerce,* Harper-Business Publishers, 1993.
2. Ibid.
3. Ibid.
4. Ibid.
5. Ibid.
6. Ibid.
7. Ramie is made from a linenlike plant native to the Philippines.
8. From a plenary speech made by William McDonough at the Habitat Green Team meeting, Atlanta, Georgia, Dec. 7, 1995. Author's notes.
9. Jane Jacobs, *Death and Life of Great American Cities,* as quoted in the *Lewis Mumford Reader*, edited by Donald L. Miller, University of Georgia Press, 1995.
10. Lewis Mumford, quoted in the *Lewis Mumford Reader,* pg. 203.
11. Luther Standing Bear, as quoted in *Through Indian Eyes*, The Reader's Digest Assn. Publishing, 1995, Inside Dust Jacket.
12. Jane Jacobs, as quoted in the *Lewis Mumford Reader*, edited by Donald L. Miller, University of Georgia Press, 1995, pg. 198.
13. U.S. Secretary of State Warren Christopher said to Jim Lehrer, December 19, 1996, PBS Evening News: "It would have been very injurious to America's security if Saddam Hussein had gained control over the oil in the Middle East."
14. Lewis Mumford, *The Lewis Mumford Reader.*
15. The Whole Foods chain in Dallas and Austin does it already, but we need it on a much greater scale.
16. Ibid., *Lewis Mumford Reader*, pg. 209.
17. Ibid., pg. 223.
18. Lewis Mumford, *The City in History: Its Origins, Its Transformations, and Its Prospects,* New York: Harcourt, Brace, 1961, pgs. 299-314; and paper by this author, "The Life and Times of the World's Great Cities," 1961.
19. Navajo song, from *Through Indian Eyes,* published by Reader's Digest Assn., 1996.
20. Ibid., *Lewis Mumford Reader.*
21. Paul Weyrich, "Conservatives and Mass Transit: Is it Time for a New Look?," as quoted in Gas Guzzler Campaign Newsletter, May/June 1997, Vol. 5. No. 3.
22. James MacKenzie, et al, "The Going Rate: What it really costs to Drive," World Resources Institute, 1992, as quoted in Gas Guzzler Newsletter, May/June 1997, Vol. 5.
23. "Getting There: Strategic Facts for the Transportation Advocate," Gas Guzzler Campaign, Washington, D.C., 1996; pg. 8, as quoted in Gas Guzzler Newsletter, May/June 1997, Vol. 5., No. 3.
24. American Public Transit Assn. Fact Sheets, 1996.
25. U.S. Office of Technology Assessment statistics.
26. William Thomas, M.D. , *Life Worth Living,* as quoted by Pat Matz in the Memorial Nursing Home Newsletter, Sidney, Nebraska, April, 1997.
27. Melissa Morrison, "American Comic Takes the Mysteries Out of Amsterdam," *Dallas Morning News*, June 30, 1996, 7G.

28. *Lewis Mumford Reader*, pg. 277.

CHAPTER 17

1. Edgar Mitchell, USA Astronaut, from *The Home Planet* by Kevin W. Kelley for The Assn. of Space Explorers, Addison-Wesley Publishing Co., 1988.

2. Frank Lloyd Wright, *The Natural House*, Horizon Press, The New American Library, 1954.

3. Bruce Anderson with Michael Riordan, *The New Solar Home Book,* Brick House Publishing Co., Inc., 1987, pg. 139.

4. Florida Solar Energy Center brochure.

5. Griffin Carrison, Thermal Conversion Technology, Sarasota, Florida (941) 953-2177.

6. Ibid., Anderson and Riordan.

7. For more information, contact EVermont, U.S. Rte. 2, Middlesex, Drawer 33, Montpelier, VT 05633. (802) 828-3246.

8. Thomas T. Volgel, Jr. , and Peter Fritsch, Staff Reporters of the *Wall Street Journal,* June 6, 1997, pgs. 1 and A11.

9. Source: French Technology Press Office, Inc., Chicago, IL., as published in *The Futurist,* July-August, 1997, pg. 13.

10. "Renewed Interest in Renewables," *Solar Today*, Sept./Oct. 1994, quoting Environmental Business Journal Inc., San Diego, CA.

11. Roy E. McAlister, President of the American Hydrogen Assn. in *Hydrogen Today*, official publication of the American Hydrogen Assn., Tempe, AZ.

12. See Appendix 17B, reference to I.F. Ivanhoe.

13. Ibid.

14. Ibid.

CHAPTER 18

1. Derivation by the author of the *V'ahavtah* prayer, keystone of Judaism, taken from Deuteronomy 6: 4-9, and Leviticus 19: 2.

2. Joseph Campbell, *The Power of Myth,* Random House, 1988.

3. Vladimir Shalatov, USSR astronaut, as quoted by Kevin W. Kelley for the Association of Space Explorers, *The Home Planet,* Addison-Wesley Publishing Co., 1988.

4. Ken Blanchard and Terry Waghorn, *Mission Possible,* McGraw-Hill, 1997.

5. Joseph Campbell, Ibid.

6. Chief Oren Boyd, notes by the author from a PBS program.

7. Michael Ryan, *"We Have to Protect What We Have,"* *Parade* magazine, Feb. 2, 1997.

8. Lawrence Kushner, *Honey from the Rock,* Jewish Lights Publishing, 1977.

9. Rainer Marie Rilke, quoted by Rashani on a card printed by *Brush Dance*, Mill Valley, California. "The Brush Dance is a Yurok Indian healing ritual where being true to yourself means giving your best to help a person in need. Being true to yourself is the one and only law."

Bibliography

Those items that the author considers will be most beneficial to beginners in Healing House design will have two asterisks (**) beside them.

SOLAR TECHNOLOGIES AND BUILDINGS:

Many books below can be ordered from the American Solar Energy Society bookstore:

2400 Central Avenue, G-1, Boulder, CO 80301 • (303) 443-3130
FAX: (303) 443-3212 • Website: http://www.ases.org/solar
e-mail: ases@ases.org • (Member prices will be less than those listed here.)

Other Ordering Codes: Real Goods Catalog (RG) (800) 762-7325

Solar Energy: Today's Technologies for a Sustainable Future, edited by Maureen McIntyre, ASES, 1997, 50+ pgs. $20.

Renewables Are Ready: People Creating Renewable Energy Solutions, by Nancy Cole and P. J. Skerrett, The Union of Concerned Scientists, Chelsea Green Publishing, 1995, 256 pgs. $19.95.

The Sunshine Revolution by Harold N. Rostvick, Sunlab, 1992, 188 pgs. $39.

***Consumer Guide to Solar Energy* by Scott Sklar and Kenneth Sheinkopf, Bonus Books, 1995, New Expanded Edition, 188 pgs. $12.95.

***Passive Solar Buildings,* edited by J. Douglas Balcomb, MIT Press, 1992, 528 pgs. $57.50.

Active Solar Systems, edited by George Lof, MIT Press, 1993, 963 pgs. $80.

Solar Building Architecture, edited by Bruce N. Anderson, MIT Press, 1990, 368 pgs. $52.50.

Fundamentals of Building Energy Dynamics, by Bruce D. Hunn, MIT Press, 1996, 538 pgs. $60.

Cooking with the Sun, by Beth and Dan Halacy, Morning Sun Press, 1992, 114 pgs. $7.95.

Residential Design

The New Solar Home Book, by Bruce Anderson with Michael Riordan, Brick House, 1987, reprinted, revised 1996, 226 pgs. $20.

***How to Build an Underground House,* by Malcolm Wells, 1991, 96 pgs. $12.

***Climatic Building Design: Energy-Efficient Building Principles and Practice*, by Donald Watson and Kenneth Labs, McGraw-Hill, 1993, 228 pgs. $34.95.

***Passive Solar Energy: The Homeowner's Guide to Natural Heating and Cooling*, 2nd Edition, by Bruce Anderson and Malcolm Wells, Brick House, 1993, 197 pgs. $24.95.

Underground Buildings, by Malcolm Wells, Raven Rock Press, 1990, 220 pgs. $14.95.

SUN-EARTH: Sustainable Design, by Richard Crowther, from a 1983 classic edition, reprinted 1994. $17.95.

**The Straw Bale House*, by David Bainbridge, Athena Steen, and Bill Steen,
Chelsea Green Publishers, 1994, 250 pgs. $30.

**Affordable Passive Solar Homes,* by Richard L. Crowther, FAIA, SciTech, 1984,
188 pgs. $20.

The Natural House, by Frank Lloyd Wright, New American Library, 1954,
22 pgs. Available at most libraries.

Adding to a House, by Philip Wenz, 1995, 263 pgs. $34. 95 RG.

**La Casa Adobe: adobe architecture and four sets of house drawings*,
by William Lumpkins, Revised Edition, 1986, 52 pgs. $11.95 RG.

Treehouses—Everything from picking the right tree to shingling the roof—
by Peter Nelson, 128 pgs., 1994. $19.95 RG.

Passive Solar House Basics, by Peter van Dresser, 136 pgs., 1995. $9.95 RG.

*New Compact House Designs: Smaller, more energy-efficient homes better suited to their
environment.* Compiled by Dan Metz, 188 pgs. 1991. $17.95 RG.

***Solar Living Sourcebook: Complete Information Compendium on the renewable energy sources of
sun, wind and falling water: Ninth Edition,* compiled by Real Goods staff, 1993 and 1996, 712 pgs.
$24.95 RG.

**The Rammed Earth House*, by David Easton, 224 pgs., 1995. $29.95 RG. Companion Video, *The
Rammed Earth Renaissance,* $24.95.

For Builders and Architects

Passive Solar Design Strategies: Guidelines for Home Building and BuilderGuide Software. Passive
Solar Industries Council, 1995, 131 pgs. $45.

Affordable Housing Through Energy Conservation: A Technical Support Document. A Technical
Guide to Designing and Constructing Energy Efficient Homes. U.S. Dept. of Energy Office of
Buildings and Community Systems, Building Systems Division, three volumes; available by calling
the Energy Efficiency Clearinghouse at (800) 363-3732.

Sun, Wind and Light: Architectural Design Strategies, by G. Z. Brown et al, 176 pgs., $45.   Order
from the Iris Catalog, (800) 346-0104.

Builder's Guide for Cold Climates, by Joseph Lstiburek and Betsy Pettit. 270 pgs. $40 plus $3 ship-
ping. Order from a form found at www.buildingscience.com or call (508) 589-5100. Also *Builder's
Guide for Mixed Climates* (and soon to come) *Builder's Guide for Hot-Humid Climates, and Builder's
Guide for Hot-Dry Climates.*

Heating, Cooling, Lighting: Design Methods for Architects, 524 pgs., $90. Order from The IRIS
Catalog, (800) 346-0104.

Daylighting: Performance and Design, by Gregg Ander, $59.95. For more info, call (800) 842-3636,
Dept. Z3820.

Energy Design Update. Monthly Publication of the Cutter Information Corp.
Call (800) 964-5118 for subscription information.

Environmental Building News. RR 1, Box 161, Brattleboro VT 05301.
Call (802) 257-7300 for subscription information, or contact them at www.ebuild.com or
e-mail: ebn@ebuild.com.

Building a Sustainable America

Buildings for a Sustainable America Case Studies, by Burke Miller Thayer, ASES, 1997, 86 pgs. $25.Video: $14.95.

Opportunities for Renewable Energy Supply in New Buildings: Performance Potential-Maps (six maps to answer your questions about how worthwhile it would be to consider solar energy applications in your area). Passive Solar Industries Council. $25.

***The Independent Home: Living Well with Power from the Sun, Wind and Water,* by Michael Potts, Chelsea Green Publishing, 1993, 320 pgs. $19.95 RG.

***A Primer on Sustainable Building.* Rocky Mountain Institute, 140 pgs., $17. Order by calling (800) 346-0104.

Laboratory Earth: The Planetary Gamble We Can't Afford to Lose, by Stephen H. Schneider, Basic Books, 10 East 53rd St., New York, NY 10022. (212) 207-7203, $20.

Earth in the Balance: Ecology and the Human Spirit, by Al Gore, Houghton-Mifflin Co. 1992, 368 pgs., $22.95.

Energy Efficiency and the Environment: Forging the Link, edited by Ed Vine, Drury Crawley, and Paul Centolella. Twenty papers from the 1990 American Council for an Energy Efficient Economy (ACEEE) Summer Study on Energy Efficiency in Buildings, includes global warming, acid rain compliance, environmental externality costs, and more. 418 pgs. $29. Available from ACEEE, (202) 429-8873 or e-mail: ace3pubs@ix.netcom.com. Ask them for free catalog of all publications.

Lean and Clean Management: How to Boost Profits and Productivity by Reducing Pollution, by Joseph J. Romm, Kodansha International, 1994, 207 pgs., $23.

The Ecology of Commerce, by Paul Hawken, Harper Business Publishers, 1993, 250 pgs., $14.

Materials for Sustainable Building

The Sourcebook for Sustainable Design. 170 pgs., $25. Order from Boston Society of Architects, (617) 951-1433 x 221.

***Guide to Resource Efficient Building Elements, Third Edition,* by Steve Leaked, Center for Resourceful Building Technology, 1991, 100 pgs+, $25. Order from IRIS Catalog, (800) 346-0104.

The World Directory of Renewable Energy Suppliers and Services, by Bruce Cross, University of Wales, James and James Science Publishers Ltd. Waterside House, 47 Kentish Town Road, London NW1 8NZ, UK. 546 Pages. e-mail: wdress@jxj.com.

The Green Builder's Catalog. Positive Energy Conservation Products. P.O. Box 7568, Boulder, CO 80306, or call (800) 488-4340.

Solar Electricity

***The Solar Electric House: A Design Manual for Home-Scale Photovoltaic Power Systems,* by Steven J. Strong with William G. Scheller. Sustainability Press, 276 pgs., 1987. $21.95.

***The New Solar Electric Home: The Photovoltaics How-To Handbook,* by Joel Davidson, aatec publications, 1990, 416 pgs. $18.95.

***Solar Electric Independent Home,* by Paul Jeffrey Fowler, Revised 1993 Edition, 200 pgs. 16.95.

Wind Energy

**Wind Power for Home and Business: Renewable Energy for the 1990s and Beyond,* by Paul Gipe, Chelsea Green Publishing, 1993, 384 pgs. $32.

Natural Landscaping

**Energy-Efficient and Environmental Landscaping,* by Anne Simon Moffat, Marc Schiler, and Staff of Green Living. Appropriate Solutions Press, 1994, 230 pgs. $19.95.

Solar Gardening. Growing Vegetables Year-Round the American-Intensive Way, by Leandre Poisson and Gretchen Vogel Poisson, Chelsea Green, 1995, 288 pgs. $24.95.

Landscaping with Nature: Using Nature's Designs to Plan your Yard, by Jeff Cox, 344 pgs., 1991. $16.95 RG.

Home Solar Gardening, by John H. Pierce, 164 pgs., 1992. $12.95 RG.

Waterscaping: Plants and Ideas for Natural and Created Water Gardens, by Judy Glattstein, 184 pgs., 1994. $18.95 RG.

Stonescaping: A Guide to Using Stone in Your Garden, by Jan Kowalczewski Whitner, 162 pgs., 1994. $17.95 RG.

Step-by-Step Outdoor Stonework: Over 20 Easy to Build Projects for Your Patio or Garden, by Mike Lawrence, 96 pgs, 1995, $18.95 RG.

The Resource Guide to Sustainable Landscapes and Gardens—Third Edition. 486 pgs., $35. Order from IRIS Catalog, (800) 346-0104.

Windows and Lighting for Energy Efficiency

**Residential Windows: A Guide to New Technology and Energy Performance,* by John Carmody, Stephen Selkowitz and Lisa Herschong, W.W. Norton & Co., 1996, 214 pgs. $22.

**NFRC Window Directory.* The Certified Products Directory published by the National Fenestration Ratings Council to compare energy performance information for windows and doors. 300 pgs. $10. Order from the IRIS Catalog, (800) 346-0104.

Lighting Listings: A Worldwide Guide to Lighting Publications, Research Organizations, Educational Opportunities and Associations, by Judith Block. Lighting Research Center, Rensselaer Polytechnic Institute. Call (518) 276-8716 or e-mail: blockj@rpi.edu.

Indoor Air Quality, Moisture Prevention, and Chemical Sensitivity Issues

**The Clean Air Guide: How to Identify and Correct Indoor Air Problems in Your Home,* by REIC Ltd., with assistance of Ed Lowans and Alicia Conrad, Research Staff at Canada Mortgage and Housing Corporation.1993, 32 pgs. To order, call (613) 748-2367.

Building Materials for the Environmentally Hypersensitive, by Oliver Drerup et al., Canada Mortgage and Housing Corporation, 1995. 238 pgs. To order, call (613) 748-2367.

Healthy House, Third Edition, by John Bower, Healthy House Institute, 1997, 381 pgs., $22. Call (812) 332-5073 to order.

The Healthy Household, by Lynn Marie Bower, Healthy House Institute, 1996, 480 pgs., $18. Call (812) 332-5073.

Moisture Control Handbook, by Joseph Lstiburek et al, Van Nostrom Reinholt, 225 pgs., $50 plus $3 shipping. Order from the form found on www.buildingscience.com, or call (508) 589-5100.

Indoor Air Quality Update. A monthly publication of the Cutter Information Corp. Call (800) 964-5118 for subscription information.

Miscellaneous Solar

The Fuel Savers, by Bruce Anderson, Morning Sun Press, 1991. $4.95.

Easy-to-Build Solar Batch Heater, TEA, 1981, 16 pgs. $7.

How to Design and Build a Solar Swimming Pool Heater, edited by Francis de Winter, Copper Development Assoc., 1975, 47 pgs. $5.

Many of the following books (those marked RG) can be ordered from the Real Goods Catalog (800) 762-7325. Others are probably available in bookstores.

General Sustainable Living

The Encyclopedia of Country Living. An old-fashioned instruction book for gardening, baking bread, delivering a baby, raising farm animals, growing herbs, churning butter, canning fruits, tapping a sugar maple, etc., by Carla Emery, 1994, 858 pgs. $27.95 RG.

Handmade Tiles, Designing—Making—Decorating, by Frank Giorgini, 141 pgs., 1994. $24.95 RG.

The Home Water Supply. Answers all your questions about your own water supply, by Stu Campbell, 1993, 235 pgs. $18.95 RG.

Finding and Buying Your Place in the Country, by Les and Carol Scher. Fourth Edition, 408 pgs., 1996. $25.95 RG.

Earth Ponds: A guide to building maintenance and restoration of country ponds, by Tim Matson. Second Edition, 1991, 150 pgs. $17.95 RG. Companion Video: $29.95 RG.

The Western Guide to Feng Shui, by Terah Kathryn Collins, Hay House, Inc. 1996, 224 pgs., $12.95. To order, call (800) 654-5126.

Feng Shui Workshop, by Stanley Aaga Bartlett. Video: 120 minutes, $34.95 RG.

Eco-Interiors: A Guide to Environmentally Conscious Interior Design, by Grazyna Pilatowicz, 171 pgs., $34.95. Order from Boston Society of Architects: (617) 951-1433 x221.

Consumer Guide to Home Energy Savings, 5th Edition, by Alex Wilson and John Morrill, 1996, 274 pgs., $7.95 ACEEE.

Symbolic Landscapes: The Dreamtime Earth and Avebury Open Secrets, by Paul Devereux, 1992, 164 pgs., $22.95. Gothic Image Publications, 7 High Street, Glastonbury, Somerset, England, BA6 9DP

Co-Housing: A Contemporary Approach to Housing Ourselves, by Kathryn McCamant and Charles Durrett. Second Edition with Ellen Hertzman, 1994, Ten Speed Press, 288 pgs., $29.95.

Rebuilding Community in America: Housing for Ecological Living, Personal Empowerment, and the New Extended Family. 432 pgs. $25. Order from the IRIS Catalog (800) 346-0104.

How Buildings Learn: What happens after they're built, by Stewart Brand, Penguin Books, 1994, 250 pgs., $20 US.

Casa, A Visual Library of Interior Adobe Detail, by Elizabeth Hilliard. Photographs by John Miller, Bullfinch Press, Little, Brown and Co., 80 pgs., $16.95.Also available by same author: *Cottage* (English), *Maison* (French), and *Villa* (Italian), all country-style decorating books.

Software

Designing Low-Energy Buildings: Energy 10 Software, by Dr. J. Douglas Balcomb and the Passive Solar Industries Council. Evaluates daylighting, passive solar heating and natural ventilation with energy-efficient envelopes, lighting and mechanical equipment. $250. Order from the IRIS Catalog (800) 346-0104.

Energy Scheming v2.5. To be used during early building design stages along with other basic architectural issues.(Minimum requirements: Macintosh II or later, System 7.0, 2.5 MBRAM, laser or ink-jet printer recommended.) $215, also from IRIS Catalog (800) 346-0104.

Sun Angle, by Christopher Gronbeck. Free software program built into the CREST WWW site. See http://solstice.crest.org/staff/ceg/sunangle/overhang/overhang.html.

Videos and CD-ROMs

The School Energy Doctor (teaches kids how to do an energy audit on their school building), Center for Renewable Energy and Sustainable Technology (CREST), 1996. Floppy Disk Set, $15.

The Greening of the White House, CREST, 1996, CD-ROM. $15

The Sun's Joules, CREST, CD-ROM, 1996. $25.

The Renewable Energy Exhibit, CREST, 1996, CD-ROM. $15.

About the Author

Barbara Bannon Harwood is committed to helping provide every American with affordable, energy-efficient, resource-efficient, environmentally friendly housing. On September 24, 1996, her company, Enviro Custom Homes, was presented with one of 14 national Building Innovation for Home Ownership awards from the Department of Housing and Urban Development (HUD) for her Esperanza del Sol project in Dallas's inner city. Her company also won both the 1996 and 1997 Energy Value in Housing Awards in a national competition sponsored by the Department of Energy, the National Association of Homebuilders, and the National Research Center; the first for the Esperanza project, and the second for a 3,300-sq.-ft. custom home, whose heating and cooling costs, since it was built, have averaged 28.3¢ a day. In 1990, she was awarded the Professional Builder Professional Achievement Award for Public-Private Partnerships in tribute to her efforts to create innovative partnerships to produce both energy-efficient low-income for-sale and rental housing.

In 1992, her company won the Best Low-Income Development in the Nation award from the Pillars of the Industry competition of the National Association of Homebuilders, and the Distinguished Appropriate Technology Award from the National Center for Appropriate Technology, for their Prince William apartment development in Oak Cliff, Texas. It recently won a Department of Energy (DOE) award for "outstanding contributions in promoting an environmentally sustainable energy future." That project serves working families earning less than 50 percent of median income. In 1994, her Esperanza del Sol community in east Dallas was awarded designation as the nation's first E-Seal recipient. E-Seal is a kind of Good Housekeeping Seal for energy-efficient housing. This inner-city development of passive solar, resource-efficient, energy-efficient, single-family detached "courtyard-style" housing guarantees that heating and cooling costs will not exceed one dollar per day, year-round.

Ms. Harwood is also a nationally known speaker on issues of energy efficiency, resource efficiency, healthy housing, and sustainable architecture and development. She recently keynoted the annual Green Buildings Conference held in Austin, Texas; and presented a paper and seminar on sustainable societies to both the American Solar Energy Society and the

Energy Efficient Buildings Association annual conventions. In 1996, she spoke to the National Association of Regulatory Utility Commissioners, the organization of all public utility commissioners nationwide; the World Renewable Energy Congress; and all the CEOs of the nation's electric utilities as keynote speaker at the Edison Electric Institute annual conference. She has keynoted, among others, the National Low-Income Energy Consortium convention; the Michigan Governor's State Energy Conference, and the Vermont Lieutenant Governor's Annual Affordable Housing Conference.

Past Chairperson of the Energy Committee of the National Association of Homebuilders, she has also served on national boards and commissions under three presidents, including a two-year term on the National Manufactured Housing Advisory Council, which decides health and energy standards for manufactured housing. She was recently appointed as a member of the "Green Team" to assist Habitat for Humanity in making its worldwide operations energy efficient and resource efficient.

Locally, she is a participant in TU Electric's pilot Service Area Advisory Group, which developed a ten-year Integrated Resource Plan for the utility to present to the Texas Public Utility Commission. She and her husband, Richard, have five children and eight grandchildren.

You may contact Barbara Harwood by writing to her in care of Hay House, or e-mail her at: **enrgyxpert@aol.com.**

We hope you enjoyed this Hay House book.
If you would like to receive a free catalog featuring additional
Hay House books and products, or if you would like information about
the Hay Foundation, please contact:

Hay House, Inc.
P.O. Box 5100
Carlsbad, CA 92018-5100

(800) 654-5126
(800) 650-5115 (fax)

Please visit the Hay House Website at:
www.hayhouse.com